The Philosophy of David Lynch

THE PHILOSOPHY OF POPULAR CULTURE

The books published in the Philosophy of Popular Culture series will illuminate and explore philosophical themes and ideas that occur in popular culture. The goal of this series is to demonstrate how philosophical inquiry has been reinvigorated by increased scholarly interest in the intersection of popular culture and philosophy, as well as to explore through philosophical analysis beloved modes of entertainment, such as movies, TV shows, and music. Philosophical concepts will be made accessible to the general reader through examples in popular culture. This series seeks to publish both established and emerging scholars who will engage a major area of popular culture for philosophical interpretation and examine the philosophical underpinnings of its themes. Eschewing ephemeral trends of philosophical and cultural theory, authors will establish and elaborate on connections between traditional philosophical ideas from important thinkers and the ever-expanding world of popular culture.

Series Editor
Mark T. Conard, Marymount Manhattan College, N.Y.

Books in the Series

The Philosophy of Stanley Kubrick, edited by Jerold J. Abrams
Football and Philosophy, edited by Michael W. Austin
Tennis and Philosophy, edited by David Baggett
The Philosophy of the Coen Brothers, edited by Mark T. Conard
The Philosophy of Film Noir, edited by Mark T. Conard
The Philosophy of Martin Scorsese, edited by Mark T. Conard
The Philosophy of Neo-Noir, edited by Mark T. Conard
The Philosophy of Spike Lee, edited by Mark T. Conard
The Philosophy of Horror, edited by Thomas Fahy
The Philosophy of The X-Files, edited by Dean A. Kowalski
Steven Spielberg and Philosophy, edited by Dean A. Kowalski
The Philosophy of Charlie Kaufman, edited by David LaRocca
The Philosophy of the Western, edited by Jennifer L. McMahon and B. Steve Csaki
The Philosophy of Steven Soderbergh, edited by R. Barton Palmer and Steven M. Sanders
The Philosophy of Science Fiction Film, edited by Steven M. Sanders
The Philosophy of TV Noir, edited by Steven M. Sanders and Aeon J. Skoble
Basketball and Philosophy, edited by Jerry L. Walls and Gregory Bassham
Golf and Philosophy, edited by Andy Wible

THE PHILOSOPHY OF
DAVID LYNCH

Edited by
William J. Devlin
and Shai Biderman

THE UNIVERSITY PRESS OF KENTUCKY

Scholarly publisher for the Commonwealth,
serving Bellarmine University, Berea College, Centre College of Kentucky,
Eastern Kentucky University, The Filson Historical Society, Georgetown College,
Kentucky Historical Society, Kentucky State University, Morehead State
University, Murray State University, Northern Kentucky University, Transylvania
University, University of Kentucky, University of Louisville, and Western
Kentucky University.
All rights reserved.

Editorial and Sales Offices: The University Press of Kentucky
663 South Limestone Street, Lexington, Kentucky 40508-4008
www.kentuckypress.com

15 14 13 12 11   5 4 3 2 1

Library of Congress Cataloging-in-Publication Data

The philosophy of David Lynch / edited by William J. Devlin and Shai Biderman.
    p. cm. — (The philosophy of popular culture)
  Includes bibliographical references and index.
  ISBN 978-0-8131-2991-4 (alk. paper) — ISBN 978-0-8131-3396-6 (ebook)
  1. Lynch, David, 1946—Criticism and interpretation. I. Devlin, William J.
II. Biderman, Shai.
  PN1998.3.L96P66 2011
  791.4302'33092—dc22   2010047403

Member of the Association of
American University Presses

CONTENTS

ACKNOWLEDGMENTS

We'd like to first thank the contributors to this work, whose diligence and insight helped to create this excellent volume on David Lynch. We would also like to thank everyone at the University Press of Kentucky—especially Mark Conard, Anne Dean Watkins, and Stephen Wrinn—who provided us with assistance throughout the process of developing this book. We are also grateful to Ila McEntire and Susan Murray for their work in the editing process. Furthermore, we'd like to thank Aeon Skoble and Steven Sanders for their wonderful advice and suggestions throughout the creation of this volume. Finally, we would both like to thank our families and friends, whose undying support of our passion for philosophy have helped to make all of our work possible. Shai would like to thank his family for their loving support, especially his parents, Shlomo and Israela, his wife, Yael, his daughter Tal, as well as Masha Yaron and Harry and Sharon Hirsch. He would also like to extend his thanks and gratitude to Yoav Ariel, William Irwin, and Daniel Dahlstrom. Bill would like to thank his family, Margaret, Robert, Rob, Katie, RJ, and Janice Wilson for their love and support. He would also like to thank Kerrie Fevold for her love and care. He would lastly like to thank Richard and Adri Howey for their dear friendship and academic support throughout the years.

INTRODUCTION

William J. Devlin and Shai Biderman

Award-winning film director, producer, and writer David Lynch is perhaps best known for his unorthodox filmmaking style. The Lynchian cinema is distinctively unique. From his cult classic film *Eraserhead* (1977) to his neo-noir television series *Twin Peaks* (1990–1991) to his abstract film *Inland Empire* (2006), Lynch distorts and disrupts viewers' expectations of a traditional approach to narrative and story line, plot points, character development, frame composing, and film styling. He presents to viewers a surreal, often nightmarish, perspective that allows us to experience the world of film in an entirely new way. While his approach to filmmaking may deter some, Lynch has attracted a wide audience over his thirty-plus years as a director.

Lynch's films are predominantly character-driven. Through the artistic and eccentric mind of Lynch, we are introduced to memorable characters through his film corpus. First, we have distinctive protagonists such as the perky, straitlaced, and incisive FBI Special Agent Dale Cooper, who is famous for his love of coffee and pie in *Twin Peaks; The Straight Story's* (1999) loveable curmudgeon Alvin Straight, who, after years of fighting with his brother, travels hundreds of miles on a riding mower to make amends; and the physically deformed John Merrick, who is willing to sacrifice his life to prove he is a human being in *The Elephant Man* (1980). Second, we have such sinister villains as the perverted and brutal Frank Booth in *Blue Velvet* (1986), whose twisted combination of ferociousness and sexual desire offends many viewers; the menacing Feyd-Rautha of *Dune* (1984), who haunts Paul Atreides' dreams; and the perplexing and appropriately named Mystery Man, whose eerie appearance in *Mulholland Dr.* (2001) challenges the notion of consistent identity (à la being in two places at the same time). Finally, we have the outright enigmatic and elusive characters, such as *Twin Peaks's* Man from Another Place, who dances and talks backward, and the Giant, both of whom leave mysterious clues for Agent Cooper to help him solve the murder of Laura Palmer; *Eraserhead's* Lady in the Radiator, who dances and sings in Henry Spencer's visions, and the Man in the Planet, who plays with mechanical levers while watching Henry's life; and the monster who lurks behind Winkie's diner, and the miniature elderly couple in the blue box from *Mulholland Dr.*

Not only are Lynch's character's memorable, but many scenes and locations are equally impressive. There are the dreamlike sequences that occur in the red room in *Twin Peaks.* There is the chicken-dinner scene in *Eraserhead.* There are the abrupt and shocking character changes in *Lost Highway* (1997) from Fred Madison to Pete Dayton. There are the multiple character identities in *Mulholland Dr.,* as Betty Elms and Diane Selwyn are both played by Naomi Watts. Then there is the abstract and surreal presentation of the life of a family of rabbits in *Inland Empire.*

Lynch's cinematic corpus thus combines what seems initially to be disharmonious and chaotic: disconnected story lines, inconsistent character identity, true stories, distorted story arches, dreamlike worlds and fantasies, bizarre characters, and both dark and psychedelic-like cinematography. The Lynchian world is a confusing labyrinth in which one can easily become lost. However, there is a thread viewers can follow to help guide them through Lynch's maze and come to understand Lynch's cinematic collection: namely, the human psyche. Lynch's central focus, whether in *Wild at Heart* (1990), *Lost Highway,* or *The Cowboy and the Frenchman* (1988), is the human mind. As such, we maintain that Lynch's philosophy is, first and foremost, the philosophy of the human being. Through the series of essays in this volume, we show that Lynch presents to his audience his own distinct philosophical account of reality, the human being, and human issues. As such, this volume is designed to assist the viewers of Lynch's films to come to understand the philosophical ideas portrayed in his body of work.

Lynch's philosophy begins with his view that, as a filmmaker, he is able to create a new reality, a new world for the audience. Lynch pulls us into his constructed reality so that the dividing line between the world on the screen and the audience members is blurred. With this in mind, part 1, "The World of David Lynch," addresses the cinematic world that Lynch creates. Philosophically speaking, what is the world that Lynch creates through his films and television episodes? Our exploration of this world begins with Robert Arp and Patricia Brace's "'The Owls Are Not What They Seem': The Logic of Lynch's World," in which they argue that Lynch plays with both valid and fallacious forms of logical reasoning to help construct his strange, and sometimes illogical, world. Next, in "Intuition and Investigation into Another Place: The Epistemological Role of Dreaming in *Twin Peaks* and Beyond," Simon Riches argues that Lynch employs an unequivocally unique take on epistemic questions and presuppositions through the character of Agent Cooper, demonstrating how Lynch plays with how we acquire knowledge by subjecting Cooper to an intertwining of the world of dreams and the real world. Sander Lee maintains, in "The Horrors of Life's Hidden Mysteries: *Blue Velvet*," that Lynch uses the suffering, violence, and misery in *Blue Velvet* to reveal that the horrors and chaos of the world are irremovable. Following the discussion of the disruption of the world's coherence, in terms of logic, knowledge acquisition, and ethics, the last two papers of part 1 explore responses to this disruption. In "The Thing about David Lynch: Reading and Enjoying the Lynchian World," Russell Manning suggests that the aestheticism of Lynch's world should not be understood through the generic Hollywood interpretation of what constitutes a good film; instead, Lynch should be understood as challenging this paradigm by attempting to capture the sublime, or the ineffable "Thing." Finally, in "The World as Illusion: Rediscovering *Mulholland Dr.* and *Lost Highway* through Indian Philosophy," Ronie Parciack turns to Eastern philosophy to help understand Lynch's films, as she claims that the nature of the world and the subject in Lynch's films are best construed through the philosophical schools of Hinduism and Buddhism.

In part 2, "Selfhood and Subjectivity: The Existential Drive toward Self-Understanding," we turn from a general philosophical account of Lynch's world to focus in on Lynch's exploration of the human individual within the context of living in a world that no longer makes the kind of sense we once thought it did. Lynch's body of work centers on the human individual—the individual's nature and psyche and the meaning of his or her life. Given that the traditional conception of the world in terms of logic, epistemology, and ethics has collapsed, Lynch provides us with an existential approach toward creating our own identity and our own meaning in life. We explain this existential drive toward self-understanding by addressing existential issues. Here we begin with "All Roads Lead to the Self: Zen Buddhism and David Lynch's *Lost Highway*," by Mark Walling, who argues that Lynch demonstrates the Zen Buddhist perspective (concerning the subject and the world) that the dualistic conception of reality divides the self and so is doomed to failure. Following the existential investigation of the self, in "City of Dreams: Bad Faith in *Mulholland Dr.*," Jennifer McMahon shows how Lynch's characters hide behind illusory and self-deceptive narratives to help make their lives bearable. Next, Tal Correm argues, in "Constellations of the Flesh: The Embodied Self in *The Straight Story* and *The Elephant Man*," that Lynch uses the physical bodies and environment surrounding his characters to help reveal how our bodies shape and structure our experiences in life. In "David Lynch's Road Films: Individuality and Personal Freedom?" Richard Gaughran turns to Lynch's exploration of individual rebellion and freedom through the characters of Sailor Ripley and Alvin Straight, suggesting that, while Sailor demonstrates inauthentic freedom, Alvin, by accepting responsibility and avoiding nihilism, lives a life of authenticity. Last, Shai Frogel continues this theme of Alvin Straight as the authentic individual in "Lynch's Zarathustra: *The Straight Story*," as he argues that Alvin is a modern American example of Friedrich Nietzsche's existential character Zarathustra.

After a comprehensive examination of the world, which is chaotic, and the individual, who must create his or her own identity, in Lynch's cinematic features, we close the volume by examining how Lynch unites the world and the individual in part 3, "The Self Confronts the World: Issues in Ethics, Society, and Religion." Here, we tackle some common issues that arise from the encounter between the self and the world, and provide a constructive and comprehensive way to understand Lynch's analysis of how the individual confronts the chaotic world. In "'There's a Sort of Evil Out There': Emersonian Transcendentalism in *Twin Peaks*," Scott Suter explores the sources of good and evil that the individual confronts in the elements of nature, using Ralph Waldo Emerson's transcendentalism to explain why good triumphs over evil. "'In Heaven Everything Is Fine': Erasing Traditional Morality," by Jason Southworth, demonstrates how Lynch evokes the philosophical lineage of nihilism, existentialism, and Ludwig Wittgenstein's morality as he rejects the traditional and common conceptions of morality. In "The Monster Within: Alienation and Social Conformity in *The Elephant Man*," Shai Biderman and Assaf Tabeka claim that Lynch provides a grim portrayal of the individual outsider who attempts to relate to society, a depiction that suggests such an individual may remain lost in alienation and estrangement. Last, William J. Devlin, in "Prophesies, Experience, and Proof: Philosophy of Religion in *Dune*," argues that Lynch emphasizes the personal and subjective experiences of religious revelation when one confronts spirituality and religion.

As a whole, this volume is intended to explore the unique and insightful philosophy of David Lynch through a careful and meticulous philosophical examination of his cinematic works. We hope these essays will help to sharpen readers' understanding of, deepen their appreciation of, and enhance their enjoyment of Lynch's cinematic corpus.

Part 1

THE WORLD OF DAVID LYNCH

"THE OWLS ARE NOT WHAT THEY SEEM"

The Logic of Lynch's World

Robert Arp and Patricia Brace

Our world is not inherently logical—we impose logic upon it to make sense of the random and absurd happenings all around us and to create a sense of order out of chaos. The beauty of the work of filmmaker David Lynch is that he not only recognizes this basic truth about the absurdity of human existence, he celebrates it to create his own unique worldview. By showcasing distortions and manipulations of reality, and logical paradoxes and fallacies used as the basis for his characters' actions, a typical Lynch film can be off-putting to many viewers. Because his films are often violent and sexually explicit with an unusual narrative structure and heavy symbolic content, repeated viewings may be necessary to grasp all of the many layers of meaning he builds in to the structure. As in the work of the Dutch surrealist Mauritius Escher (1898–1972), who manipulates the rules of perspective to create the appearance of three-dimensional space on a two-dimensional surface, the logic of Lynch's world at first appears twisted and chaotic. But for those existing within it, everything makes perfect sense. In Lynch's works, we often find the filmmaker manipulating the viewer by playing an illogical (even nonsensical) scene perfectly straight. The characters within the narrative do not see any humor or irony in their beliefs or actions, just as the man walking up the stairs to nowhere in an Escher work (*Relativity,* lithograph, 1953) doesn't realize his world is visually illogical; he just keeps walking up and down the steps. In a Lynch film, as in an Escher print, reality is carefully planned and controlled for maximum effect, even when it seems uncontrolled and illogical to the viewer. As the filmmaker, Lynch imposes his brand of logic upon the story to make sense of the random and absurd happenings all around his characters and to create a sense of order out of chaos within the film itself.

In David Lynch's *The Cowboy and the Frenchman* (1988), an episode for the French series *The French as Seen By . . .* (1988), Lynch tells an absurdist story involving, as the title suggests, cowboys and a Frenchman. Driving the comedic tone of this show is Lynch's play on the modern stereotypes of cowboys, Indians, and Frenchmen. The cowboys, led by the almost stone-deaf Slim (Harry Dean Stanton), are all decked out in cowboy hats, plaid shirts, and chaps. They drink longneck bottles of Budweiser, appear to be trigger-happy gunslingers (even going so far as to shoot at a bird for tweeting) and speak in Western slang. The Indian, "Broken Feather" (Michael Horse), wears a feather in his long hair, is bare-chested (clothed only in buckskin breeches and a loincloth), and speaks in pidgin English, beginning phrases with "Me no." Meanwhile, Pierre the Frenchman (Fredric Golchan), who speaks only French, has a thin mustache, wears a dark suit, a beret, an ascot, and carries with him a suitcase full of French souvenirs: bottles of wine, loaves of baguettes, packs of cigarettes, a replica of the Eiffel Tower, and, to the cowboy's horror, a dinner plate of snails. The cowboys finally stumble onto this strange man's national identity when they find a plate of French fries in the magical bag.

This meeting between the Frenchman and the cowboys is reduced to seeming absurdity by the end, as we see cowgirls and French girls dancing together to a cowboy rock song, while Pierre learns how to say "Yippee-kay-ay" and cowboy Slim learns how to say "Ooh la la." As Slim sings "Home on the Range," accord between the two groups is symbolized by Pierre's presentation of a small replica of the Statue of Liberty, echoing the original friendship gift between the two nations, as the whole party shouts "Vive la France" and trigger-happy Slim shoots off his pistol. The final scene, set the next morning, finds Slim has traded his cowboy hat for Pierre's beret, while Pierre, in perfect English, rhapsodizes about pancakes, and the Indian, also in perfect English, wishes he had a suitcase like the Frenchman's.

This short film, whose actual title is *The French as Seen by David Lynch*, may be read as a subtle comment on the ubiquitous and often overpowering nature of *American* culture. The American cowboy Slim is literally deaf to all comments and criticism; U.S. politicians are often referred to as "cowboys" by foreign leaders—in 1988, Ronald Reagan (who often played a cowboy onscreen in his first career) had just finished his last term as president.

Immigrants to the United States are told everyone should speak English, and by the end of the film, everyone is. The Frenchman is lucky because he can pack his bag and leave, but the Indian has no suitcase so he can't. When we first meet Broken Feather, Slim orders one of the other cowboys to apologize and pay off his gambling debt to the Indian, a double allusion to the reparations Native Americans have sought from the U.S. government for treaty violations and to their profitable reservation casinos. A hint of Lynch's ambivalence about the French also peeks through at the end in the final image: a dead snail is stuck to Slim, and he plucks it off and throws it to the ground, saying, "damn!"

The people in the film, as seen by Lynch, are on the surface an absurdist humorous play on stereotyping. Stereotyping is a form of jumping to a conclusion. For example, there is the stereotypical cowboy, as portrayed in Lynch's episode. This depiction of the cowboy—trigger-happy, beer-swilling, lassoing farm men—is rooted in the assumption that if one, a few, or most are like this or that, then they must *all* be like this or that. If we are told about a cowboy, someone might think that, because this person is a cowboy, he and anyone else who is a cowboy must love shooting, the great outdoors, horses, and wide-open spaces. "After all," thinks the stereotyper, "this person is a cowboy, and they're all like that." Broadening the analogy to all Americans versus all Frenchmen or all Indians or even all women (who are also stereotyped in the film as dancing sex kittens who bring food and beer to the men), we see Lynch's ability to take what on the surface seems an illogical absurdist comedic short and make a deeper social comment.

Lynch plays with the notion of stereotyping in *The Cowboy and the Frenchman,* humorously alluding to the moral and logical harm that stereotyping does to people in real life. Consider all of the racism, sexism, ageism, and every other negative "ism" that results from people inappropriately jumping to negative conclusions about groups of people. Lynch, too, recognizes the harm that can result from stereotypes. Take, for instance, *The Elephant Man* (1980), a film based on the real-life story of Joseph Merrick (named John Merrick in the film and played by John Hurt), a man who suffered from a congenital disorder that severely altered his physical appearance. In the film, we find that Bytes (Freddie Jones), the man who manages the Victorian freak show of which Merrick is a part, treats Merrick's oversized deformities as a disability and labels Merrick a "freak." Labeling Merrick a freak coincides with Bytes's brutal treatment of Merrick—using such a label,

Bytes is able to see Merrick as less human and therefore unworthy of being treated with kindness and respect.

The logical harm of typecasting or stereotypes occurs because the conclusion drawn isn't supported by the reasons given for that conclusion. The conclusion that they're all like that or they all must have that same feature, quality, or characteristic doesn't follow from, and cannot be fully supported by, reasons having to do with one or a few instances being like that or having the certain feature, quality, or characteristic. It is likely that there are cowboys who are trigger-happy, beer-swilling, lassoing farm men, but you could never legitimately draw the conclusion that *all* cowboys are like that. Likewise, not *all* people (or any, for that matter) with deformities can be labeled "freaks." Stereotyping is bad *and* it is due to bad reasoning.

Logicians, those who study the principles of correct reasoning, have a term for the kind of bad reasoning involved in our examples of typecasting and stereotyping from Lynch's work. They call it a *fallacy,* and the thinking involved, *fallacious reasoning.* Fallacies occur whenever we jump to a conclusion, namely, when we incorrectly, illegitimately, or inappropriately draw a conclusion from reasons that don't support the conclusion. Fallacious reasoning is much too common in the real and film worlds. Racists think that just because they have had a bad experience with a person of a particular race, creed, or color, then everyone of that race must be like that. Instead of seeking to become an authority in a particular matter ourselves, we too often blindly accept what someone tells us because we perceive him or her to be an authority concerning that particular matter. Think of all of the people who came to see Merrick and believed that he must be a freak because Bytes said he was a freak. As we, the viewers, notice, these people were not justified in concluding either that they're all like that or that it's true just because Bytes said so. In these cases, the conclusions drawn don't follow from the reasons given as supposed support. In other words, these are all examples of fallacies.

In this essay, we explore Lynch's take on logic in his films. This approach entails further discussion of Lynch's strange use of logic through famous examples in his works, appreciating the bizarre, paranoid, and often fallacious reasoning associated with Lynch's characters. We argue that a Lynch work doesn't always abide by the principles of correct reasoning and often operates within a world of fallacies, yet his characters usually find a way to function within their illogical worlds.

Argumentation Is an Art—Just Not a Visual Art

Logic is the study of the principles of correct reasoning concerning the formation and evaluation of arguments. As we've seen already, people don't always abide by these principles. The way characters and people reason has consequences for how they live their lives in the film and real worlds alike. Good and bad reasoning affect the beliefs people are willing to die for, the policies we adhere to, the laws we make, and the general way in which we live our lives. For the most part, it seems as though Lynch's characters try to abide by reason to determine how to live their lives. In order to see how Lynch's characters follow the forms of good reasoning, we need to discuss the basic elements of logical reasoning. First, we describe the basic components and types of arguments. Second, we discuss two common types of arguments. Finally, we examine the evaluation of arguments.[1]

BOTH REAL AND IMAGINED PEOPLE NEED TO PUT FORTH
GOOD ARGUMENTS

An argument is made up of two or more statements, one of which is called the *conclusion*. The conclusion is the statement in the argument that is supposed to be justified by, warranted by, supported by, shown to be the case by, demonstrated by, or proved to be the case by the premise or premises. A *premise* is a statement in the argument that is supposed to justify, warrant, support, show, demonstrate, or prove the conclusion. The basic goal of an argument is to convince or persuade oneself or others of the truth of the concluding statement. Now, Lynch makes use of logical arguments in his films, as, on many occasions, his characters attempt to rationalize the best decision or course to take in their life.

Take the character Sailor Ripley (Nicholas Cage) and his lover, Lula Pace Fortune (Laura Dern), from *Wild at Heart* (1990) as one example. Sailor has just been released from prison after serving time for manslaughter. Lula's jealous wicked-witch mother, Marietta Pace Fortune (Diane Ladd), tried to have him killed but, instead, Sailor killed the assassin in self-defense. Marietta has forbidden Lula to see Sailor, but she defies her mother and picks him up at the Pee Dee Correctional Institution, and they head out for New Orleans and then California, violating his parole. Marietta puts out another hit on Sailor, something he suspected she would do, so they make a stop in the humorously named town of Big Tuna, Texas (not many tuna swimming in the desert). This small town is populated by the usual bizarre

Lynchian characters (such as the twitchy, dog-obsessed Bose "Double Aught" Spool, played by Jack Nance, who actually references Dorothy's dog Toto) and is also where his old "friend" Perdita (Isabella Rossellini) lives. We are never clear on the exact nature of their past relationship, but Sailor reminds her that she owes him a favor, which he has come to claim. Sailor wants to confirm that there is a contract out on him. Perdita is connected, as it were, so she knows about the network of hit men. Unfortunately for Sailor and Lula, Perdita's new boyfriend, the loathsome Bobby Peru (Willem Dafoe), is the hit man hired to carry out Marietta's contract, so Perdita lies, telling Sailor he is safe.

Sailor's reasoning pattern was correct. From his two initial premises, namely that (1) if I want help, I'll contact an old friend who'll help me; and (2) if I contact an old friend who'll help me, then I'll need to go to Texas, Sailor concludes necessarily that if I want help, then I'll need to go to Texas. But he was mistaken in the facts: Perdita is no longer his friend (in Spanish *perdita* means loss). And so Sailor and Lula find themselves stranded at the Hotel Iguana in Big Tuna, Texas, where their lives are now in jeopardy.

Now, arguments are made up of statements, a concluding statement (the conclusion) and at least one supporting statement (the premise). A *statement* is a claim, assertion, proposition, judgment, declarative sentence, or part of a declarative sentence—resulting from a belief or opinion—that communicates that something is or is not the case concerning the world, self, states of affairs, or some aspect of reality. Statements are either true or false and, again, are the results of beliefs or opinions that people have about what they perceive to be reality. Our beliefs and opinions are made known through statements, either in spoken or written form. For example, in the context of *Wild at Heart,* the statements "Bobby shoots two clerks during the bank robbery" and "Johnnie Farragut (Harry Dean Stanton) is a private detective" are true, whereas the statements "Sailor came on to Lula's mother" and "Sailor murdered a man in cold blood" are false.

Statements are shown to be true or false as a result of *evidence,* which can take the forms of either direct or indirect observation, the testimony of others, explanations, appeal to definitions, appeal to well-established theories, appeal to appropriate authority, and good arguments, to name just a few. So, that Bobby shoots two clerks is shown to be true by observing *Wild at Heart,* and that Johnnie Farragut is a private detective is defined by his creator, Lynch. Also, that Sailor came on to Lula's mother is false because of observation, and Sailor murdered a man in cold blood is false because of the testimony of others and authorities, observation as well as the judicial theory of self-defense and first-degree murder.

Critically thinking adults have beliefs or opinions that they think are true and that they express in written or spoken statements. However, we can't stop there. We must defend why we hold these beliefs, and so we must give a reason (the premise of our argument) for why we hold to a particular belief (the conclusion of our argument). Take, for example, Henry Spencer's (Jack Nance) moral dilemma in *Eraserhead* (1977). There, Henry learns that his girlfriend, Mary X (Charlotte Stewart), has just had a baby. Upon this discovery, he decides to marry Mary. But why did Henry decide to marry her? We can gather that his decision stems from his belief that marrying one's girlfriend is morally the right thing to do and that he should always do what is right. In this respect, you might put forward an argument on behalf of Henry that looks like this. Henry begins with three premises: (1) My girlfriend, Mary, has a baby; (2) marrying one's girlfriend when she has a baby is the right thing to do; (3) these two factors necessarily contribute to what I ought to do. Now, from these premises, Henry is able to infer that he ought to marry Mary.

THE TWIN PEAKS OF ARGUMENTATION

There are two basic types of arguments, *deductive arguments* and *inductive arguments*. With deductive arguments, the speaker intends the conclusion to follow from the premise(s) with certainty so that, if all of the premises are true, then the conclusion must be true without any doubt whatsoever. Also, the conclusion of a deductive argument is already found in the premise(s) in a way that there is absolutely no other conclusion that could be inferred from the premise(s). To say that a conclusion *follows* from a premise means that we are justified in having reasoned from one statement (the premise) to another statement (the conclusion).

In the television series *Twin Peaks* (1990–1991), Special Agent Dale Cooper (Kyle MacLachlan) is assigned to investigate the murder of Laura Palmer (Sheryl Lee). During his investigation, he looks into *One-Eyed Jacks,* a brothel and casino just north across the border into Canada. He is first tipped off about this place by a note placed anonymously at his hotel room door that reads "Jack with one eye" (season 1, episode 4: "Rest in Pain"). Agent Cooper is able to deduce that Audrey Horne (Sherilyn Fenn) wrote him this note with the following deductive argument. First, he begins with three premises: (1) If Audrey Horne's handwriting sample matches the handwriting of the mysterious note and if the note is not a forgery, then Audrey wrote the note; (2) Audrey Horne's handwriting sample matches the handwriting of the mysterious note; (3) the note is not a forgery. From these claims, Agent Cooper deduces that Audrey wrote the note. Provided that the three premises are true (and we know they are from season 1, episode 3: "Zen, or the Skill to Catch a Killer"), we can see that the conclusion absolutely must be true. We can also see that there's no other conclusion that could possibly follow from the premises—from looking at the premises alone you can recognize the conclusion before even seeing it. The previous argument about Henry marrying Mary is also a deductive argument. Just like with Cooper's mystery note argument, if all the premises are true, then the conclusion has to be true. There isn't any other conclusion that could possibly be drawn from the premises, and you can figure out what the conclusion is without even seeing it.

Unlike deductive arguments, in inductive arguments the speaker intends the conclusion to follow from the premises with a degree of likelihood or probability *only* so that, if all of the premises are true, then the conclusion likely or probably is true. But it's still possible that the conclusion is false. As we continue to follow Agent Cooper's investigation, we notice that he is able to quickly connect Laura Palmer's murder to a murder that occurred a year ago: namely, the murder of Teresa Banks (Pamela Gidley). His reasoning that leads to the connection is as follows. First, Agent Cooper accepts two claims: (1) In the past murder case of Teresa Banks, a letter on a tiny piece of paper was found under her fingernail; (2) a letter on a tiny piece of paper was found under Laura Palmer's fingernail. Second, from these premises, he concludes that it is likely that Laura Palmer's murderer is also Teresa Banks's murderer.

We can see that, provided the premises are true, the conclusion is probably or likely true, but it is not definitely true. It makes sense to conclude that the murderer is the same in both cases given the similarities between the two cases. But the truth concerning the evidence garnered from both cases does not guarantee that, with absolute certainty or without a doubt, the same murderer struck in both cases. It's still possible that there is a copycat murderer in Laura Palmer's case or that Laura placed the letter under her fingernail herself. So, the conclusion is merely probable or likely.

Consider the kind of reasoning Agent Cooper utilized with his chess game with Windom Earle (Kenneth Welsh), in which innocent lives were at stake. There, Earle played a maniacal game of life and death with Cooper where, for any chess piece Earle captures, he kills a person. Furthermore,

Earle, who laid away in hiding, would notify Agent Cooper, in one way or another, what his next move would be so that the game could continue. Because Earle had followed the rules of this twisted game for several rounds, Agent Cooper concluded that Earle would continue to follow these rules. As he tells Sheriff Truman (Michael Ontkean), "Earle has a perverse sense of honor" about following the rules (season 2, episode 23: "Slaves and Masters"). However, later we find that Agent Cooper is no longer confident that he can understand Earle's reasoning; he tells Sheriff Truman: "There was a time where I could comprehend with a high degree of clarity Windom Earle's twisted logic, but his actions of late have left me completely bewildered. He is changing the pattern of the game board. Any hope of deducing his next move has evaporated" (season 2, episode 26: "On the Wings of Love"). Finally, as he realizes that Earle has stopped notifying him of his next move, Agent Cooper accepts that his original conclusion—that Earle will follow the rules—is mistaken. As he tells Sheriff Truman: "He's taken another pawn, but he didn't tell us his move. Windom Earle is playing off the board" (season 2, episode 27: "Variations on Relations"). This is an example of inductive reasoning where it seemed as if the conclusion were going to be true, but it turned out in the end to be false.

EVALUATING ARGUMENTS

The goal for any rational creature—from Lynch to Laura Palmer—isn't simply to form arguments. We need to form *good arguments,* and we need to evaluate the arguments of others. In both the deductive and inductive realms, there are good and bad arguments. In either realm, a good argument has to meet two conditions: (1) the conclusion must logically follow from the premises, and (2) all of the premises must be true. If either (or both) of these conditions is missing, then the argument is bad and should be rejected.

In the deductive realm, the term *valid argument* is reserved for an argument where a conclusion does, in fact, follow from the premises (if a conclusion does not follow, then an argument is considered to be an *invalid argument*). When an argument is valid and all the premises are true, the argument is a good, *sound argument.* The conclusion, then, is without a doubt, absolutely, positively true. In the inductive realm, the term *strong argument* is reserved for an argument where a conclusion likely will follow from premises (if a conclusion is not likely to follow, then an argument is considered to be a *weak argument*). When an argument is strong and all the premises are true, the argument is a good, *cogent argument.* The conclusion most likely or probably is true. Absolute truth and probable truth are good things, so sound arguments and cogent arguments are, by definition, good arguments in the deductive and inductive realms, respectively.

Thus, as critically thinking creatures, we must always go through the two-step procedure of checking our own arguments—and the arguments of others—to see if: (1) the conclusion follows from the premises (Is the argument deductively valid or inductively strong?); and (2) all of the premises are true (Has evidence been provided to show the premises to be true?). If the argument fails to meet either (1) or (2) or both, then we should reject it, thereby rejecting the person's conclusion as either absolutely false or probably false.

For example, take Dorothy Vallens's (Isabella Rossellini) line of reasoning used in *Blue Velvet* (1986) when she discovers Jeffrey Beaumont (Kyle MacLachlan) hiding in her closet. Because she believes that all people who hide in closets are practicing voyeurism, Dorothy concludes that Jeffrey broke into her apartment and hid in her closet just to watch her undress. But her first premise, that all people who hide in closets are practicing voyeurism, is obviously false. We, the viewers, know that her conclusion is wrong because of this premise. Jeffrey broke into her apartment to snoop around to find clues regarding the severed ear he had found earlier, not to watch her disrobe. Thus, Jeffrey's own case is a counterexample to her first premise. In the case of this particular deductive argument, the conclusion "Jeffrey broke into her apartment and hid in her closet just to watch her undress" is false and unsupported by one of the reasons given (again, the first premise is false).

On the other hand, Agent Cooper's deduction that Audrey wrote the mysterious note is a good argument. It's true that if there is a match between Audrey's handwriting sample and the mysterious note, and if the note is not a forgery, then Audrey wrote the note. And given this fact, plus the fact that Cooper does discover that there is a match and that the note is not a forgery, Cooper is justified in concluding that Audrey did, indeed, write the mysterious note. In fact, we can see that this conclusion necessarily follows from the premises. And, since the premises are true, the conclusion must be true.

Fallacy Is Fact: The Logic of David Lynch

As we've seen, Lynch seems to invoke the use of good reasoning in his characters' use of logic. However, when we delve deeper into the Lynchian universe, we uncover a richer and more bizarre approach to reasoning. For instance, in *Twin Peaks,* we find that Agent Cooper, the quintessential example of applying deductive methods to FBI investigations, twists logic by employing a deductive Tibetan technique that he intuitively grasps in his dreams. Not only does he employ this strange form of Tibetan mysticism, but he also relies heavily upon his dreams (which include the Man from Another Place, the Giant, Laura Palmer, Bob, Mike, the red room, etc.) to provide him with clues that he uses deductively to solve the case of who murdered Laura Palmer.

It seems prima facie that Agent Cooper fails to employ good reasoning—his reliance upon nonrational methods, such as intuitions and dreams, would not allow him to bring about proper conclusions under the standard norms of logic. However, this need not be the final analysis of Lynch's use of logic. Instead, one can argue that Lynchian logic is twisted and chaotic, similar to a surrealist visual artist's approach. The work of the Dutch artist Mauritius Escher—with its transformations of things like farm fields into white birds and then those into black birds (*Day and Night,* woodcut, 1938) and the aforementioned stairways to nowhere—is often visually illogical, yet it is also carefully planned and controlled for maximum effect, much like the work of David Lynch. Escher also uses a visual twinning technique, which he called a *tessellation,* to entirely fill the picture plane of his drawings. An object, animal, or person, was created in such a way that its outline was able to symmetrically interlock with itself so that in repetition the form was both positive and negative (*Reptiles,* lithograph, 1943). One can also see this idea in repeated tile patterns or wallpaper designs. In the real world, one would have great difficulty finding such perfectly interlocking twins, but David Lynch often uses twins in his work to show the same interlocking positive and negative aspects of a character. In the television show *Twin Peaks* (1990–1991), dead blonde Laura Palmer has an identical cousin, the living brunette Madeline, as innocent as Laura was corrupt, both played by Sheryl Lee. This mirror image is used to create tension and confusion when Maddy impersonates Laura to try to lure her killer into revealing himself.[2]

Escher also did a series of self-portraits in which he appears as a reflection in a spherical mirror ball that he is holding (*Self-Portrait in Spherical Mirror,* lithograph, first printing January 1935). His own reflection and that of the room beyond him, which includes a bookshelf that seems to bend and rise as a stairway and a framed Indonesian shadow puppet, are recognizable, but distorted. Lynch creates distorted Escher-like landscapes, such as the red room in Agent Cooper's dreams and visions, with appearances by a dwarf and a giant—distortions of normal human scale, and a black-and-white checkerboard or chevron-patterned floor. In the final episode of *Twin Peaks*, the hero, Agent Cooper, after escaping the red room, is revealed to be the equivalent of the evil twin, as he looks at his reflection, sees the image of evil, Bob (Frank Silva), staring back at him, and then repeatedly bashes his head into his bathroom mirror.

Lynch also appears in his own work as an exaggerated and distorted reflection of himself. In real life, he is a soft-spoken, rather introspective man, but his alter ego, appearing in both *Twin Peaks* and its movie sequel, *Twin Peaks: Fire Walk with Me* (1992), is FBI Regional Bureau Chief Gordon Cole, Agent Cooper's superior (played by Lynch himself). Like Slim in *The Cowboy and the Frenchman*, Cole is almost totally deaf and subsequently yells most of his dialogue and comically misinterprets what people tell him; yet he is a canny investigator. In the opening scenes of *Twin Peaks: Fire Walk with Me*, a very odd character, the red-wigged Lil (Kimberly Ann Cole), does an even odder gestural dance, after which the mostly deaf Cole yells: "She's my mother's sister's girl" to a newly arrived FBI special agent. It's only after his fellow agent, who works with Cole, explains that the dance is a coded message that we realize that the dance was a clever and memorable warning about the difficult situation they are about to walk into: namely, the investigation of the death of Teresa Banks. For example, that shout about relatives is interpreted as referring to a missing *uncle*, since the male relative isn't mentioned. Lynch chooses to open the film with a reflection of himself—odd, quirky, but adhering to an internal logic for the world of that film.

Faulty Reasoning and Fallacies on Film or for Real

Like Escher, Lynch is trying to present a picture of reality as distorted and illogical. The best way to demonstrate Lynch's attempt to provide such a picture is through his use of fallacies in his films. As noted in the beginning of this essay, a *fallacy* occurs when we incorrectly or inappropriately draw a conclusion from a reason or reasons that don't support the conclusion. In what follows, we will see that Lynch's characters commit several common fallacies in logic that further help to reveal the bizarre absurdities lurking within the Lynchian world.

One common fallacy that Lynch uses to reveal absurdities in his work is the *argument from inappropriate authority*. This fallacy occurs when we incorrectly draw a conclusion from premises based upon an illegitimate, noncredible, nonqualified, or inappropriate authority figure. We have to be careful about which authority we trust. Take, for instance, the Log Lady (Catherine E. Coulson) in *Twin Peaks*. In normal circumstances, the Log Lady would be a freaked-out quasi-religious kook, *definitely* to be considered very unreliable. It's hard to imagine a more illegitimate, noncredible, non-qualified, or inappropriate authority figure than a woman who talks to a log. But Lynch confounds our expectations by having her tell an important truth about the murder of Laura Palmer to Agent Cooper, Dr. William Hayward (Warren Frost), Sheriff Truman, and Deputy Hawk (Michael Horse) when they visit her remote cabin in season 1, episode 6: *"Cooper's Dreams."* Our first impression is that she is a backwoods eccentric. However, far from being unreliable, the Log Lady's inward turning has given her unique insight and perceptions. The men recognize this and treat her with the same respect given to prophets and Native American "holy people," as indicated by Deputy Hawk's remarks and Cooper's decision to address his questions not to her, but to her log. For Lynch, the very fact that she is the best witness makes perfect sense. Again, this is an absurdity; in real life, a Log Lady is about as reliable as an Ouija board. However, in the Lynchian world, where logic and proper reasoning offer only one way to describe reality, a lady listening to a log is as credible as the top FBI investigator.

Another common fallacy that Lynch makes use of in his works is the *false dilemma*. The false dilemma is the fallacy of concluding something based upon premises that include only *two* options, when, in fact, there are three or more options. In *The Elephant Man*, the conclusions drawn by most people about Merrick's mental competency are based on his disease-altered physical appearance and the way he was forced to live like an animal when he is, in fact, an intelligent, gentle soul. Even his patron, Frederick Treves (Anthony Hopkins), the doctor who discovers him in the sideshow, believes that he is limited. He teaches him to repeat certain stock phrases, such as "I am very pleased to meet you," in preparation for an interview with a hospital administrator. But when it goes badly, Merrick surprises them both with a perfect reading of the Twenty-third psalm. His shocked patron asks:

TREVES: Why did you let me go on like that, teaching you what you already knew? Why didn't you tell me you could read?
MERRICK: You did not ask me.
TREVES: I never thought to ask. How can you ever forgive me?

Treves's conclusions were drawn from a false dilemma, where he begins with two premises: (1) Merrick can repeat the phrases being taught to him or Merrick is an imbecile; (2) Merrick cannot repeat the phrases being taught to him. From here, he deduces that Merrick is an imbecile. The idea that the "Elephant Man" was intelligent, educated, and, as we find out later in the film, even urbane, witty, and artistic had simply never occurred to him. Lynch uses this concept of false face because he always wants us to see beyond the outward appearances of people and things. Laura Palmer's beautiful and seemingly innocent face masks a dark and disturbed soul, created from years of sexual abuse, who courted death with her out-of-control lifestyle. Merrick's physical deformity brought him physical and psychological abuse, but his soul is somehow able to remain pure. Both defy our initial expectations based on physical appearance, and both are innocent victims who just want their pain to end.

A false dilemma is set up by Alvin Straight (Richard Farnsworth), the main character in *The Straight Story,* when he decides that he will either (*a*) drive his lawnmower from Iowa to visit his ailing brother in Wisconsin, or (*b*) not go at all. In fact, his pride and anger allow his stubborn mind *only* those two choices. However, he could have (*c*) asked someone for a ride (but he doesn't want handouts), (*d*) taken a bus, (*e*) taken a plane, (*f*) ridden the lawnmower to the Iowa state line and then taken a bus, (*g*) ridden partway, and then taken a plane, (*h*), (*i*), etc. It's rare that we're given *just* two choices or that things are simply black-or-white, *totally* right or *totally* wrong, *completely* true or *completely* false, about anything in life. You can see how the stubborn illogic of Alvin's quixotic quest, a true story, would have appealed to Lynch. Lynch, the filmmaker, doesn't need to use his usual bag of surrealist tricks because the whole *situation* is surreal! For Mr. Straight, the false dilemma fallacy is his fact. Driving a John Deere lawnmower hundreds of miles at a top speed of 5 mph is how he chooses to deal with what he sees as the facts of the situation. The Lynchian touches are mostly in the quirky characters he encounters on the road who reinforce his reason for the quest. For instance, there's Crystal (Anastasia Webb), the pregnant runaway he calmly counsels to return to her family by having her see the strength in a bundle of sticks. Then there is the Deer Woman (Barbara E. Robertson) who has hit thirteen deer in seven weeks on her drives to and from work. She loves deer, but she has to get to work (when a policeman later questions him about the deer's antlers that he has prominently displayed on the trailer he pulls, Straight tells him it was roadkill, in response to which the officer muses, "Must've been one slow buck"). Finally, there are the twin Norwegian tractor repair-men, Harold Olsen (Kevin P. Farley) and Thorvald Olsen (John Farley), who Alvin gets to reduce their labor charge by shaming them about their constant bickering, saying: "No man knows your life better than a brother near your age. He can know who and what you are better than most anyone on the earth. A brother is a brother."

Another common fallacy that receives a unique treatment in the Lynch-ian universe is *ad hominem.* In this fallacy, one inappropriately concludes that a person's statements or arguments aren't worth listening to or the conclusion is false because of premises that deal with an attack on the ac-tions, personality, or ideology of the person putting forward the statement or argument. *Ad hominem* is Latin for *to the man.* In other words, instead of focusing on the person's issue, statements, or argument, one attacks the person. This strategy is used when we try to discredit a person's argument by discrediting the person. But notice, the person and the person's arguments are two distinct things—to attack one isn't necessarily to attack another.

For example, in *Twin Peaks,* Agent Albert Rosenfield (Miguel Ferrer) criticizes the methods and results of the initial autopsy of Laura Palmer, performed by Dr. Hayward, as well as the general method of practicing law in Twin Peaks, by attacking the characters of Hayward and Deputy Andy Brennan (Harry Goaz). He snidely remarks to Agent Cooper that the au-topsy was "amateur hour." With respect to Deputy Brennan's presence, he tells Agent Cooper: "I do not suffer fools gladly and fools with badges never. I want no interference from this hulking boob, is that clear?" Here, Agent Rosenfield fails to address any weaknesses in the methods of the autopsy or investigation that he may notice. Instead, he attacks the individuals who are part of the autopsy and investigation. Agent Rosenfield sticks with this fal-lacious strategy even when Sheriff Truman tells him that he's had enough of this; Agent Rosenfield responds by saying: "Well, I've had enough of morons and half-wits, dolts, dunces, dullards and dumbbells. And you chowderhead yokel, you blithering hayseed, you've had enough of me?" (season 1, episode 4: "Rest in Pain"). In addition, Agent Rosenfield's use of an ad hominem attack makes us fallaciously infer that *he* is simply a misanthrope, when in fact, as he tells Sheriff Truman, he is a peaceful person who aspires to be like Gandhi and Martin Luther King Jr. (season 2, episode 10: "Coma").

The *slippery slope* is another fallacy often utilized regularly by people in their bad thinking. This fallacy happens when one inappropriately concludes that an unavoidable chain of events, ideas, or beliefs will follow from some initial event, idea, or belief and, thus, we should reject the initial event, idea, or belief. For an example of this, we can look at the end of *Wild at Heart*. When Sailor returns from serving a five-year-and-ten-month prison term for his part in the Big Tuna bank robbery, he rejects Lula and his six-year-old son, Pace (Glenn Walker Harris Jr.), believing that he will only bring them heartache: "I'm a robber and a man slaughterer and I haven't had any parental guidance. . . . I'm wild at heart." In his mind, it is best for his son and the woman he still loves to go on without him because he has falsely concluded that he is an irredeemable corrupting influence. He wants them to reject the idea of having him in their lives because only bad things will follow. All of a sudden we're at the bottom of the slope! To counter this fallacy, Lynch employs a fantastical deus ex machina, in keeping with the movie's *Wizard of Oz* motifs, and has Glinda the Good Witch (played by none other than Laura Palmer herself, Sheryl Lee) arrive in her bubble to counter Sailor's false conclusion with her contention that Lula loves him and that's all that matters. That he has just been mercilessly beaten by Marietta's thugs may have something to do with this rather hallucinogenic apparition, but Sailor is convinced. Regaining consciousness, he races back to Lula and Pace and they are reunited.

The End

In this essay, our goal was to explore Lynch's take on logic within his films. As we've seen, Lynch's characters don't always abide by the principles of correct reasoning and often operate in a world of fallacies, yet they usually find a way to function within their illogical worlds. Alvin Straight finds forgiveness and reconciliation with his brother Lyle in a poignant front-porch reunion after positively affecting the lives of many of those he meets on his seemingly absurd journey; after a bloody and vengeance-filled odyssey of their own, Sailor Ripley, Lula Pace, and their son find forgiveness in each other and live happily ever after under their self-made rainbow despite all the odds against them. However, Lynchian characters don't always get a stereotypical cinematic happy ending: Agent Cooper finds Laura Palmer's murderer (albeit in a place he never expected), then paradoxically *becomes* the murderer he sought as the evil Bob takes him over; Merrick's humanity is "saved" as he asserts himself and finds a measure of fulfillment in his friendships, books, and models, but nothing the physicians do can save his life, and he still dies as a result of his physical condition. Lynch films remind us that our world is not inherently logical—we impose logic upon it to make sense of the random and absurd happenings all around us and to create a sense (perhaps only the illusion of?) order out of chaos. Good people continue to die for no good reason, evil continues to exist, the French still eat snails, and the owls are not what they seem.

Notes

1. For further readings on logic, see Anthony Weston, *A Rulebook for Arguments* (Indianapolis: Hackett, 2000); Robert Johnson, *A Logic Book: Fundamentals of Reasoning* (Belmont, Calif.: Wadsworth, 2006); Patrick Hurley, *A Concise Introduction to Logic* (Belmont, Calif.: Wadsworth, 2006); and Gregory Bassham, William Irwin, Henry Nardone, and James M. Wallace, *Critical Thinking: A Student's Introduction* (New York: McGraw-Hill, 2004).

2. To explore Escher's aesthetics further, see the seminal, Pulitzer Prize–winning work by Douglas R. Hofstadter, *Gödel, Escher, Bach: An Eternal Golden Braid,* 20th anniversary ed. (New York: Basic Books, 1999); J. L. Locher, ed., *The Magic of M. C. Escher* (New York: Harry N. Abrams, 2000); and Doris Schattschneider, *M. C. Escher: Visions of Symmetry,* 2nd ed. (New York: Harry N. Abrams, 2004).

INTUITION AND INVESTIGATION INTO ANOTHER PLACE

The Epistemological Role of Dreaming in *Twin Peaks* and Beyond

Simon Riches

If there is one thing that viewers remember about David Lynch's hit ABC television series *Twin Peaks* (1990–1991), it is surely FBI Special Agent Dale Cooper's (Kyle MacLachlan) dream at the culmination of "Zen, or the Skill to Catch a Killer" (season 1, episode 2). Amid a succession of characters, Cooper encounters a dancing, backward-talking lounge-lizard dwarf in a strikingly vivid red room—an enigmatic figure known as the Man from Another Place (Michael J. Anderson). Among its multifarious array of imagery and wordplay, Cooper's dream supposedly held the answer to the series' enduring question: the mystery of who killed the severely troubled homecoming queen Laura Palmer (Sheryl Lee), who, as we discover in the pilot episode, was brutally murdered and left floating in a river, iconically wrapped in plastic.[1]

Understood in its wider context, this dream scene represents two themes that recur throughout Lynch's work: the nature of the *experience* that a person has while dreaming, often in comparison with the experience of waking, or "genuine," reality; and the idea of gaining knowledge through some form of investigation. Frequently employing a conventional crime narrative (though commonly subverted with supernatural themes), Lynch often presents characters searching for clues, accumulating evidence, and making inferences. This essay focuses on the philosophical context in which Lynch ties these forms of knowledge acquisition to dreaming. The idea of there being some underlying *meaning* to the dreams, as epitomized in Viennese founder of psychoanalysis Sigmund Freud's (1856–1939) theory of explicit or veiled wish fulfillment, will also be broached but will not be the central focus.[2]

Dreams and Investigation

Let us first consider the theme of dreaming. *Blue Velvet* (1986), *Twin Peaks*, *Twin Peaks: Fire Walk with Me* (1992), *Lost Highway* (1997), *Mulholland Dr.* (2001), and *Inland Empire* (2006) all cross the boundaries of the natural world in order to embrace otherworldly themes, appearing, to varying degrees, to occur in what one might think of as a "dream reality." This Lynchian distortion of our conventional understanding of the natural world tends to home in on a special, seemingly inaccessible location: a dream space (or "another place"), which gets perhaps its most vivid expression in *Twin Peaks*'s red room, a symbolic precursor to *Mulholland Dr.*'s Club Silencio; but it is also present in *Lost Highway*'s cabin and in the multiple spatial distortions—the switching of corridors and their adjacent rooms—in the *Inland Empire* house.[3]

Mulholland Dr., for instance, is commonly interpreted as consisting almost entirely of central character Diane Selwyn's (Naomi Watts) dream, one doubtlessly intended to represent genuine delusion in her waking life. A clue supporting this reading is provided in the mid-title-sequence point-of-view scene of an otherwise unidentified woman murmuring and then lowering herself onto a red pillow. Comparing this to another memorable Lynch scene, film critic Graham Fuller observes that "we need only recall the unconscious plunge into the severed ear of Jeffrey Beaumont (Kyle MacLachlan) in *Blue Velvet* to recognize this brief scene as a portal to a dream."[4] From this, one might judge that everyday objects, such as pillows and ears, function for Lynch as *portals* to a dream, whereas distinctively Lynchian constructions like the red room and the red-curtained Club Silencio—Lynchian in their aesthetics and their atmosphere—are symbolically representative of the dream as a whole.

On this reading of *Mulholland Dr.*, viewers are then unwittingly watching a dream rather than a tale representing the character's genuine reality; although, of course, the great strength of the film—as with so much of Lynch's work—lies in its ability to blur that distinction. The potency of blurring this dream/reality distinction is nowhere more apparent than in the arresting abruptness with which *Mulholland Dr.*'s Club Silencio singer

Rebekah Del Rio stops lip-synching (in stark contrast with *Blue Velvet*'s lip-synching performer Ben [Dean Stockwell], who is so *obviously* acting) and reveals to the audience—in this case, to both those characters observing *and* the film's viewers—a fact of which they were until now unaware: that her performance was *all* an act. "No hay banda!" Club Silencio MC (Geno Silva) repeats hypnotically, compounding the disorientation both on- and offscreen, breaking through what Fuller describes as "the dream fabric of the film," and highlighting "the fragility of cinema's hallucinating power."[5]

The Club Silencio revelation has a deeply distressing effect on audience member Betty Elms (Naomi Watts), the dreamed "version" of Diane. Awakened from the fiction of her idealized Hollywood life as an emerging starlet, staying in her affluent aunt's Hollywood apartment ("this dream place," as she remarks tellingly on her arrival), she is compelled to accept the deception of her dreamed experience. Like Cooper's dream, this revelation serves to generate profound change and convey an otherwise inaccessible truth. Just as Laura Palmer's murder could only be fully understood through dreams, Diane's true identity is revealed by the proceedings in Club Silencio.[6]

The second theme of investigation as a means of knowledge acquisition, where characters take the form of knowledge *seekers,* has long been of fascination to Lynch. Consider, for instance, *Blue Velvet*'s amateur investigator Jeffrey, and the collaborative efforts of friends Donna Hayward (Lara Flynn Boyle), James Hurley (James Marshall), and Laura's cousin Maddy Ferguson (Sheryl Lee) in *Twin Peaks,* as well as that of intimately connected strangers Betty Elms and Rita (Laura Elena Harring) in *Mulholland Dr.,* all of whom go to great lengths to uncover concealed information.

But whereas the investigation undertaken by *Blue Velvet*'s Jeffrey Beaumont (Kyle MacLachlan), for instance, involved gaining knowledge of facts about his surrounding environment, *Twin Peaks* is different because it directly combines investigation with dreams. The unconventional Cooper—a character that film writer Chris Rodley describes as "unique in the detective genre, because he uses his mind, his body and most importantly his intuition"—appears to gain knowledge through the red room's coded messages, information he then uses in his quest to discover Laura Palmer's killer.[7] In this regard, film writer Angela Hague observes that Cooper places trust in what she calls "the intuitive dimension of his unconscious," and, importantly, makes the point that "his use of intuition is what distinguishes him from both classical and hard-boiled versions of the detective."[8] Hague draws attention to the post-dream breakfast scene at the Great Northern Hotel, in which Cooper recalls to Sheriff Harry S. Truman (Michael Ontkean) and his receptionist and assistant Lucy Moran (Kimmy Robertson) his dreamed meeting with the Man from Another Place, who introduced his "cousin" Laura Palmer; and the images of demonic host characters BOB (Frank Silva) and MIKE, occupant of the one-armed man Phillip Gerard (Al Strobel). Comparing another dream from three years earlier about the plight of the Tibetan people, Cooper informed his stunned partners: "I awoke from the same dream realizing that I had subconsciously gained knowledge of a deductive technique involving mind-body coordination operating hand in hand with the deepest level of intuition." He believes that the red room dream holds the solution to the murder of Laura Palmer and interprets it as simply a code that needs to be broken. The phrase "crack the code, solve the crime" becomes Cooper's mantra, thus inverting Hague's stereotypical characterization of an altogether more conservative FBI agent.

Of course, Cooper is by no means the only Lynchian character who might be said to gain knowledge through dreams. One might also think, for example, of Henry Spencer's (Jack Nance) "Lady in the Radiator" nightmare in *Eraserhead* (1977); John Merrick's (John Hurt) haunting juxtaposition of childhood scenes with elephant imagery and sounds in *The Elephant Man* (1980); Paul Atreides' (Kyle MacLachlan) visionary dreams in *Dune* (1984); and the aforementioned dreamworld of Diane in *Mulholland Dr.* Yet *Twin Peaks*'s Cooper is a particularly interesting example because he is able to incorporate this seemingly supernatural ability for gaining knowledge—in the context of a genuinely mysterious murder case—within his otherwise strong capacity for considered reasoning and rational thought.

The area of philosophy that attempts to provide a theoretical understanding of human knowledge and knowledge acquisition is known as *epistemology*. While a conception of epistemology that involves knowledge gained through dreams may hold for the *Twin Peaks* universe, one might consider to what extent this Lynchian understanding of the relation between knowledge and dreaming presents a cogent understanding of how knowledge can be gained, at least as it is traditionally conceived in contemporary analytic philosophy.[9]

The term *analytic philosophy* tends to cover the exploits of philosophy mostly in Britain and the United States, predominantly in the twentieth and twenty-first centuries. Closely allied to scientific methodology, analytic philosophy has engendered a growing interdisciplinary trend toward *naturalism,* according to which the methodological boundary between traditional theoretical philosophy and the investigative work of empirical science is no longer clearly defined (or, on some particular versions of naturalism, it is held that philosophy is subservient to the discoveries of science). *Naturalism* is a widely and variously employed term, but, broadly understood, naturalists are generally skeptical of anything resembling the supernatural and believe that all phenomena can be explained through features of the natural world. So in the case of the specific epistemological question under discussion here, naturalists may be willing to grant that Cooper can gain knowledge about his surrounding environment by a variety of means, but they may question *how it is possible* to gain knowledge through dreams, or they may at least find it questionable unless a natural explanation is provided.[10]

Human Knowledge and Epistemology

As viewers of Lynch's work, we are frequently invited to decipher plot through coded messages delivered in the form of characters' dreams (or dreamlike experiences), but the example of Cooper reveals that there are also occasions where Lynch's characters themselves are required to examine their dreams as a way of gaining knowledge. This idea of there being a particular way or, more generally, various ways that knowledge can be gained is one studied by epistemologists. An understanding of this area of philosophy will therefore enable us to gain a deeper understanding of *Twin Peaks* because it raises an important epistemological question: Can evidence from dreams provide human beings with a legitimate way of gaining knowledge?

When considering this question, it is important to emphasize the distinction between gaining knowledge of the external world and gaining knowledge of one's own mental states. Freud's work on dream interpretation reveals how dreams might be understood as providing us with knowledge about ourselves, but this is not the central issue in *Twin Peaks*. Rather, what makes Cooper such an interesting character, and his method of detection so compelling, is the fact that dreams appear to provide him with knowledge of the world outside of his mind. For it seems plausible that dreams might provide us with knowledge of ourselves, but how dreams are supposed to provide us with knowledge of the world external to our minds seems to be a genuine mystery.

Authorities in a wide range of academic fields study the topic of human knowledge. It is of interest to psychologists, sociologists, anthropologists and linguists, to give just a few examples. Distinctively philosophical questions about human knowledge however are commonly arranged into those that consider the broadly *metaphysical* issue of the precise nature of *what we know* and those that consider the broadly *epistemological* issue of *how we know* what we know. Notice that the key words to identify on each side of this arrangement are *what* and *how*: when we consider the issue of *what we know*, we are addressing a question about *what* knowledge human beings possess or about *what* human beings can be truly said to know. The metaphysical task is generally held to account for the collected body of human knowledge. The epistemological issue of *how we know what we know*, on the other hand, considers *how* the knowledge possessed by human beings is acquired: how people come to know—and continue to know—the things that they know.

The idea of *how we know* in a given case of knowledge might be termed the *way of knowing*. So in any single instance of a person's knowledge—for example, a proposition that the person knows—analysis of the way of knowing reveals *how* the person knows the proposition of which he or she has knowledge. Note that when I refer to a person's knowledge, I am exclusively concerned with what philosophers call *propositional knowledge,* rather than *practical knowledge.* Propositional knowledge, as it is often put, is knowledge *that* rather than knowledge *how.* So the fact that Cooper knows *that* Laura Palmer is dead is an example of his propositional knowledge, whereas the fact that he knows *how* to operate the tape-recording machine in his continual updates to his never-seen assistant Diane is an example of his practical knowledge. As the contemporary British philosopher Crispin Wright puts it, propositional knowledge is "knowledge of truths," where "truths" simply means "true propositions," and so is not the kind of knowledge one might associate with practical know-how.[11]

So how should we understand such ways of knowing, where they pertain specifically to true propositions like "Laura Palmer is dead"? We might begin by saying that if a person knows something, then there is a *specific way* in which they know. Another contemporary British philosopher, Quassim Cassam, has a way of articulating this idea. On his formulation of the issue, a question with regard to how a person *comes to know* a given proposition *p* is "a question about the *source* of his knowledge or his *route* to the knowledge that *p*."[12]

In the pilot episode of *Twin Peaks,* consider how Cooper comes to know that Laura's secret boyfriend, James Hurley, was at the picnic recorded in the home movie. He *sees* the reflection of his motorcycle in the camera lens. Consider how Cooper connects Laura's murder to that of Teresa Banks (Pamela Gidley). He *remembers* the letter inserted under the fingernail in the Banks murder case. *Seeing that p* or *remembering that p* may therefore be specific *ways* of *knowing that p*. This methodological approach highlights a person's knowing that *p* in a specific instance and, by association, the specific way by which one knows that *p*.

To fully explain specific ways of knowing, we might need to understand how it is *possible* to gain the kind of knowledge that is possessed. Questions that ask how a certain kind of knowledge is possible are epistemological examples of what Cassam calls "how-possible questions." Of course, questions of the "how is it possible?" variety need not apply exclusively to knowledge. It is feasible to ask, "How is it possible?" on a range of topics. "How is it possible that Ronette Pulowski (Phoebe Augustine) managed to escape?" and "How is it possible for Audrey Horne (Sherilyn Fenn) to work at One-Eyed Jacks?" are examples of nonepistemological how-possible questions. And, as Cassam observes, how-possible questions imply an *obstacle* to the possibility of the deed in question.

So epistemologists may ask how it is possible to gain a particular kind of knowledge. Of course, there are various ways of knowing, and there may be many ways to know a single proposition. We are not limited to just *seeing* and *remembering*. The contemporary American philosopher Alvin Goldman articulates the point in terms of what he calls "pathways to knowledge": "I do not conceive of knowledge as being attained by just a single pathway, or even a handful of pathways, but by a wide variety of sometimes independent and sometimes interconnected pathways. The upshot is that epistemology, by my lights, is not a narrow subject but a highly rich and diversified subject."[13]

Imagine the many ways that a person might gain knowledge. From the brain-wracking remembering of *Mulholland Dr.*'s amnesiac Rita, to the surreptitious seeing and hearing of *Blue Velvet*'s wardrobe spy Jeffrey, accounting for these many pathways is a large and complex project beyond the scope of any single essay. However, epistemologists throughout the history of philosophy have invoked the role of *experience* in connection with understanding how knowledge is gained. They argue that whether it is gained in a way that is either dependent on or independent of experience is of crucial importance when classifying types of knowledge.[14]

In the next section, we consider how the epistemological role of dreaming in *Twin Peaks* might seem at odds with this model founded on experience and how this in turn raises important philosophical questions about the nature of the dreaming experience. This should then serve to highlight the fact that gaining knowledge of the world outside of one's mind through dreams is a particularly mysterious idea.

Knowledge, Experience, and Dreams

Cooper vows to solve the crime by cracking the code. The code acts as a kind of obstacle to his knowledge of the killer. How then can he gain access to that knowledge? Consider MIKE's poetic coded message heard in Cooper's dream:

> Through the darkness
> Of future past
> The magician longs to see.
> One chants out between two worlds
> FIRE
> Walk with me.

Academic film writer and well-known Lynch scholar Martha Nochimson provides this analysis of the poem: "The magician is Cooper. The heart of detection is the magic of boundary crossing. Cooper's longing to see the One (BOB) who "chants out between two worlds" will enable him to cross the limits of the ordinary world into the darkness where future and past conflate."[15] Perhaps the most obvious reason that Nochimson views Cooper as the magician is his special ability to gain some kind of intuitive access into the supernatural red room dreamworld. Cooper seems to have a capacity for intuition that allows him, like BOB, to cross the limits of the ordinary, natural world—in MIKE's poetic phrase, to "chant out between two worlds"—into the red room world of his dream. Given Cooper's *reliance* on this apparent capacity for intuition, Angela Hague writes: "Clearly, Twin Peaks is not the place for viewers in search of brilliant logical deductions, high-tech forensics, and comforting rational solutions. Cooper's unorthodox crime-solving techniques, which include clairvoyance, precognitive and 'shared' dreams, visions, and an obsession with Tibetan Buddhism, not only violate traditional ratiocinative detection but also generally fail to provide any real solutions to the 'crimes'; as discussed earlier, his revelations more frequently lead to a set of larger, more unanswerable questions."[16]

Although correct to highlight the unorthodoxy in Cooper's crime-solving techniques, Hague's analysis seems to unfairly misconstrue Cooper's overall approach. In many ways, with his Jimmy Stewart-esque enthusiasm and predilection for the plain facts, Cooper recalls *Blue Velvet*'s Jeffrey, who accumulates evidence solely through observation and who literally acts out his boyishly earnest exclamation to love interest Sandy Williams (Laura Dern) that "there are opportunities in life for gaining knowledge and experience."[17]

Cooper and Jeffrey are alike in their natural propensity for inquisitiveness and willingness to investigate a mystery. After all, Cooper does his research on the facts available from his experience of the surrounding environment. With no assisting visual aid, Cooper is able to recall Leo Johnson's (Eric Da Re) entire list of felonies when he and Sheriff Truman initially question the trucker outside his home. And Cooper is hugely perceptive with regard to the body language of people he barely knows. He immediately recognizes the romantic involvements between Big Ed Hurley (Everett McGill) and Norma Jennings (Peggy Lipton), and between Sheriff Truman and Josie Packard (Joan Chen)—relationships that, like so much in the town of Twin Peaks, were being kept secret.

The important point is that Cooper is not constrained in his investigative abilities. Other Lynchian "detectives" like *Blue Velvet*'s Jeffrey—much like *Twin Peaks*'s Donna, James, and Maddy, who go in search of Laura's secret tapes and secret diary; as well as *Mulholland Dr.*'s Betty and Rita, who scour the newspaper and break into an apartment searching for information—are limited by the fact that they can only consult the facts presented to them in their worldly experience: what philosophers refer to as *empirical facts*. Cooper stands apart from them in this regard. He seems to have an intuitive capacity for gaining knowledge in a special way that they lack, a way not solely dependent on the facts of his worldly experience. After all, if the red room is not of this world, and Cooper is able to gain knowledge through his dreamed visits there, then his knowledge does not straightforwardly seem to depend on experience of worldly facts, even if it is dependent on a kind of experience.

With this in mind, let us further consider how this idea of experience has figured in standard epistemological thinking about human knowledge. On the standard view, the category of *empirical* (or experiential, or a posteriori) *knowledge* is diametrically opposed to that of *a priori knowledge*. Empirical ways of knowing *depend* upon the worldly experience of the person, and a priori ways of knowing are *independent* of such experience. A paradigm species of empirical ways of knowing is the category of perceptual ways of knowing (since perceptual experience is one sort of experience). Subspecies of perceptual ways of knowing include visual and auditory ways of knowing.

Many philosophers think that some knowledge is based on experience in this way, and that there are other kinds of knowledge that do not seem to be. These kinds of knowledge are deemed nonempirical, or a priori. Clearly perceptual ways of knowing are not suitable routes to a priori knowledge. Instead, philosophers tend to think of mathematical knowledge and knowledge of basic principles of logic as a priori. The basic idea is that this kind of knowledge can be gained purely by our powers of intellection, solely by working it out in our minds, and without consulting worldly experience.[18]

In the context of this distinction, consider the kind of introspective knowledge that Cooper gains when reflecting on his own life, for instance, the thought—subsequently tape-recorded for his assistant Diane—that he would like to purchase real estate in Twin Peaks. Consider also the fact that Cooper comes to know that Laura worked at One-Eyed Jacks because Audrey told him so. And consider again his memory of the Teresa Banks case that enabled him to connect the two murders. How should these kinds of knowledge be classified? Traditionally, introspective knowledge and knowledge gained by testimony or memory are empirical because in different ways, it has been claimed, introspection, testimony, and memory may be said to depend on the experiences of the person, albeit—in these cases—experiences not directly involving perception.

Against this background of how the notion of experience has aided classification of types of knowledge, some epistemologists argue that perception and introspection may count as legitimate means of knowledge acquisition by virtue of being reliable mechanisms. Though these mechanisms are potentially fallible, we can still rely on them to produce knowledge the vast majority of the time. A criterion like reliability has proven useful to epistemologists in deciding which mechanisms count, and which do not count, as legitimate ways of gaining knowledge. On this model, there would be acceptance granted to ways of knowing that proved reliable, and skepticism extended to ways of knowing that proved unreliable.

The notion of experience has brought about certain difficulties for the conception of knowledge sketched here. Some commentators argue that memory and introspection represent borderline cases. After all, although one might argue that there is a kind of experiential input in memory, there also seems to be a sense in which such knowledge is gained purely through thought and without consulting any further experience. In addition, although some philosophers claim that introspective ways of knowing depend on a kind of *inner* experience, this seems to be in stark contrast to many of our paradigm cases of empirical knowledge, which depend on what may be loosely dubbed "outer experience"—experience of the external world, such as perceptual experience.

The contemporary American philosophers Paul Boghossian and Laurence BonJour take opposing views over this issue. According to Boghossian, the divide between experiential and nonexperiential places inner experience on the a priori side. Boghossian has "always found it natural to regard a priori knowledge as encompassing knowledge that is based on no experience as well as knowledge that is based purely on *inner* experience."[19] BonJour disagrees. He argues that introspective knowledge is a species of empirical knowledge: "The justification of introspective knowledge pertaining to one's own states of mind should surely count as empirical, as should . . . knowledge of past events deriving, via memory, from previous episodes of perception." He goes on to consider the legitimacy of more unusual cases: "Moreover, if it should turn out (surprisingly) that there is genuine knowledge that results from parapsychological or extrasensory capacities such as telepathy and clairvoyance, it seems apparent that its justification should also count as empirical, and not a priori, from the standpoint of the traditional distinction."[20]

Evidently a clearer understanding of this issue depends on how we understand the notion of experience. Perhaps BonJour might categorize Cooper's dreaming experience along with telepathy and clairvoyance and claim that it qualifies as a kind of inner experience. On this model, it could be argued that Cooper's knowledge gained through his dreams is a species of empirical knowledge. Yet it is clear that a philosopher like Boghossian models his category of the empirical on worldly experience. On this model, knowledge gained through dreams—like that gained by telepathy and clairvoyance—might be more strongly aligned with the category of the a priori.

Perhaps this issue is complicated further still by the visions of BOB experienced by Maddy, Laura's mother Sarah Palmer (Grace Zabriskie), and—as we later find out in the prequel *Twin Peaks: Fire Walk with Me*— Laura herself, where it is unclear whether the visions are of genuine worldly experience or are figments of these characters' imaginations. In this case, we face philosophical questions about what constitutes a genuine worldly experience and what is merely imagined, and about the possibility of discerning such different experiences.

Though classifying knowledge according to experience might be "partly a matter of tradition," as Cassam claims, a fully satisfying account of the a priori/empirical distinction would endeavor to go beyond some of the approximations clearly employed in this field. Perhaps Cassam's view that "the notion of an experiential way of knowing can no more be defined than that of experience itself" is correct. But, as he continues, "This doesn't mean that we have no idea whether it applies in particular cases. Intuitively, seeing or feeling that a particular cup is chipped are paradigmatically experiential ways of knowing that the cup is chipped, whereas calculating that $68 + 57 = 125$ is a paradigmatically nonexperiential way of knowing that $68 + 57 = 125$. The appropriate classification of other cases depends on their similarities to these paradigms. So, for example, if we don't know whether to classify introspection as an experiential or nonexperiential source of knowledge, that is because it seems to fall somewhere between the paradigms."[21] So we do have paradigm cases to work with, and, despite the skepticism ordinarily extended to unconventional ways of knowing such as telepathy and clairvoyance, *Twin Peaks* seems to represent Cooper's dreaming as a reliable mechanism for knowledge. But the dreaming experience on which Cooper's knowledge depends certainly seems to be situated somewhere—in Cassam's words—between the paradigms. How then are we to explain this kind of experience and its relation to the empirical/a priori distinction in order to further understand this way of knowing?

The Lynchian Dreaming Experience

Suggesting adherence to a curious brand of subjectivity, *Lost Highway*'s Fred Madison (Bill Pullman)—discussing his aversion to video cameras with two Los Angeles detectives—remarks, "I like to remember things my own way." Fred's ensuing breakdown into madness, much like Diane's in *Mulholland Dr.* and Laura Palmer's as depicted during her last seven days in *Twin Peaks: Fire Walk with Me*, is brought about because he can no longer distinguish a seeming reality from a genuine one.[22]

Twin Peaks, like *Mulholland Dr.*, employs dreams as the vehicle to pose questions about the nature of reality. In a striking scene from *Twin Peaks: Fire Walk with Me*, the missing, seemingly in limbo FBI Special Agent Philip Jeffries (David Bowie) briefly returns to headquarters before disappearing again, leaving behind the message "We live inside a dream." Jeffries' message and his mysteriously unclear location, seemingly outside of the natural world, tie dreams to the supernatural. This scene recalls a question posed by Donna to Harold, in *Twin Peaks*'s "The Orchid's Curse" (season 2, episode 5), when, like her best friend, Laura, Donna begins to fall under his spell. "How do we know that our dreams are not real?" she inquires, raising a serious philosophical question about their perceived reality.[23]

In his explanation of how Lynch playfully distorts basic facts about our experience in order to conflate the categories of genuine reality and dreams, Greg Hainge cites Lynch's "deliberate obfuscation and contravention of logic at the diegetic level" and likens Lynch to the artist Francis Bacon (1909–1992) in the sense that his "aesthetic vision fractures narrative."[24] Much as in the knowingly unreal universe of *Twin Peaks*, evidence throughout *Blue Velvet*—from the exaggerated coloration, the slow-motion fire interludes, and the subversive narrative—supports Hainge's contention that we are clearly in an "artificial realm."[25] This is made apparent when Jeffrey appears to awaken (from a dream?)—the camera retracting from his ear—toward the end of the film. With an obviously artificial robin eating the unpleasant bugs, has Sandy's dream of love finally, though somewhat unconventionally, come true, heralding in this moment (though clearly satirically) what the British writer J. G. Ballard calls "a return to morality"?[26]

In various respects becoming the soap opera that it first endeavored to satirize (no more so than in the serial-within-serial *Invitation to Love*), the supposedly postmodernist dreamlike unreality of *Twin Peaks* reached farcical levels by the culmination of season 2. In the Lynch-directed final episode, "Beyond Life and Death" (season 2, episode 22), various characters are needlessly killed off in freakish events. Audrey, Pete Martell (Jack Nance), Andrew Packard (Dan O'Herlihy), and two bank workers are apparently blown up in an underhanded revenge attack from beyond the grave by Andrew's old nemesis Thomas Eckhardt (David Warner); and Donna's father, Dr. William Hayward (Warren Frost), appears to accidentally kill roguish tycoon Benjamin Horne (Richard Beymer), following the bizarre revelation that Ben is actually Donna's father.[27]

Like several plot strands in the second season, all this was entirely superfluous to the main thrust of the story line and to the culmination of the series: the search for the Black Lodge, which was ultimately discovered as the location of the red room from Cooper's dream. This quest, which so intrigued *Twin Peaks* enthusiasts, was eventually realized with the discovery of the Black Lodge at a temporal location in Glastonbury Grove. The evidently mysterious and magical Black Lodge, or "the dwelling place of spirits," in

Deputy Hawk's (Michael Horse) words, does much to substantiate Jeffries' hazily asserted juxtaposition of dreams with the supernatural.

Despite certain superficial similarities between *Twin Peaks* and *Blue Velvet*—both depict idyllic scenes of lumber-town suburbia concealing sinister forces beneath the surface—there is a crucial difference. Fearsome as he might be, *Blue Velvet*'s Frank Booth (Dennis Hopper) is just a man. As Rodley observes, "the new element" in *Twin Peaks* is "that evil is not even of this world. It literally comes from beyond."[28]

Central to this idea of evil located in the beyond is the distinction between our genuine experience and the dreaming experience. Discussing the moving picture sequence in *Twin Peaks: Fire Walk with Me* when Laura enters the framed photograph on her wall, Nicholas Rombes argues that understanding the Lynchian dreaming experience demands acceptance of contradictions and impossibilities.[29] Cooper's dreaming experience constitutes an entry into another world: the dreamworld of the red room. It could be argued that this world exists in a nonphysical location. Some philosophers are skeptical about the existence of such nonphysical realms. As naturalists, many analytic philosophers are skeptical of anything that is not part of the natural world or that could not be explained in natural terms. But the *Twin Peaks* universe evidently countenances such apparently questionable supernatural phenomena. Cooper *is* able to cross the two worlds and gain intuitive insight into this apparently existent nonphysical realm. But in order to further understand the explanatory issue of *how it is possible* to gain knowledge in this way—a way of knowing that depends on Cooper's experience of the dream reality—we might consider how this fits within the a priori/empirical distinction.

The dreaming experience in *Twin Peaks* is not experience of worldly facts. It is a supernatural experience of the supposed facts of an otherworldly nonphysical realm. So it does not seem to be empirical in Boghossian's sense. On his view, it would seem to be a priori, although it would certainly not be one of the paradigm cases of a priori knowledge. BonJour might ally the dreaming experience with the experience involved in telepathy and clairvoyance, in which case he may therefore classify it as empirical, although of course its association with such dubious means to knowledge would lead to questions about its legitimacy. One might take Cassam's view that the dreaming experience places knowledge gained through dreams between the paradigms, although even this view may be further complicated by the apparently fluctuating nature of Cooper's dreaming experience. After all, he does eventually manage to physically travel to the Black Lodge, a place he at first only visited in his dreams. We are left to wonder how we should understand the notion of experience given this fact.

Knowledge, Intuition, and Naturalism

In a humorous scene in *Twin Peaks*'s "Zen, or the Skill to Catch a Killer" (season 1, episode 2), Cooper proceeds to display a deductive technique involving throwing rocks at bottles while the names of potential murder suspects are announced, a technique that he explains is drawn from his understanding of the plight of the Tibetan people. Cooper accepts the answers that this technique yields without question, suggesting his faith in its reliability.

There can be no doubt that Cooper is an extremely spiritual character. In "Arbitrary Law" (season 2, episode 9), during the final moments of Leland Palmer's (Ray Wise) life, as he confesses to Laura's murder and explains how BOB possessed him as a young boy, Cooper urges Leland to move "into the light" and acts as his spiritual guide. As Nochimson writes, "this scene . . . is a crystalline visual, emotional, and narrative realization of Cooper's Tibetan Method."[30] Cooper is unrelenting in his commitment to such abilities, and to their cogency, and the *Twin Peaks* universe appears to justify this confidence. It is with this degree of spirituality that Cooper trusts the special capacity for intuition that allows him to gain knowledge through his dreams.

One of the problems that might be raised by analytic philosophers is the lack of empirical evidence that such a faculty of intuition exists. Take the related worry with regard to intuition-based explanations of a priori knowledge, where such explanations have sometimes gone by the name *rational insight*. Without further evidence of its existence, such a special faculty is deemed mysterious. Perhaps Boghossian puts the point best in the following passage: "The single most influential consideration against rational insight theories can be stated quite simply: no one has been able to explain—clearly enough—in what an act of rational insight could intelligibly consist. . . . If the theory of rational insight is to serve as a genuine explanation for how we are able to have a priori knowledge, rather than simply acting as a placeholder for such an explanation, it must consist in more than a suggestive label; it must somehow lay bare, in appropriate detail, how some capacity that we have gets to work on the properties we are able to think about so as to disclose their natures."[31] This criticism focuses on the issue of explanations. It does not question whether it is really possible to gain knowledge in the proposed way. Rather, it questions the proposed explanation for how it is possible to gain knowledge in this way. Some analytic philosophers are skeptical about intuition-based explanations, querying the degree to which these explanations satisfy our need to understand the way of knowing in question.

Much like the supposed objective existence of a nonphysical dreamworld, it is in this sense that Cooper's special intuitive insight into the dream reality makes *Twin Peaks* appear at odds with the naturalistic trend in analytic philosophy. And yet several *Twin Peaks* inhabitants—perhaps most notably the Log Lady (Catherine E. Coulson), Major Garland Briggs, and Hawk—hold the unshakeable belief that there is something out there in the woods, some mysterious force that makes *Twin Peaks* such a special place; and as we discover in season 2, Major Briggs's Air Force–related research substantiates this fact. But, despite this level of belief, for a clearer understanding of Cooper's abilities we would still require a more thorough explanation of how he is able to gain knowledge in this way. Compounding this point, potential critics may also have reason to emphasize the criterion of reliability. Analytic philosophers have frequently observed how in the history of philosophy supposed insights and intuitions have frequently been proven wrong; and so any purported intuition-based way of knowing must be subject to intense scrutiny with regard to its reliability.

So some analytic philosophers might argue that intuition is an unreliable mechanism for knowledge, that intuitions do not possess the degree of reliability that we associate with perception, for example. Again, the apparent reliability of Cooper's intuitions in *Twin Peaks* does seem to present a different conception of epistemology, one where intuition does reliably yield knowledge but only for those with Cooper's special cognitive capacities. In fact, the verbal cues of the Man from Another Place in the red room dream—the chewing gum coming back in style, the fact that Laura's arms sometimes bend back, and the fact that there's always music in the air—all prove crucial in Cooper's finally solving the murder.

Notes

I would like to thank Sophie Archer, Gareth Fitzgerald, Anna Ferguson, Craig French, Jill Riches, David Tait, and especially the volume editors Bill Devlin and Shai Biderman for helpful comments and suggestions on earlier drafts.

   1. Originally unnamed, the *Twin Peaks* episodes were given titles by German

television, which have subsequently been widely employed. I adopt that convention throughout this essay, adding the series and episode numbers in parentheses.

2. See Sigmund Freud, *The Interpretation of Dreams* (Hertfordshire: Wordsworth, 1997).

3. Its status as a symbolic precursor is supported by fan speculation about an unnamed woman in Club Silencio who bears a significant resemblance to Laura Palmer (who after her death appears to reside in the Black Lodge). In terms of the unity between the Lynchian dream spaces, consider also the external similarity between *Blue Velvet's* Slow Club, as seen on Jeffrey's second visit (when Frank is also present), and Club Silencio.

4. Graham Fuller, "Babes in Babylon," *Sight and Sound* (December 2001): 14.

5. Ibid., 16.

6. What makes the Club Silencio scene so compelling is its capacity to represent Diane's self-deception through our own susceptibility to illusion and deception. We are repeatedly told that everything in Club Silencio is an illusion, and yet the incredible power and apparent authenticity of Rebekah Del Rio's performance still manages to deceive us. Earlier in *Mulholland Dr.*, the complexity of this dream/reality distinction is further compounded in an apparently extraneous scene. Two peripheral characters discuss a dream about a hideous man behind Winkie's diner, in which they are sitting. Following this recollection, the two characters then unwittingly enact the dream with apparently fatal consequences, seemingly rendering it true via its recollection. Understood as a segment of Diane's dream, this scene symbolizes (in her dream reality) her own later moment of realization in Club Silencio—a further level on which Lynch employs the notion of dreaming to induce reflection on the nature of the reality with which we are presented.

7. Chris Rodley, ed., *Lynch on Lynch*, rev. ed. (London: Faber and Faber, 2005), 169. This feature is certainly what made Cooper original, but it is worth noting that this idea has been developed in Johnny To's *Sun taam* (*Mad Detective*, 2007).

8. Angela Hague, "Infinite Games: The Derationalization of Detection in *Twin Peaks*," in *Full of Secrets: Critical Approaches to Twin Peaks*, ed. David Lavery (Detroit: Wayne State University Press, 1995), 136.

9. For an excellent introduction to epistemology, see Duncan Pritchard, *What Is This Thing Called Knowledge?* (Oxon: Routledge, 2006).

10. For further reading on naturalism, see David Papineau, "Naturalism," *Stanford Encyclopedia of Philosophy*, February 22, 2007, http://plato.stanford.edu/entries/naturalism/.

11. Crispin Wright, "Intuition, Entitlement and the Epistemology of Logical Laws," *Dialectica* 58, no. 1 (2004): 156. For the knowledge *how*/knowledge *that* distinction, see Gilbert Ryle, *The Concept of Mind* (London: Penguin, 2000). For a recent challenge to this distinction, see Jason Stanley and Timothy Williamson, "Knowing How," *Journal of Philosophy* 98, no. 8 (2001). For general reading on propositions, see Mathew McGrath, "Propositions," *Stanford Encyclopedia of Philosophy*, May 29, 2007, http://plato.stanford.edu/entries/propositions/.

12. Quassim Cassam, *The Possibility of Knowledge* (Oxford: Oxford University Press, 2007), 5, my italics.

13. Alvin I. Goldman, *Pathways to Knowledge* (New York: Oxford University Press, 2002), xi.

14. In fact, this classification in terms of experience is one of the central issues according to which philosophers have drawn the traditional distinction between *rationalism* and *empiricism*. For further reading on rationalism, see the writings of Descartes (1596–1650), Spinoza (1632–1677) and Leibniz (1646–1716). See Laurence BonJour, *In Defense of Pure Reason* (Cambridge: Cambridge University Press, 1998); and Christopher Peacocke, *The Realm of Reason* (Oxford: Oxford University Press, 2005) for a contemporary defense of rationalism. For further reading on empiricism, see the writings of Locke (1632–1704), Berkeley (1685–1753), and Hume (1711–1776); and in the twentieth century, the logical positivists of the Vienna Circle. See A. J. Ayer, *Language, Truth and Logic* (London: Penguin, 2001) for a well-known expression and defense of the logical positivist view.

15. Martha P. Nochimson, "Desire under the Douglas Firs: Entering the Body of Reality in *Twin Peaks*," in *Full of Secrets: Critical Approaches to Twin Peaks*, ed. David Lavery (Detroit: Wayne State University Press, 1995), 148.

16. Hague, "Infinite Games: The Derationalization of Detection in Twin Peaks," 136.

17. It is in this scene of *Blue Velvet* that Jeffrey relays the details of his stakeout to Sandy. As in *Mulholland Dr.*, *Twin Peaks*, and elsewhere, Lynchian characters so often seem to hatch plans and discuss their investigations in those iconically American diner booths.

18. For further reading on a priori knowledge, see the collected articles in Paul K. Moser, ed., *A Priori Knowledge* (Oxford: Oxford University Press, 1987); and in Paul Boghossian and Christopher Peacocke, eds., *New Essays on the A Priori* (Oxford: Clarendon Press, 2000).

19. Paul A. Boghossian, "Analyticity," in *A Companion to the Philosophy of Language*, ed. Crispin Wright and Bob Hale (Oxford: Blackwell, 1997), 363n.

20. BonJour, *In Defense of Pure Reason*, 7–8.

21. Cassam, *The Possibility of Knowledge*, 189, 209.

22. For discussion of contemporary debates about skepticism, see Duncan Pritchard, "Recent Work on Radical Skepticism," *American Philosophical Quarterly* 39 (2002).

23. With season 2's emphasis on the search for the Black Lodge and the twin exploits of Major Garland Briggs (Don S. Davis) and Windom Earle (Kenneth Welsh), *Twin Peaks* spawned a succession of television programs, from *The X-Files* (1993–2002) to *Lost* (2004–2010), preoccupied with the paranormal. Rather than straightforwardly sci-fi, like *Star Trek* (1966–) and its spin-offs, for example, these programs specifically exploited the idea that our everyday reality might be other than it appears (see Rodley, ed., *Lynch on Lynch*, 184, for his discussion with Lynch on this aspect of his work).

24. Greg Hainge, "Weird or Loopy? Specular Spaces, Feedback and Artifice in *Lost*

Highway's Aesthetics of Sensation," in *The Cinema of David Lynch: American Dreams, Nightmare Visions*, ed. Erica Sheen and Annette Davison (London and New York: Wallflower Press, 2004), 142.

25. Ibid., 137.

26. J. G. Ballard, "Blue Velvet," in his *A User's Guide to the Millennium: Essays and Reviews* (London: HarperCollins, 1996). It is in this short article that Ballard famously called *Blue Velvet* "the best film of the 1980s" and drew attention to its Oedipal aspects. With regard to the exaggerated coloration and subversive narrative, one might also view *Twin Peaks* as an ancestor of TV shows like *Desperate Housewives* (2004–).

27. This scene also includes the brief and bizarre reappearance of Ben's wife. Throughout much of season 2, one could be forgiven for forgetting that Ben is even married. Film writer Thomas Caldwell claims that, disenchanted with the show, Lynch set out to punish it by killing off characters (see his "David Lynch," *The Senses of Cinema* [May 2002], online).

28. Rodley, ed., *Lynch on Lynch*, 178. Depending on whether one reads *Blue Velvet* as one of the dream films, Rodley's claim may be worth further consideration. Just as *Mulholland Dr.*'s Louise Bonner (Lee Grant) might be said to exist both inside and outside the dreamworld (her dialogue seems particularly pertinent when understood from outside the dream: "someone is in trouble, something bad is happening") and just as Rita seems to dream of Club Silencio within Diane's dream (she even seems to conjure up its existence within the dream with her waking cries of "Silencio! Silencio!"), there is evidence in *Blue Velvet* that Frank is another character who traverses both the dreamworld and real world as an accentuated aspect of Jeffrey's character. One of the most significant aspects of *Blue Velvet* is that Frank's violence to Dorothy Vallens (Isabella Rossellini) is replicated by Jeffrey. Then, later, with characteristic menace and intensity, Frank says to Jeffrey, "You're like me," before sparing his life. Perhaps there is a sense in which Frank steps forth from the dream and reveals his relationship with Jeffrey when he recites the Roy Orbison lines: "In dreams I walk with you/In dreams I talk to you/In dreams you're mine/All of the time." For an interesting discussion of this relationship, in the context of an account of Lynch's portrayal of evil, see the final section of David Foster Wallace, "David Lynch Keeps His Head," in his *A Supposedly Fun Thing I'll Never Do Again: Essays and Arguments* (London: Abacus, 2009).

29. Nicholas Rombes, "*Blue Velvet* Underground: David Lynch's Post-Punk Poetics," in *The Cinema of David Lynch: American Dreams, Nightmare Visions*, ed. Erica Sheen and Annette Davison (London and New York: Wallflower Press, 2004), 72.

30. Nochimson, "Desire under the Douglas Firs: Entering the Body of Reality in *Twin Peaks*," 155.

31. Paul A. Boghossian, "Inference and Insight," *Philosophy and Phenomenological Research* 63, no. 3 (2001): 635.

THE HORRORS OF LIFE'S HIDDEN MYSTERIES

Blue Velvet

Sander H. Lee

Many of us are lucky enough to live ordinary, comfortable lives untouched by the violence and disasters we hear about on the news. But what if there exists a horrific, violent, and evil reality hiding just below the surface of even the most seemingly secure lives? After the events of 9/11, Americans need no convincing that normal life can be shattered in an instant and that nowhere is completely safe. David Lynch's 1986 film *Blue Velvet*, which he wrote as well as directed, shows us that there is, and always will be, a frighteningly violent and sleazy underside to human life.

What Lies Just Beneath the Surface

Lynch communicates these underlying themes in the film's opening sequence. The credits appear against the backdrop of a heavy curtain of blue velvet while Angelo Badalamenti's haunting music plays, the screen dissolves to solid blue and then to roses wavering in the wind before a white picket fence. The color is lush and vivid, reminiscent of the rich colors we tend to associate with films shot in the 1950s. The combination of color and music is reminiscent of great films like *Rear Window* (1954) and *Vertigo* (1958) directed by Alfred Hitchcock with their unforgettable scores composed by Bernard Herrmann. This nostalgic motif continues as we hear Bobby Vinton's 1963 original version of the song *Blue Velvet* and see slow-motion scenes of a small American town, including children crossing the street and a bright red fire truck complete with a waving fireman and his traditional Dalmatian dog. We next see a middle-aged man (Jeffrey Harvey) watering the lawn of his typical middle-class small town home while his wife sits on the sofa in the living room watching a TV screen filled with the image of a hand holding a gun.[1]

Suddenly, the man's water hose becomes tangled and, as he turns his head to discover the cause of the stoppage of water, some form of stoppage within himself strikes him. He grabs his neck and collapses to the ground. The hose, now untangled, spurts a fountain of water from which a frolicking puppy drinks, while an infant happily dances near the apparently lifeless body of the man. The camera now dramatically moves away from this scene and into a clump of grass on the lawn. Suddenly, where once there was silence, we hear a buzzing sound that gets louder and louder. At first, we have trouble identifying the picture and the sound, but soon we realize that we are watching a swarm of large, disgusting black bugs feeding and fighting among themselves. This image dissolves and the movie's story begins.

Ostensibly, the purpose of this opening scene is to explain the return of the stricken man's son, Jeffrey Beaumont (Kyle MacLachlan), to his hometown of Lumberton. Jeffrey has left home to attend college, but is called back because of his father's sudden illness. However, much more is communicated in these opening shots. Indeed, we are presented with the film's basic themes. While these themes may be associated with more than one worldview, they share many elements of the philosophy of Arthur Schopenhauer (1788–1860). Schopenhauer believed that everything that exists is a manifestation of a force he calls *the Will*. This Will is fundamentally spontaneous and irrational. There is only one Will, and it pervades all reality while determining every action. By making these claims, Schopenhauer is opposing his philosophy to those of Immanuel Kant (1724–1804) and G. W. F. Hegel (1770–1831), the most influential German thinkers of his time. For Kant, the inner Will is rational. By following our common intuition of duty (which derives from the Will), all of us are freely able to act morally. In Hegel, this force becomes an all-encompassing rational spirit that drives human history progressively toward a better, more moral future. Schopenhauer reacts negatively to such optimism. Turning these ideas upside down, Schopenhauer's Will is made up of our worst impulses, the irresistible violent and sexual drives that most of us try to hide behind a veneer of civility. These impulses are evil and overpowering. While we like to pretend that we are strong enough to overcome these instincts through rational action, the sad truth is that we can never escape their grip. The most we can do is lie to ourselves that all is well when we know in our hearts that it is not.[2]

   In the opening scene, we see that humanity attempts to pretend that life is beautiful, serene, purposeful, and happy. The little town wears a facade of bright colors and smiling faces that conceal the truth. In fact, for Schopenhauer, human life, like all animal life, is best characterized by a senseless brutality, by nature's seemingly uncaring processes of violence, illness, and death. The puppy and child happily frolic in the presence of the stricken man while bugs fight and die in the endless struggle for existence. Humans try to hide these sordid truths through happy fantasies of religion and love, but, in fact, we are powerless to control the savage forces of nature, forces that exist not only outside of us but also in our very essence as human animals. We pretend that human nature is fundamentally caring and good, but the reality is that we are secretly fascinated by the barbaric and the violent. Thus, our feeble attempts to impose rationality and order on the world are doomed to failure.

   In the next scene, Jeffrey goes to visit his father in the hospital. When we see his father lying in bed with tubes running from his nose and arms and his head surrounded by a metal apparatus, unable to speak, we are struck both by the fragility of human life and by the machinelike nature of the physical processes upon which our lives depend. Lynch is masterful at encapsulating hints of life's coarseness in ways that initially go unnoticed but that prefigure later scenes of obvious savagery. The tube running from Jeffrey's father's nose prefigures the inhaler used by Frank Booth (Dennis Hopper) later in the film. We hear the radio announcer of station WOOD in Lumberton jokingly refer to all the trees out there waiting to be chopped (killed) just before Jeffrey finds a severed human ear in a field. We entertain ourselves by images of violence even as we pretend that the human soul is basically peaceful and loving.

   The rest of the film replays these themes vividly. The ear itself plays a role in communicating these themes. The camera lingers on the ear sitting in the field, discolored and covered with crawling bugs, as though it were just another object in a world of objects, but we are forcefully aware that it is not. It is part of a human body that has been sliced off. When Jeffrey brings the ear in a paper bag to Detective Williams (George Dickerson) at police headquarters, we are struck by the nonchalant manner in which Williams receives and discusses the ear. Williams is a man inured to life's viciousness. He shifts from polite chitchat to discussion of the ear without surprise or change in tone. Similarly, the coroner discusses the ear in the same bored tone of voice. No emotion is displayed as he reveals that the ear was cut off with scissors and that its owner is probably still alive. In the next shot, we see scissors cutting the police line in the field where the ear was found.

Jeffrey is filled with curiosity about the ear. Yet he keeps its existence a secret from his mother and aunt. When he leaves his house to go over to the Williams house to find out more, he lies by saying that he is just going for a walk around the neighborhood. He is warned by his aunt to stay away from Lincoln, a nearby street. The suburban streets are familiar yet menacing. A man walking his dog appears weird and frightening. Jeffrey pictures the ear in his mind, and with him we examine it microscopically. Metaphorically, we, along with Jeffrey, enter into the frightening world that the ear represents. The ear symbolizes Schopenhauer's world of inexplicable evil, a place where the discovery of severed human body parts merely confirms a brutal and violent reality of irresistible impulses. We do not emerge from this world until the end of the film, when Lynch brings us out of Jeffrey's own ear.

At the Williams house, he is welcomed with polite chitchat by Mrs. Williams (Hope Lange). Detective Williams refuses to tell Jeffrey more about the ear. He understands Jeffrey's curiosity and admits that his own curiosity brought him into police work, but he is a full participant in the conspiracy to hide the brutal underside of human reality from those not directly confronted with it, especially women and children. Yet when Jeffrey exclaims that police work must be "great," Detective Williams remarks, "it is horrible, too."

Outside the Williams house, Jeffrey hears a female voice ask, "Are you the one who found the ear?" Out of the darkness slowly steps Sandy (Laura Dern), the detective's daughter, a vision of innocent loveliness and purity. Sandy reveals that she knows a few details of the case, despite the fact that her father has attempted to hide them from her. However, following Schopenhauer's philosophy, one could argue that the conspiracy to shield the "innocent" from life's harshness can never fully succeed because we are all too "curious." Sandy is enticed into showing Jeffrey the apartment house of a woman involved in the case named Dorothy Vallens (Isabella Rossellini). Sandy and Jeffrey use their discussion of the case as a way to flirt, the whiff of danger and violence being as seductive as the suggestion of sex.

Of course, the apartment is located on the dangerous Lincoln Street we heard about earlier. Sandy and Jeffrey tune out the crude advances addressed to her by men in a passing car, yet another indication of our tendency to ignore life's seamier side. Dorothy Vallens's apartment house is called "Deep River Apartments," a name suggesting that setting foot into the building will throw Jeffrey and Sandy into the deep currents of human torment below the still waters of supposedly "normal life." There is also the suggestion that one crosses the river Styx and enters into Hell.

The next day, Jeffrey succeeds in getting Sandy to come with him to a diner despite her fear that her boyfriend, Mike, will find out. Jeffrey reveals that he has a plan to infiltrate Dorothy Vallens's apartment in order to discover more about the case. Sandy is initially reluctant, but Jeffrey convinces her seductively. In this scene, Jeffrey begins by explaining: "there are opportunities in life for gaining knowledge and experience. Sometimes it is necessary to take a risk. I got to thinking that I guess someone could learn a lot by getting into that woman's apartment." Here the film equates knowledge with an experience of the dark underside of human behavior. Jeffrey's initial motivation is to gain knowledge. He does not yet realize that his search for knowledge, like that of mythic Faust, will bring him into contact with demonic forces.

The seductive attraction of this darkness is revealed in Dorothy Vallens's performance at the Slow Club the next night. The fiery neon of its sign subtly suggests the hellish aspects of this club, as do the antlers (devilish horns) displayed between the words "Slow" and "Club." Inside, horns are also attached to the front of the stage. Dorothy is introduced as the "Blue Lady." She emerges wearing a black backless dress with blue eye shadow and bright red lipstick. Blue neon bathes her as she begins the song "Blue Velvet." Although Jeffrey and Sandy were flirting adolescently before Dorothy's entrance, as soon as she begins to sing, we become immediately aware of Dorothy's more sophisticated sexual attractiveness for Jeffrey. His eyes open wide, and Sandy suddenly appears awkward and uneasy. Dorothy's rendering of the song is in jarring contrast to the original version of the song heard at the film's beginning. Then it sounded upbeat and happy, but the way Dorothy sings it conveys a melancholy message.

As Jeffrey leaves Sandy to sneak into Dorothy's apartment, Sandy betrays the dual nature of Jeffrey's obsession with the case when she says, "I don't know if you are a detective or a pervert." Jeffrey responds, "That's for me to know and you to find out." Throughout the rest of the film, an ambiguity exists between these two possible interpretations of Jeffrey's behavior. We are never fully sure of Jeffrey's motivation. Again, like Faust, Jeffrey's search for knowledge becomes distorted into a need for sensual gratification. We are reminded of Schopenhauer's claim that the Will is composed of primal instincts that motivate all human behavior. In this belief, Schopenhauer prefigures Sigmund Freud's (1856–1939) later claim that all of us are driven by our most basic desires, especially our need for sexual gratification.

Seeing without Being Seen

The important role of seeing in the film now becomes apparent. The French philosopher Jean-Paul Sartre (1905–1980) describes what he calls the *Look* in his famous pioneering work of existential philosophy *Being and Nothingness*. The act of looking makes one the subject and objectifies the world. Those who watch control those who are watched.

Sartre famously gives the example of a man on his knees looking through a keyhole into a hotel room. While he is alone in the corridor, he is the subject of all he sees. Motivated perhaps by jealousy, he judges the meaning of the events he observes on the other side of the door. But suppose someone else (say, a woman) should turn down the corridor and see the man. Realizing that he is being seen by the other person, the man immediately becomes aware of how he must look, down on his knees spying through the keyhole. Self-consciously, he leaps to his feet and hurries away, anxious to disappear before the other person has the chance to confront him. While he was alone, the man was in control of his identity, but once he becomes aware of the other's look, he realizes that she may see him quite differently than he sees himself. While he may have thought that his actions were justified, he is very aware that the woman might see him instead as a voyeur, a Peeping Tom, or, that most pathetic of creatures, the jealous lover.[3]

Hiding in the closet in Dorothy's apartment, Jeffrey is in control of the situation. He is able to gain clues and see Dorothy at her most vulnerable. He watches as Dorothy removes her clothes and wig. He listens as Dorothy receives a phone call from Frank, whom she calls "sir." He learns that Frank is holding some people, including a child named Donny, prisoner. After the phone call, she pulls a picture from under the couch and hugs it.

However, it is also in Dorothy's apartment that Jeffrey moves from spectator to participant in the case. When Dorothy discovers him in the closet, Jeffrey pretends to be a sexual voyeur. At some level we realize that this is not entirely a pretense. Jeffrey really is a voyeur, but he is a voyeur who seeks gratification not just from sex but from danger as well. Choosing a punishment that fits the crime, she orders Jeffrey to undress at knifepoint. As a show of her domination over Jeffrey, she commands him not to look at her and not to move. When he shows defiance by refusing to reveal his last name, she cuts his face with her knife. This red cut on the cheek initiates Jeffrey into Dorothy's world of violence. The mark disappears in the next scene in the comfortable surroundings of Jeffrey's home, yet it appears soon afterward when Jeffrey returns to the Slow Club.

Dorothy toys with Jeffrey sexually to discover his hidden quirks. She harshly threatens to kill him if he touches her and then seductively asks if he likes that kind of talk. Suddenly, there are three knocks on the door. Dorothy pushes Jeffrey back into the closet with his clothes and again he becomes the unseen voyeur. What follows is the most powerful scene in the film. We are introduced to Frank Booth, Jeffrey's evil double, a man incapable of hiding his inner brutal forces. Jeffrey has lived his life maintaining the pretence that people are fundamentally good. Now Jeffrey's search for knowledge forces him to confront the sordid inner drives within us all. Jeffrey's discovery of Frank is the inevitable culmination of his search.

Frank embodies the fierce savagery within all of us, what Freud famously called the *Id*. He does and says exactly what he feels. While he is in the apartment, he dominates Dorothy completely. His language and actions are shocking in their selfishness and spontaneity. Dorothy speaks only five words in this scene while Frank delivers a torrent of angry and obscene demands and threats. Frank's nature is clear in this monologue. As he storms into the apartment, Dorothy says, "Hi, Baby." Frank replies, "It's Daddy, you shithead! Where's my bourbon? Can't you fucking remember anything? Now it's dark. Spread your legs! Wider! Show it to me! Don't you fucking look at me!" Like Sartre's man in the corridor, Frank knows he is vulnerable to the other's look. If he can control Dorothy's look he remains dominant. Aware of the bizarre nature of his acts, Frank is terrified of seeing himself reflected in her eyes.

At this point, Frank pulls out his green plastic inhaler and sucks it furiously. This action, repeated by Frank before every event of great ferocity, reminds us of Jeffrey's father's apparatus in the hospital. His constant need for oxygen, the very essence of life, emphasizes the fragility of the human body, especially at moments of extreme emotion. Frank continues his diatribe: "Mommy, baby wants to fuck! You fucker! Don't you fucking look at me!" The repetition of this final phrase over and over again (twelve times in this one scene) indicates once more the power of seeing without being seen. Frank repeats it regularly throughout the film to those whom he attempts to control, including, eventually, Jeffrey. Frank must be in control of the way he appears to others or he risks losing his power over them. Frank's greatest terror is that he will be forced to see himself as others see him. He

takes out a pair of scissors and waves them while rapidly opening and closing them. This demonstration of power and control chills us as we realize
that Frank was the one who sliced off the ear. Frank now sucks a piece of
blue velvet he has cut from Dorothy's robe as he violently engages in some
form of sexual release.

As Frank leaves, his words to Dorothy are equally brutal: "You stay alive,
Baby! Do it for Van Gogh!" We now fully realize that Dorothy is Frank's
victim, forced to engage in these horrible acts to protect the lives of those
she loves. Yet we soon see that Dorothy is not a completely unwilling victim.
As Jeffrey comforts her following Frank's departure, Dorothy insists that he
hold and fondle her as she softly talks to him: "See my breast? . . . You can
feel it. Do you like the way I feel? Feel me! (*pause*) Hit me! (*pause*) Hit me!
Hit me! Hit me!" As she says, "Hit me!" the first time we see a close-up of
her red lips, and we feel her deep depravity. Jeffrey is initially too inhibited
to comply with her demand, yet, later in the film, he will be able to do so.

As Jeffrey leaves the apartment, he is surrounded by blackness and enters
a surrealistic world in which his father's face distorted in pain transforms itself
into Frank's face contorted in rage. We then see the flame of a candle burning
brightly followed by Dorothy's red lips saying, "Hit me!" Frank's disturbed face
reappears, and his fist strikes out at us. Jeffrey wakes with a yell in his own bed
and points toward a primitive-looking head with large, bared fangs hanging
from his wall, a symbol of the primeval emotions overtaking him.

Jeffrey and Sandy drive to a churchyard, where Jeffrey summarizes his
encounters with Frank and Dorothy, taking care to leave out the sexual nature
of the events and his participation in them. Sandy is amazed at how much
Jeffrey has learned and urges him to tell her father. Jeffrey says he can't do
this because he obtained his information illegally and because Sandy would
get in trouble. Overcome with emotion, Jeffrey asks Sandy, "Why are there
people like Frank?" Sandy responds with her romantic dream that someday
robins will descend from heaven and the blinding light of love will chase
away all evil. Celestial organ music plays in the background as she speaks.
This dream is so naive and unrealistic that we are not surprised when we
see Jeffrey knocking on Dorothy's door in the very next shot. Sandy's lovely
innocence is no competition for Dorothy's powerful sexual allure.

Jeffrey, like her father, wants to shield Sandy from the harsh realities of life,
but he can't resist the darkness within himself. Unlike Sandy, Dorothy directly
expresses her animal instincts. She tells Jeffrey that she looked for him in the
closet again that night. She tells him that she likes him and she enjoys being

with him. In this film, only the characters that have given in to their dark impulses are able to be completely honest. Again, Lynch equates openness and truthfulness with a recognition and acceptance of inner drives and passions. The pretence of inherent goodness is equated with lying and self-deception.

Another philosopher, Friedrich Nietzsche (1844–1900), while a great admirer of Schopenhauer, believes our primal instincts, what he called the *will to power*, transcend morality altogether.[4] Where Schopenhauer describes the desires of the Will as evil, Nietzsche famously celebrates what he calls the *Dionysian* virtues of a *master morality*. He actively encourages strong-willed individuals to transform themselves into superior people who will be untouched by the weapon of guilt used by those in the *slave morality*. Such individuals will overcome the self-deception practiced by those who accept traditional morality and religion. Thus, from a Nietzschean viewpoint, Jeffrey's metamorphosis as the film processes is a positive one.[5]

Jeffrey is now intoxicated with Dorothy. He goes alone to the Slow Club to watch her sing. When he observes Frank in the audience fondling his piece of blue velvet, Jeffrey waits for him and his friends outside the club and then follows them in his car. We learn what he discovered as he reports to Sandy at the diner. It is a tale of a murdered drug pusher, a "yellow man" (a man wearing a yellow jacket), and a "well-dressed" man with an alligator briefcase. But we don't really care about the details of the case. We don't mind that we hear them secondhand or that Jeffrey runs through them too quickly for us to take them in. The criminal case in this film is a Hitchcockian "MacGuffin," existing only as a superficial excuse for the story. Lynch is no more interested in it than we are.

When Sandy asks Jeffrey why he persists in pursuing the case without the police, Jeffrey returns to his Faustian obsession with mysteries. "I'm seeing something that was always hidden. I'm involved in a mystery. I'm in the middle of a mystery." "You love mysteries that much?" Sandy asks. "Yeah!" Jeffrey responds enthusiastically. He distracts Sandy from his darker motives by lying to her. "You're a mystery," he exclaims, as he moves to kiss her, yet we are well aware that it is Dorothy who embodies mystery and excitement for Jeffrey, not Sandy.

Desire, Suffering, and Buddhism

In the next scene, Jeffrey and Dorothy make passionate love, and this time Jeffrey hits her. As they writhe in ecstasy, we again see a bright flame, this time erupting into a blazing blast furnace as we hear a roaring sound. After their lovemaking, we hear loud thundering outside; even the elements respond to their passion. Dorothy tells Jeffrey that she knows he thinks she is crazy, but "she is not crazy, she knows the difference between right and wrong." There is a subtle indictment of Jeffrey in this statement. Dorothy is obviously in a psychological state of extreme vulnerability. In the guise of helping her, Jeffrey is actually exploiting her in a manner not totally unlike that of Frank. Both men are using Dorothy to gratify their lust outside the context of a romantic relationship. Dorothy later accuses Jeffrey of this when she repeatedly tells Sandy, "he puts his disease in me."

Lynch's use of fire imagery to represent strong passions provides another link to Schopenhauer's philosophy. Schopenhauer was very interested in Eastern philosophy, especially Buddhism. The first two Noble Truths of Buddhism state that all life is suffering, and suffering is caused by desire. In Buddhism, it is common to associate this desire with the image of fire. Giving in to one's desires is like adding fuel to the fire, making it stronger and harder to quench. If no more fuel is added to the fire, it will eventually burn itself out and die. In the same way, to extinguish desire one must stop giving in to it. For example, I may love to eat chocolate. Yet, if I give in to my desire to eat chocolate whenever I want, my appreciation of the taste will diminish to the extent that I find myself eating more and more and enjoying it less. In addition, my overeating will eventually make me feel sick and bloated. Thus, my desire for the pleasure of eating chocolate has instead led me to pain and suffering. For Buddhists, this is life's unavoidable pattern. We desire something, so we seek it. Yet when we get it, it is never everything we dreamed it to be so we seek more. But we never get enough and the pursuit of pleasure always leads to suffering. Desires can never be fully fulfilled. The only way to escape suffering is to escape desire altogether.[6]

The sound of the storm has stopped by the time Frank and his friends dramatically and frighteningly appear outside the door of Dorothy's apartment just as Jeffrey is leaving. Dorothy tries to explain Jeffrey away as "just a friend from the neighborhood." From this point on, Frank calls Jeffrey "neighbor." As we saw earlier, Jeffrey's Aunt Barbara spoke of Lincoln Street as though it was not a part of the neighborhood, as though the events there did not relate to the lives of the "nice people" living in the neighborhood. By emphasizing the fact that Dorothy's apartment is located very near to both Jeffrey's and Sandy's homes, and by having Frank refer to Jeffrey as "neighbor," Lynch emphasizes that the brutal aspects of the human spirit are in all of us; they are not simply carried within those who live in a certain part of town or are members of a certain class.

Frank forces Jeffrey and Dorothy to go on a "joy ride" in his black Dodge Charger to a place called "This Is It." Frank mistakenly fails to take Jeffrey for a serious adversary. Evidence of this mistake lies in the fact that Frank and his friends think they can humiliate Jeffrey by questioning his virility and discussing his assumed virginity. Little do they know that Jeffrey just had sex with Dorothy and that Jeffrey knows that Frank is impotent. At "This Is It," a sleazy place of uncertain purpose run by a swishy homosexual named Ben (Dean Stockwell), Frank and his associates harass and beat Jeffrey. We also learn that Dorothy's husband and son are being held in the club and that Frank's accomplice, Detective Gordon (Fred Pickler), has killed the drug dealer mentioned earlier.

Frank demands that Ben lip-sync Roy Orbison's song "In Dreams." The lyrics of this song are of mystical significance to Frank. He later repeats them to Jeffrey as a sign of his power. These scenes exemplify Lynch's trademark strangeness with the unexplained presence of a middle-aged overweight women and the bizarre behavior of Frank's friends, especially Paul (Jack Nance) and Raymond (Brad Dourif). Raymond even dances with a live snake as Ben pretends to sing. Frank abruptly turns off the song and announces that it is time to continue Jeffrey's joyride. Frank has totally entered the frenzied state of mind in which we first saw him. He repeats as before, "Now it's dark." Then he screams, "Let's fuck! I'll fuck anything that moves!" As he laughs hysterically, his image magically vanishes from the room.

Obscene language is very important to Frank. He wishes to scream out the obscene that is normally hidden in polite society. His constant use of the word *fuck* demonstrates his rage. He has Ben toast, "here's to your fuck, Frank." Frank's relationship to Ben has sexual overtones. Just as Frank is Jeffrey's dark double, Ben is Frank's homosexual side. Frank can't stop telling Ben how "suave" he is.

We return to Frank's black Dodge Charger as he drives maniacally at speeds of over a hundred miles an hour. Frank pulls off the road and turns his attention to Jeffrey. When he sees Jeffrey looking at him, he reasserts his power of seeing, asking him, "What are you looking at?" "Nothing," responds Jeffrey. When Frank commands, "Don't you look at me, Fuck!" Jeffrey lowers his eyes. Frank then confirms his identity with Jeffrey by saying, "You're like me." He pulls out his inhaler and his eyes bulge as he rapidly sucks. But when Frank starts to make sexual advances to Dorothy, it is Jeffrey who becomes aggressive. Frank looks at Jeffrey with shocked surprise. Jeffrey then punches Frank in the face! We in the audience are as surprised as Frank. Jeffrey has no fear of Frank whatsoever because Frank is right. Jeffrey is like Frank. As was suggested earlier, Frank is Jeffrey's evil double, a man incapable of hiding his inner brutal forces. Jeffrey's search for knowledge has brought him face to face with his sordid inner drives.

Frank responds by having his friends drag Jeffrey from the car. Frank smears lipstick on his lips, as he drags on his inhaler and murmurs, "pretty, pretty." He then kisses Jeffrey repeatedly on the lips. As Paul plays "Candy-Colored Clown" on the car stereo, Frank tells Jeffrey, "You're fucking lucky to be alive. Candy-colored clown. Don't be a good neighbor to her. I'll send you a love letter straight from my heart. Do you know what a love letter is? It's a bullet from a fucking gun. You receive a love letter from me and you're fucked forever! Do you understand, Fuck? I'll send you straight to Hell, Fucker!" He speaks the words of the song as it is playing: "In dreams I walk with you. In dreams I talk to you. In dreams you're mine all the time." Frank takes his piece of blue velvet and puts it in Jeffrey's mouth. After showing Jeffrey his muscles, he beats Jeffrey brutally. As this action ends, we see the flame again burning brightly, representing intense rage.

Jeffrey decides that it is time to report to Detective Williams; however, when he arrives at police headquarters he finds the "yellow man" in Williams's outer office. He now realizes that the yellow man is Detective Gordon, the man Frank mentioned to Ben. To avoid Gordon, he goes to the Williams home in the evening. He tells Williams some of what he has discovered, but he lies about Sandy's involvement and does not mention his sexual relationship with Dorothy. We see Williams's flash of surprise as he recognizes Gordon as the man with Frank. Could Williams be another of Frank's accomplices?

Dreams of Life's Innocent Purity

Time passes. We see Jeffrey out watering the lawn in a posture reminiscent of his father's collapse. Reading our mind, Lynch then shows us Jeffrey and his mother visiting his father in the hospital. When Jeffrey arrives on Friday at the Williams house to pick up Sandy for a date, he is surprised to see Gordon there. Williams encourages Jeffrey to play along (telling him, "Easy does it, Jeffrey. Behave yourself. Don't blow it") and act as though he does not recognize him. For the second time, Gordon fails to recognize Jeffrey as the pest-control man he first saw in Dorothy's apartment. Gordon's repeated failure to recognize Jeffrey demonstrates his inability to "see." While Gordon on three occasions clearly is shown looking at Jeffrey, on none of these occasions does he really see Jeffrey. Yet every time Jeffrey encounters Gordon, he recognizes and reacts to him. In fact, it is because Jeffrey photographs Gordon and Frank together (photography being a very powerful form of seeing in the sense that it isolates and captures a single moment of perception) that Jeffrey is able to convince Detective Williams of their guilt. Thus, we are not very surprised when, in the end, Frank manages to double-cross and kill Gordon. Frank understands the power of "seeing" while Gordon does not.

At a party, Jeffrey and Sandy dance, kiss, and pledge their love as celestial choir music again plays. On the way home from the party, a dark car follows and bangs their rear fender. Afraid that it is Frank, Jeffrey races to his home. Sandy and Jeffrey are both relieved to find that it is just Mike, Sandy's old boyfriend, drunk and seeking revenge. Yet, our relief quickly ends as a naked, beaten Dorothy emerges from the front porch of Jeffrey's home. Jeffrey runs to embrace Dorothy as Sandy is horrified in her recognition of Dorothy Vallens. Sandy and her mother watch in shock as Dorothy hugs Jeffrey and exclaims, "My secret lover. Don't get the police. Stop him! I love you! Love me!" She turns to Sandy and her mother, and explains, "He puts his disease in me. Tell me it's all right! Help him! Promise me you'll help him! He puts his disease in me."

Sandy responds by slapping Jeffrey's face as he tells her he should go to the hospital with Dorothy. We next see Sandy in her room sitting under a huge poster of Montgomery Clift as she cries into the phone at Jeffrey, "You lied to me! I love you, but I couldn't watch that." This scene confirms the contention that Sandy wants to be protected from the dark underside of life. She has a poster of Montgomery Clift hanging on her wall as a romantic idol, yet it is common knowledge that the actor was gay. Perhaps Sandy could live with the suspicion that Jeffrey's relationship with Dorothy was more than he admitted; it is seeing it she can't stand. Sandy later appears to completely forgive Jeffrey as though the incident with Dorothy never happened. She is willing to engage in self-deception to maintain her dreams of life's innocent purity.

At Dorothy's apartment, Jeffrey enters a truly bizarre scene. Tied to a chair is the dead body of Dorothy's husband with blue velvet in his mouth. We know it is he because he is missing an ear. Tom Gordon, the "yellow man," stands wavering with blood pouring from his head as his police radio crackles. Gordon shoots out a hand as the police radio begins to talk. Suddenly, we hear Ketty Lester's 1962 song "Love Letters" as the scene cuts to a gunfight between the police and what we assume are Frank's associates in a warehouse. Jeffrey says to himself, "I'm going to let them find you on their own," and turns to go.

As he descends the stairs, he sees the "well-dressed man" coming up and realizes it is Frank in disguise. He runs back to Dorothy's apartment and radios Detective Williams and tells him his location before realizing that Frank probably has a radio as well. He then misinforms Williams that he is hiding in the back bedroom and returns to his original hiding place, the closet. It is fitting that the final encounter with Frank takes place with Jeffrey in the closet, his place of power. Here Jeffrey can see without being seen. Again Frank underestimates Jeffrey because he doesn't fully understand that Jeffrey shares his capacity for brutality. Frank thinks Jeffrey will be overcome with fear and will put up no fight. Frank speaks out loud to Jeffrey in a disparaging manner, grabs the blue velvet, and uses his inhaler again as a stimulus. Sounding like a parrot, Frank again yells, "Pretty, pretty!" as he goes into the bedroom to kill Jeffrey.

Jeffrey uses Frank's absence to run to Gordon's body, remove his gun and return to the closet. When Frank can't find Jeffrey, he shoots out the TV screen, and then Gordon. Finally, he realizes that Jeffrey must be in the closet and inhales happily to prepare himself for the kill. However, once more, as in the car, it is Jeffrey who acts aggressively, shooting Frank in the forehead as he opens the closet door. Frank's surprise is complete. Sandy and Williams rush in, and Williams points his gun around the room as he takes in the situation. He then tells Jeffrey that it's all over. The screen is filled with the image of two lightbulbs burning brightly that go out with a great whoosh. The primal flames of desire and brutality are temporarily extinguished. Sandy and Jeffrey kiss as celestial music plays again.

In the last scene, we again see an ear, but this time it's Jeffrey's living healthy ear. He is reclining outside on a beautiful day. As he opens his eyes he sees a robin in a tree. He is called to lunch as we see Jeffrey's father, now, in his own words, "feeling much better," talking to Detective Williams at the Williams home. In the kitchen, Sandy, Aunt Barbara, and Jeffrey see the robin again, this time standing in the window. Jeffrey says to Sandy, "maybe your robins have come." Yet Aunt Barbara notices that the robin is eating a large, live, black bug, like the ones we saw at the film's opening. "I don't know how it can do that," Aunt Barbara says, looking like a predator herself as she takes a bite of meat. "It's a strange world," Sandy says smilingly to Jeffrey.

The film closes as it began, with shots of waving flowers before a white picket fence, and a fireman waving from the side of his fire truck. We then see Dorothy playing with her young son. Yet as Dorothy hugs her son we hear the last words of her rendition of "Blue Velvet" ("and I still can see blue velvet through my tears"). The camera rises through the trees to the bright blue sky that transforms into the curtain of blue velvet and the musical score that opened the film.

Schopenhauer or Nietzsche

In *Blue Velvet*, David Lynch tells us that our feeble attempts to pretend that rationality and order can be successfully imposed both on nature and us are doomed to failure. Those who hold these beliefs, such as Sandy, are portrayed as living in a world of fantasy. Even the best of us are irresistibly drawn to the degrading, the brutal, and the violent. People who will be most successful, like Jeffrey or Detective Williams, are those who can control their drives, hiding them when it's to their advantage and yet satisfying them when they can get away with it. Whether Lynch paints a depressing picture or a joyous one depends on whether you prefer Schopenhauer or Nietzsche. A follower of Nietzsche might claim that these inner forces are necessary to drive the most talented and courageous of us to acts of great imaginative intensity. Schopenhauer, on the other hand, sees life as a cycle of pain and suffering in which each of us is determined by irresistible evil impulses we can hide but never escape.

Notes

This essay is a revised and expanded version of a film review that originally appeared in the conference proceedings *Inquiries into Values and Ethical Views: The Inaugural Sessions of the International Society for Value Inquiry.* Printed by permission of The Edwin Mellen Press, 1988.

1. *Rear Window* may have inspired David Lynch in his creation of *Blue Velvet,* especially in its treatment of the power of watching without been seen (see my essay, "Philosophical Themes in Hitchcock's *Rear Window*," in "Film and Philosophy," special issue, *Post Script: Essays in Film and the Humanities* 7, no. 2 [Winter 1988]).

2. For more information on these philosophers, see Roger Scruton, Peter Singer,

Christopher Janoway, and Michael Tanner, *German Philosophers: Kant, Hegel, Schopenhauer, Nietzsche* (New York: Oxford University Press, 2001).

3. Jean-Paul Sartre, *Being and Nothingness*, trans. Hazel Barnes (New York: Washington Square Press, 1993), 340–400.

4. *The Stanford Encyclopedia of Philosophy* explains Nietzsche's position this way: "Alternatively, Nietzsche philosophizes from the perspective of life located beyond good and evil, and challenges the entrenched moral idea that exploitation, domination, injury to the weak, destruction and appropriation are universally objectionable behaviors. Above all, he believes that living things aim to discharge their strength and express their 'will to power'—a pouring-out of expansive energy that, quite naturally, can entail danger, pain, lies, deception and masks." (http://plato.stanford.edu/entries/nietzsche/).

5. For Nietzsche's account of morality, see Friedrich Nietzsche, *On the Genealogy of Morals*, trans. Walter Kaufmann and R. J. Hollingdale (New York: Vintage Books, 1989); and Friedrich Nietzsche, *Beyond Good and Evil*, trans. Walter Kaufmann (New York: Random House, 1966).

6. Turning again to *The Stanford Encyclopedia of Philosophy*, we find that:

Schopenhauer believes that a person who experiences the truth of human nature from a moral perspective—who appreciates how spatial and temporal forms of knowledge generate a constant passing away, continual suffering, vain striving and inner tension—will be so repulsed by the human condition, that he or she will lose the desire to affirm the objectified human situation in any of its manifestations. The result is an attitude of the denial of our will-to-live, which Schopenhauer identifies with an ascetic attitude of renunciation, resignation, and will-lessness, but also with composure and tranquillity. In a manner reminiscent of traditional Buddhism, he recognizes that life is filled with unavoidable frustration, and acknowledges that the suffering caused by this frustration can itself be reduced by minimizing one's desires (http://plato.stanford.edu/entries/schopenhauer/).

THE THING ABOUT DAVID LYNCH

Enjoying the Lynchian World

Russell Manning

This whole world is wild at heart and crazy on top.
—*Wild at Heart* (1990)

Let's begin by arguing there are movie experiences that, at first take, are very difficult to put into words. Whether they inspire us to be deliriously happy or bone-shakingly frightened, there is something about these extraordinary films that fills us with a heightened emotional response, what we could call awe or wonder. In philosophy we can ask ourselves, What is it to be awed? Why is such a feeling so attached to films we see as awe-some, with a power to generate such heightened and inspiring feelings as awe or wonder? To explain, if we imagine the difference between watching some amazingly powerful waves at the beach and actually surfing one of those powerful waves, we derive a sense of the feelings of awe and wonder. When this feeling is great enough, we start to lose the vocabulary to explain it; the emotional response seems to defy words. In fact, we could say this elevated feeling, like that of riding a monstrous wave, could be almost overwhelmingly emotional; perhaps even *sublime*. That is, there must be some *Thing* that gives rise to this feeling of awe. Artists have tried for centuries to capture it in music or painting. Now, can we capture it on film? Can we somehow encounter this emotion on the film screen? If we called this heightened emotional response something that arises at an intense emotional encounter, what exactly is this Thing we are trying to articulate?[1]

The psychoanalyst Sigmund Freud (1856–1939) argues that the Thing we are describing here is a psychoanalytic name to explain what is, in simple terms, the feeling you get when you are scared witless at a horror movie, or on a roller coaster, or, indeed, surfing that huge wave. We all know the feeling, but it is almost impossible to fully explain in words, and so, like Freud, we label it the *Thing*. He said this arises because of some primal anxiety of being overwhelmed. In simple terms, psychoanalysis suggests that when we become socialized into language (as toddlers), the being we were changes forever, and, as a result, we spend the rest of our lives searching and desiring to return to that pre-language state. Of course it is impossible to do so, but this effect gives rise to how we attach emotional feelings to people, objects, and places, how we love, desire, or are repulsed by some things and not others. Consider the surfer: the thrill is not just the ride but the feeling that he could come to serious grief at any moment. In the horror movie, the fear arises through the imagined feeling of the possibility of the monster coming to life. What we imagine is accompanied by an actual feeling. This feeling comes to us (via the Thing) as joy, fear (of losing rationality), anxiety, and so on.[2]

The Slovenian philosopher Slavoj Žižek (1950–) follows the Freudian assessment when he describes this curious Thing as "a permanent failure of the representation." In other words, the Thing is something that cannot be fully put into words, or that is beyond our full comprehension. When we try to explain the full import of the wave or describe the meaning of the work of art, we get to a point in which the words don't seem to capture how strong the feeling is and we are left with a gap between what we experience and the words we use to express this experience. This gap is the location of the Thing.[3]

The question I pose in this essay, then, is: Can we be filled with awe by the cinema of David Lynch? That is, does Lynch create cinematic pieces that are sublime? And, if so, in what sense can Lynchian cinema be talked about in terms of the Thing? The world of David Lynch is a cinematic world where the Thing comes to the forefront, almost leaping from the screen. It is in Henry Spencer (Jack Nance) and Mary X's (Charlotte Stewart) baby, in Bobby Peru's (Willem Dafoe) sneer, in Mr. Eddy's (Robert Loggia) maniacal outburst against tailgating. It is a visit to the White Lodge or a car ride with Frank Booth (Dennis Hopper). This is not real terror, but its most artistic equivalence. Yet it is one of the reasons we go to the movies.

In this essay, I pursue the claim that Lynch attempts to capture the Thing through his films. What I aim to show is that film reviews that accuse Lynch of being deliberately obscure, weird for weird's sake, self-indulgent, and so on, simply confuse weird with Lynch's attempt to capture the Thing. Lynch's films are, indeed, weird, but they are not weird for weird's sake.

Lynch's cinema should be understood as his ongoing attempt to capture the Thing, to be an encounter with the sublime. I explore Lynch's attempt by offering a new way to approach Lynch's films. Here, I examine Lynch's unique cinematic method as a philosophical criticism and challenge to the standard paradigm for Hollywood films (what I refer to as the "Hollywood film machine"). I show that Lynch challenges the Hollywood film machine most specifically by reinterpreting the cinematic notions of character and narrative. I then close by offering an examination of the Thing in *Mulholland Dr.* as an example of how to approach Lynch's films.[4]

Rethinking Film: Lynch's Cinematic Method

The first step in our exploration of the way Lynch tackles the Thing (which cannot be spoken of, but only experienced as the sublime) requires a brief assessment of our method of inquiry. It is evident to me (and, for that matter, should be evident to anyone who ever watched a film by Lynch and has found himself bewildered yet fantastically exhilarated) that Lynch's films, and especially the elusive and indefinable Thing that stands for their sublimity, require a new and broader method of interpretation of film (and maybe even a new and bolder way of delineating the experience of viewing films). In order to do so, we may want to adopt a more inquisitive and open attitude toward films in general and to the films of Lynch in particular. Such an attitude should embrace the unspoken experience not as a flaw, but as an advantage. It will allow us to experience the Lynchian world in its entirety, overlook the narrow and limited traditional interpretation (which ends up with "weird for weird's sake" judgments), and instead adopt a broader and more comprehensive approach to film appreciation and viewing. This approach will make different sense of the way Lynch's enigmatic films might be thinking, and will thus illuminate the true genius of Lynch as a filmmaker.[5]

A new method of interpretation of film should answer the desire that lies at the basis of every method: namely the desire to know what the film, its scenes and characters, might mean. In other words, we try to make sense of films because we are eager to know what it is all about. Commonly, we would try to track down the logic of the film's narrative, understand the characters (their actions and motivations), and contemplate the plot's twists and turns in order to make sense of the film. However, Lynch presents us with a body of cinematic work that constantly ignores this method of inquiry and accordingly defies this line of interpretation. What, then, should we do? How are we to determine what the Lynchian film is about?

To help us determine this, we can turn to Jean Baudrillard (1929–2007), a French thinker who provides us with a new way of approaching art and so, for our purposes, film. Baudrillard would see any attempt by a film critic to tell us what a character or a narrative *should be* as an attempt to "alter the real," or an attempt to transform the true nature of the cinematic world. This attempt is the struggle for dominance of ideas that can be won, for example, by the media with its powerful distribution capacities telling us what a real film is supposed to be. Yet there is a way to fight back. Following Baudrillard, we can develop our own set of rules for the real, a way of thinking about Lynch as a filmmaker who challenges the typical Hollywood way of thinking of films that comes across as preprogrammed and often very soft in its challenge to the audience.[6]

Lynch forces us to experience his films in a new and unique way and, accordingly, to make our own new rules (to paraphrase Baudrillard) regarding what the films are really about. Consider Fred Madison's (Bill Pullman) transfiguration in *Lost Highway* (1997), Agent Dale Cooper's (Kyle MacLachlan) uncanny reaction to the Log Lady (Catherine E. Coulson) in *Twin Peaks* (1990–1991), or the manmade-chicken scene in *Eraserhead* (1977). If we understand these scenes as a deliberately incomprehensible attempt to force us into an active viewing experience, then everything starts to make some sense. With his weird, incomprehensible scenes and characters, Lynch forces us to let go of our reflective disposition and concepts, and instead to actively create the film for ourselves and set its interpretation as an extension of our own feelings of uneasiness and bewilderment.

These feelings, which accompany (and maybe define) the experience we have when we watch a typical Lynchian scene, are the result of Lynch's attempt to film what we find so difficult to put into words and concepts, that is, the Thing. There is something in each of these scenes that evokes that anxiety-laden feeling that is uniquely associated with the unapproachable nature of the Thing. But exactly what might Lynch be trying to accomplish with such initially bizarre scenes? In order to explore these manifestations of the unspeakable Thing, we might want to let Lynch's scenes speak for themselves.

Let us therefore begin with a few predominant examples. Take, for instance, the location of Club Silencio in *Mulholland Dr.* (2001). A traditional interpretation of the club's cinematic meaning might point out that its name suggests silence, and so stands for a kind of secrecy and perhaps conniving. While this is a valid interpretation, the full meaning of this scene lies not in our reflections, but in our feelings. It will not suffice to just talk about the scene. We must experience it, too. While doing so, we cannot escape the feeling of disoriented appreciation. This disorienting feeling is that of the Thing; the Thing is present in the club, but exactly how we can understand it is not immediately to be known.

Another predominant example is the Mystery Man's (Robert Blake) desert shack in *Lost Highway*. The Mystery Man may be a dual materialization of both something within the space of the film as a symbolic form of evil (or as the portent of cataclysmic change). But, equally important, he is the materialization of an idea from Lynch's personal creative reservoir. The Mystery Man becomes an idea Lynch offers but cannot, nor has to, fully explain (perhaps this is why he films it). In short, this enigmatic character is a Thing in the film space that is something more than a stereotypical filmic character. He is a true Thing in some way connecting Fred's (impossible) desire to resolve his relationship with Renee (Patricia Arquette). As such, this character opens up the field of contested meaning to try to articulate this Thing, which is of course an unattainable task left only for theory, the real space for a creative form of philosophy. The Mystery Man therefore is never the one unitary stitching point for meaning, but the space at which the dialogue for interpretation opens. And we can conclude that, although ultimately uncanny and terrifying, his appearance and the unease it generates might possibly be akin to the malevolent nature of an entity that always has the possibility to disturb us.

As we reflect on Fred's guilt, we sense how uncanny and powerful this feeling called guilt can ultimately be. Lynch's skill is in rendering this uncanny feeling on the screen, a visually poetic filmed depiction of Fred struggling, after murdering Renee, with the disorienting nature of his deteriorating psyche. The Mystery Man becomes the filmed Thing, the terrifying defiance of spatio-temporal logic (he is in two places at once) or the harbinger of doom (he appears just before Fred morphs into Pete Dayton [Balthazar Getty] and before Pete morphs back into Fred). As such, Lynch uses the Mystery Man to palpitate terror and embody the Thing so that it is as if we, the viewers, are staring the Thing in the eye.

Another primary example can be traced in the character of Frank Booth (Dennis Hopper) in *Blue Velvet* (1986). According to the traditional reflective interpretation, which attempts to close down this space and asphyxiate discussion through imposing single points of view on the world of film, Frank is merely a psychopath, an eccentric (yet cinematically ordinary) movie character who serves the purpose of making us scared. However, when Sandy Williams (Laura Dern) sadly wonders why there are people like Frank Booth, she echoes the viewer's same question, a question that cannot be satisfactorily answered by tracking down the psychological profile of the character. Frank exists because he is an embodied Thing that can possess (or scare) us all. And this revealing moment of pure sensation is the core of Frank's role as a character in the film.

As we have seen in the above examples, a traditional reflective way of interpretation, whereas valid in its own right, is nevertheless oppressive and, in Lynch's case, somewhat ineffective. Nullifying the space for creative ideas, it restricts any possibility of a dialogue, and, as a result, the freedom to fully experience the film is lost. Here, then, the reflective method fails to capture the Thing. It fails to speak about that which cannot be spoken of. With our new method, we focus on film experience rather than on its contemplated meaning. As such, we have a greater liberty to speak our mind (and feelings) about the film instead of forcedly speculating about its pre-given meaning.

Lynch's Cinematic Method in Focus: Characters and Narrative

Now that we have a general presentation of Lynch's cinematic method, we can take a closer look at this method at work. Particularly, in this section, I focus our interpretative lens on two areas of Lynch's films: his unique use of characters and narrative.

"I LIKE TO REMEMBER THINGS MY OWN WAY": THE LYNCHIAN CHARACTER

Lynch's characters are infamous for their outlandish and bizarre nature. There is nothing typical in Lynch's characters, as they fail to conform to the common prototype of a mainstream Hollywood character. Consider again the Mystery Man in *Lost Highway* or the Cowboy (Lafayette Montgomery) in *Mulholland Dr.* or practically every character in *Eraserhead*. What immediately strikes us as outrageously unique with these characters, and therefore leaves a residue of perplexity that seems, at first viewing, puzzling at the very least, can be traced back to the traditional role of characters in a narrative fiction. The traditional role of film characters is that of an anchor. Film characters, through their actions, motivations, and thoughts, carry the plot forward to help construct and support the narrative and to bring the film to a conclusion. Now, on the basic level, Lynch's characters resonate with this traditional role of characters. On a deeper and more unique level, however, Lynch's characters employ a more concrete expression of the inherent logic of the plot: namely, their ability to *move* an idea in a direction against convention or expectation. In other words, the Lynchian characters embody the abstract ideas that Lynch aims to convey in his films. The characters are designed not only to move the story in a certain direction, but also to actually stand for a specific idea within the narrative. Such a role, when embodied within the otherwise stylistic Lynchian atmosphere, is a very powerful cinematic tool that captures and explicates the experience of the Thing.

To illustrate this claim, we can turn to the manmade-chicken scene in *Eraserhead*. As we watch Henry's attempt to carve them (thus seemingly portraying them as objects of his desire), one cannot overlook the feeling of disgust that arises from watching the scene. The scene is indeed repulsive: the legs move and putrescent fluid oozes from the cavity, while Henry looks on in horror. What is the purpose of this scene? What does Henry's character stand for in this scene? The idea Lynch is moving around here grows from both Henry's displacement and our discomfort. Henry's inner and outer worlds are clashing, and so are, to a certain extent, our worlds. The chickens are therefore the best way to capture this absurdity and disorientation; in this sense, the chickens *do* fit the scene simply because they don't. It is Henry who does not quite fit, as all the action in the filmed space around him appears to be normal. The tables are turned, as Henry appears as the abnormal component of the scene. It is as if his craving of the manmade chicken is much more plausible and normal than, say, his craving a standard succulent chicken. In this world, and in complete contradiction with normal expectation, it is as if Lynch's bizarre characters have *invaded* the real space of the screen, instead of the fictitious space of the film being imposed on normative characters.

Through the chicken scene, we can see how the Lynchian cinematic method echoes Žižek's philosophy. Žižek discusses at length the methods we employ when we experience our day-to-day problems, those everyday troubles we encounter and try to work through for ourselves. Žižek labels the mental process we employ in order to keep these problems under control as *fantasy*, a term used to depict our first-person point of view and the way these mundane problems appear to us.[7] Now, the chicken scene is basically a straightforward depiction of a mundane encounter with the world. At least it should have been, and probably still is, under the surface of the Lynchian magic show. Henry's problems (his relationship with Mary, caring for his baby, etc.) are as mundane as they come, at least to the extent that they can occupy real space, both in real life and onscreen. However, the Lynchian portrayal of these seemingly mundane problems is anything but conventional. Instead, Lynch tries to film the fantasy, namely, Henry's first-person perspective of his existence and his troubles. In other words, Lynch tries to put the elements of the fantasy normally associated with the unconscious up on the screen for us. He aims to disclose the fantasy and unveil the direct and unmediated experience of Henry's reality to the viewers. It is important to stress here that this first-person point of view of fantasy is not to be confused with an attempt to mask the true perception of reality with fleeting daydreams and distorted realities. On the contrary, with this instantiation of the mundane through the bizarre, Lynch aims to show us the way the mind deals with problems by constructing conscious and unconscious processes to manage these everyday realities. Because we have to exist in the world, we need a fantasy screen to help us do so. And the Lynchian characters exemplify this very need to exist.

We all employ such methods of fantasy when we "see ourselves" in the world, as we use fantasy to keep anxieties at a manageable distance. In other words, our fantasies are the "space" we create in order to shield and protect us from the horror of the world itself; from the Thing getting out "into public." The fantasies thus act as a filter between us and the world. This filtering process is what I would claim guides Lynch in the portrayal of his characters. In many of his films, his characters are forced to confront the Thing.

We can see this filtering process of fantasy in at least two predominant examples. First, in *Wild at Heart,* we see Bobby Peru as an obnoxious lecher, but clearly that is not how he imagines himself. From the first-person point of view, Peru sees himself as a powerful ladies' man. In the controversial rape scene of Lula (Laura Dern), in true Lynchian fashion, as the scene reaches its dramatic conclusion, Lula relents, shifting her own fantasy from one of repulsion to desire. What we see in this controversial scene is Lynch turning the tables on film cliché, shifting the sentiments of repulsion from the audience toward Peru over to curiosity as to why Lula makes such a shift. The fantasy worlds of both Lula and Bobby thus become the actual content of the scene, as does our first-person perception, which faces the task of extrapolating their perspectives.

A second example can also show this task at play. In *Mulholland Dr.,* we are confronted with Diane Selwyn's (Naomi Watts) fantasy world when we are asked to make sense of a seemingly typical love story between Diane and Camilla Rhodes (Laura Elena Harring) that has gone wrong. Lynch allows us to peek into Diane's first-person perspective in order to see how insane jealousy might actually look through her fantasy filter. The multiple story lines in the film, along with the attempt to bring Diane's fantasies onto the screen, create a mixture that defies the standard objective narrative and instead unfolds a new and subjective point of view, which is what the film is all about.[8] We could say the multiple narratives invite us to look beyond, to seek out the Thing that drives us to being curious filmgoers.

Thus, through Lynch's cinematic method, a method that follows Žižek's use of fantasy, the unconscious—that strange mechanism that shapes human desire—is on the screen before us. As Žižek reminds us, the "unconscious is outside," and, by employing this interpretation, we start to see that the structural logic of Lynch's films is not that perplexing. Instead, it is seen more as a series of floating layers of the world of characters' fantasies as they exist in stories of an increasingly fragmented and dissociated meaning. Just as the abstract artists attempted to paint the human dilemma in the early twentieth century, Lynch attempts to film the ideas that flow from the troubled mind. His narratives attract us because through his articulation of the Thing (or at least its presence in the film), we are drawn to them; drawn to engaging with the ideas he invites us to pursue. By following Lynch through Žižek's philosophy, along with a smidgen of Baudrillard's ideas, we begin to see his characters as symptoms of this fragmented and disoriented potential of the world.[9]

WHAT IS A NARRATIVE SUPPOSED TO BE?

Our investigation of Lynch's characters through Žižek's philosophy may lead one to conclude that Lynch's films are *only* fantasies, perhaps just details of the characters' nightmares to which we have privileged access. But this conclusion is far too simple and writes off much of what we can get from Lynch's films. Lynch provides us with more than just fantasy and nightmares. The illusion consists of more than just the nightmarish aspects of Lynch (such as the grotesque baby in *Eraserhead*, the evil that lurks behind Winkie's in *Mulholland Dr.*, or the Mystery Man's desert shack in *Lost Highway* where the Thing literally appears). It also includes the seemingly everyday world as it struggles to contain the psychic implications of trauma and violence, of getting too close to the Thing, such as Mr. Eddy's (Robert Loggia) road-rage reaction to being tailgated in *Lost Highway*. This trivial activity of driving in the everyday world paradoxically masks the traumatic world to which we have to cling to stop us from encountering the monsters that do lurk in the background. These monsters are real. They are the fears of losing your job, of getting cancer, of the plane's wing falling off, etc. The power of creating these illusions, this thin fabric of normality to fight off the nightmares, also has its flip side. Here, Lynch challenges the typical narrative by allowing what lurks under the surface loose.

In order to understand this challenge, we need to flesh out what the traditional cinematic narrative entails. Such narratives entail a regular, rationally ordered pattern with all the clues and conventions of orthodox film technique. They work because they fall into patterns we have grown up with and are used to. They tend to be singular in the sense that diverse readings are more difficult (but not impossible) to achieve.[10]

Following the Lynchian cinematic method, however, we see that Lynch plays with the traditional cinematic narrative to suggest that if we see Hollywood films as the be-all-and-end-all image of what narrative *should* be, then we are seduced into letting Hollywood make this real. Here, we can see that Lynch once again echoes the philosophy of Žižek. We can say that the traditional cinematic narrative includes what Žižek refers to as a *symbolic order* of contemporary society, or a set of unwritten codes of what a film narrative (and character) should be. The symbolic orders are the set of unwritten rules by which we operate. Žižek maintains that when we speak or listen, we ground our action in a network of complex rules and presuppositions. These facilitate communication and social cooperation and are, as such, a symbolized order. But they are not merely a set of learned operating procedures like a how-to manual for being; they are what we constantly measure ourselves against. For example, we have to learn the rules of social grace (don't sniff in public, do help the elderly cross the street), the rules of fashion (denim is *in*, florescent spandex is *out*), and so on. The symbolic order is therefore a mediating process, a guideline for expressions of personality.[11]

Furthermore, there is a controlling voice of the symbolic order, which Žižek labels *the big Other.* He uses the capital O to emphasize the law-giving power of this voice. Thus, when we construct our point of view of the world, the big Other is that imaginary observant entity that we look to for governing decisions. The big Other comes in many forms: it is the spectral voice of your parents reprimanding you for actions that violate social grace; it is the voice of fashion trends that dictate what you should wear; and so on. Such a voice is powerful, personal, subjective, and, above all, open to be challenged and contested.[12]

When we turn to the issue of film narrative, we find that the big Other, or the dominating voice that determines what film narrative is, is none other than the Hollywood film machine itself. Here, the Hollywood film machine, as the big Other, sets down the alleged rules for the symbolic order of the film narrative, thereby establishing a cookie-cutter paradigm for what a film's narrative should be like. Lynch, however, is a director who challenges and contests the Hollywood film machine. Here is where viewers typically get into difficulty understanding Lynch because he has confronted and usurped the rules of narrativization from *Eraserhead* to *Inland Empire* (2006) by suggesting (quite correctly) that there is no official big Other in film narrative. The Hollywood film machine attempts to set the rules of narrativization and characterization. But, as Baudrillard might have observed, the exponential rise of Hollywood films' use of computerized graphics and the enhanced use of makeup techniques, filmed death, explosions, etc. are conveyed with such authenticity that the magic of cinema ceases to hold us. It is replaced by these dominant and ubiquitous demands on our senses, demands from the big Other, to just watch rather than be reflective about the film. As such, it becomes harder to engage with a film at a deeper level than the visual with the appreciation of explosions, gruesome deaths, and strong sex scenes dominating.

Baudrillard's thinking encourages us to watch cinema, such as Lynch's films, as a challenge *against* Hollywood's imposed conception of what is real for the cinematic world. If Hollywood encourages us to merely buy the idea that films should be cut from the same template, then the challenge is to resist this attitude by developing counter-readings, counter-theories, and therefore counter-realities from which to consider.[13] Lynch's application of Žižek's and Baudrillard's philosophy can perhaps be best exemplified in the dialogue between Adam (Justin Theroux) and Vincenzo Casitliane (Dan Hedaya) in *Mulholland Dr.*:

ADAM: Hey!!!!! That girl is not in my film!!!
VINCENZO: It is no longer your film.

"Whose film is it?" therefore might be the definitive question we must pose when we watch or talk about Lynch's narrative. But since Lynch challenges the Hollywood film machine (through his challenge of the traditional cinematic narrative), the answer to this question will not follow a traditional style. Under the traditional cinematic approach, we can say, for example, that *Lost Highway* is, at least on one level, a narrative concerning desire, obsession, death, fidelity, etc. This, of course, can be supported by evidence provided in the film. Nothing provided from Lynch in this film (and the other two under consideration here) is that straightforward. Since there are no fixed interpretations, the viewer cannot entertain a clear-cut meaning. This is a philosophical position itself, suggesting that meaning is not necessarily fixed and immutable, but open to the vagaries of contested perspectives. Instead of attempting to control the debate over what the film means, we can choose to stay within what is occurring on the screen, what the material itself says to us. Then we can quite legitimately conclude that we have an interpretation of a particular character or scene in the film. We don't control the film space; we simply interpret it, letting Lynch's ideas seep into each other like an abstract painting that demands initial attention to itself, not to some conceptual and colonizing interpretation. So when Fred morphs into Pete in *Lost Highway*, we don't respond by asking, "What does this mean?" but "How does this work for us?" or "Where could this be going in Lynch's terms?" Through such questions, we see whose film it is: it is ours, it is Lynch's, and it is nobody's all at the same time.

Following Lynch's cinematic method, we can now ask ourselves not what the film means, precisely, but where our thoughts are led by Lynch's narrative. We can operate reflexively, challenging and questioning ourselves about how we came to the conclusions we did about narrative and, more important, about who is controlling these conclusions. It is therefore not Hollywood that seduces us. If this happens we are dead, Baudrillard tells us, because the reactions to the film are not our reactions, but ones that have been encoded into the Hollywood films. As such, we become automatic and respond only to stimulation of the violent or sexual images rather than to the challenge of the film understood symbolically.[14]

Therefore, from this premise, Fred's journey in *Lost Highway*, as he transmogrifies into Pete Dayton, certainly has philosophical resonances replete with questions of what it is to be a (sane) self. This is not what the film is about but merely an idea to play with, one to initiate a challenging dialogue about the ideas that arise from such an interpretation and may lead us to many points on the interpretative compass. Of course we can come to a conclusion or a resolution, as Žižek most certainly does, on *Lost Highway*. But the conclusion is not to totalize meaning—it is to create a clearing in which contestation and argument can be encouraged rather than stifled. In Baudrillardian terms, this keeps us alive because we are no longer such easy targets for the marketers. We are now starting to enjoy the Lynchian world.[15]

What If? *Mulholland Dr.* as Thought Experiment

To help facilitate such enjoyment, let's zero in on Lynchian characterization and narrativization in *Mulholland Dr.* and see how the universe of the film is structured. The film presents Diane Selwyn (Naomi Watts) and her journey either as a wannabe or failed actress, depending on which "entry point" of the narrative you choose. In the wannabe trajectory, she arrives in Hollywood as a naïve, starstruck country girl and is quickly embroiled in the mystery of Rita (Laura Elena Harring). In the failed-actress reading, Diane is overcome with jealousy as she is left alone and distraught. From there, we track Diane's life as it goes out of control. Lynch has severely disrupted the linear nature of the narrative, filming the haphazard path tracking how the mind itself bounces ideas around, running in and out of fantasy and reality like a competition between two strong forces.

You can see here that both stories are equally relevant and contain equal status in the film's narrative. In both versions, Diane's life is destabilized by what we could theorize as symptoms that emerge into the frame of the movie. These are the Lynchian "what ifs" that we need to think simultaneously, not allowing either story to take precedence, but letting them both unfold as equal narratives. To the aspiring actress, Rita materializes to work as what could be a symptom of Diane's repressed desire. In the failed-actress entry point, Rita emerges as the antithesis to Betty's mundane life, a fanciful imagining of what could be. Here we can see the Lynchian thought experiment moving ideas around. It is as if we are viewing the contents of both characters' unconscious desires as they spin out of control, as strong desires can do to anyone when confronted by a rampaging Thing.

However, what if what frightens, disturbs, or disgusts us most appears in concrete reality? A man fantasizes about killing his boss, and the next moment he finds himself standing over his boss's body? In *Mulholland Dr.*, we see Lynch's philosophical attempt to film the answer to this question. In what unfolds, we see multiple fantasies of interconnected lives experiencing these materialized scenarios. We can now provide a reasonable account for this in *Mulholland Dr.* in the seemingly incongruous sequence that takes place in the Winkie's diner as Dan (Patrick Fischler) explains his dream to Herb (Michael Cooke): "You're in both dreams and you're scared. I get even more frightened when I see how afraid you are and then I realize what it is—there's a man . . . in back of this place. He's the one . . . he's the one that's doing it. I can see him through the wall. I can see his face and I hope I never see that face ever outside a dream." Here, Dan's fears take on a concrete form, ending with the confrontation with the man located behind the restaurant.

Now, if we take into consideration what I have said above, searching for a sole interpretation here can lead us astray. It is better to just hold this scene for what it says. It has no coherent interchange in the narrative but to add to the dizzying swirl of nightmarish aspects of the film. And just as nightmares often spring out of the blue, this scene stages this exact feeling. Yet here this filmed symptom can indicate the beginning of a discussion of why it is on the screen at all. Why can we be so in thrall of this scene when it has little direct connection to the rest of the narrative? But the appearance of the symptom used not only connotes the Lynchian narrative, but also the modern filmmaker's stock in trade. That is, these symptoms often disturb us at a more fundamental level, and that is why they work so effectively/nightmarishly on the screen. For example, we could see Bobby in *Wild at Heart* as a symptom of masculine violence and Frank in *Blue Velvet* as a symptom of the hostility of the (drug) market. Such examples suggest that Lynch uses these symptoms, which are disconnected from the narrative, to bring forth that deeper disturbance; to confront the Thing.

Furthermore, following Žižek's philosophy, we can approach *Mulholland Dr.*'s multiple narratives as refreshed expressions of a re-marked symbolic order where narrativization is more fluid and volatile, rather than fixed and predictable where the two (or three) narratives can be thought through simultaneously. In this approach, we start within the Lynchian universe and discuss the relationship between Diane and Rita and see the subtleties and nuances of this relationship that flags certain Lynchian motifs for sexuality, fantasy, and desire. After Rita wanders away from the car crash into Betty's world, Lynch manages to materialize something in Rita that is the concrete embodiment of Betty's (Diane's) failure to completely integrate the magical world of Hollywood as a smooth unified whole. Here, something is never quite right and, underpinned by Angelo Badalamenti's haunting score, we sense this. Consider the imbecilic grins on Betty's two travel angels and the dog crap in Coco's (Ann Miller) courtyard. They all seem to stain the scene, but Rita appears the uncanniest stain of all and becomes more disorientating as the film progresses with her uncanny status shifting as she occupies a place in both concurrent narratives. In other words, Rita becomes the filmed Thing. This is exactly the same feeling produced anytime something disturbs us that we cannot put into words.

Now Rita is not just the simple presence of some disruptive influence like the menacing existence of the shadowy criminal, but the disquieting something other that we cannot fully frame into language or, as Žižek would say, account for in the symbolic order. If the symbolic order is the set of unwritten rules through which we filter our personal versions of reality, then the symbolic order of the Hollywood film machine would decree that the cinematic stains Lynch throws into the mix have to be justified by accounting for them as archetypal dream sequences, or expressions of the aberrations of the characters involved. They of course can be. But they can also be explained as elemental disruptions to the frame of the filmmaker himself, intended not to complicate the thematic structure of the film but to add to its texture—to accumulate ideas to be dealt with at a more literal level, at the level of the question, "What if?"

With this in mind, the stains become something we must confront at a far less abstract level. Betty's world is dislocated because it is too much a reproduction of Hollywood, idealized to the point of breakdown. The grinning grandparents disrupt this idealized image; the dog crap disrupts Coco's idealized starlet accommodation, and so on. Now we can see that the disruption to the scene, this staining feature so prominent in the Lynchian world, is equivalent to our human mind. The feeling that something is not quite right, or that something just doesn't quite fit, is common to us all. Hence our relationship with the big Other is never completely secure and harmonious because we will always have to confront the Thing. It is a necessarily bumpy ride because, just when we seem to have our desires in order and under control, it shifts, slipping away as we attempt to control it. We must thank Lynch for filming it.

Notes

1. Philosophers from the ancient Greeks onward have theorized over the notion of the sublime, or the Thing. Plato (427–347 BCE), for instance, suggests that the sublime is a quality located in the soul, and thus beyond human interpretation. The German philosopher Immanuel Kant (1724–1804) argues that the sublime is an aesthetic quality, defined as "that which is absolutely great" and is awe-inspiring because of the human faculties' incapacity to articulate the vast beauty and power of nature and art. Both Plato and Kant claim there must be something to talking about the sublime.

2. This is a condensation of Freud's perspective. For more on the Thing, see M. Sharpe and J. Faulkner, *Understanding Psychoanalysis* (Stocksfield: Acumen Books, 2008), 23.

3. Slavoj Žižek, *The Sublime Object of Ideology* (London: Verso Books, 1997), 203.

4. For examples of the generic criticisms against Lynch, see the collection of reviews for *Eraserhead* found at www.rottentomatoes.com/m/Eraserhead.

5. To be sure, films don't think, since thinking requires a cognitive agent. However, we can speak of films thinking, metaphorically. I thus propose here that if we imagine that Lynch's films are a "mind in action," we have a much better chance of seeing how they work.

6. For an excellent précis on employing Baudrillard to challenge the real, see Rex Butler, *The Defence of the Real* (London: Sage, 1999), chap. 3.

7. Slavoj Žižek, *How to Read Lacan* (London: Granta Books, 2006).

8. We can see this filtering process of fantasy occur in at least two other examples in Lynch's films. First, in *Lost Highway,* sex plays an integral part of structuring the relationships of Fred/Pete, yet this is no *ordinary love story* as Fred's love for Renee turns nightmarish, and Lynch allows these fantasies to bleed into Fred/Pete's reality. Second, in *Eraserhead,* Henry's relationship with Mary seems to not have any strong rational premise at all, as if his life has turned into a reflection of the machinist and ascetic world in which he finds himself trapped.

9. Slavoj Žižek, *The Plague of Fantasies* (London: Verso Books, 1997), 13. We can also think here of a symptom as what Sigmund Freud conceived it to be, which was masking something deeper in the unconscious, a repressed dilemma to be resolved. For Freud's account of symptoms, see Sigmund Freud, "Inhibition, Symptom and Fear," in *Beyond the Pleasure Principle and Other Writings,* ed. John Reddick (New York: Penguin, 2003).

10. The traditional cinematic narrative can be best exemplified, for instance, through the works of Steven Spielberg, who often constructs his narratives to tease out some (historical) issue (*Schindler's List* [1993], *Amistad* [1997], *Saving Private Ryan* [1998]) to accommodate in the viewer a heightened sense of historical urgency in the human condition (the trauma of the Holocaust, the horror of slavery, the insanity of war, etc.).

11. Žižek, *How to Read Lacan,* 9.

12. Jean Baudrillard, *The Ecstasy of Communication* (New York: Semiotext[e], 1987), 98.

13. See Jean Baudrillard, *Simulacra and Simulation,* trans. Sheila Faria (Ann Arbor: University of Michigan Press, 1994).

14. Jean Baudrillard, *Fatal Strategies* (New York: Semiotext[e], 1990), 15.

15. Slavoj Žižek, *The Art of the Ridiculous Sublime* (Seattle: University of Washington, 2000).

THE WORLD AS ILLUSION

Rediscovering *Mulholland Dr.* and *Lost Highway* through Indian Philosophy

Ronie Parciack

This essay addresses the shaping of the *phenomenal world*, or the world of experience, in two films by David Lynch: *Lost Highway* (1997) and *Mulholland Dr.* (2001). These films form an interpretational challenge due to their unclear narratives, characterized by fluid characters, winding, unstitched structures, nonlinear time, and incoherent space. I argue that Lynch's work is a philosophical act that calls for a significant upheaval in the Western spectator's apprehension of the phenomenal; it constitutes an epistemological change regarding both the nature of the phenomenal world and the nature of the subject within it.

This issue is widely discussed in various traditions of Indian philosophy, in particular by the prominent Advaita-Vedānta school of Indian philosophy that considers our normal, everyday understanding of the phenomenal as ignorance, and defines the phenomenal world as ontologically dilapidated. Through the Indian debate on the concept of *ātman* (essence, self) and the rejection of *essentialism* (the assumption according to which entities are stable and are endowed with a firm essence) in early Buddhist traditions, I discuss the aspirations for the elaboration or the breaking of the boundaries of the self and the idea that the phenomenal is an essence-less, empty world. I use these notions to discuss the philosophical significance of deviations from the conventions of the realist style in cinema employed by David Lynch in these two texts.

Who Dunnit? Philosophical Premises and Narrative Conventions

Lost Highway and *Mulholland Dr.* are similar in some pivotal narrative aspects, which make these films difficult to follow. In order to shed light on the philosophical qualities that might lie behind this difficulty, I begin by endowing these films with an apparent comprehensibility in the terms of Western cinematic narrative. As I show, this interpretation is opposed to the Lynchian philosophical view.

Both films present a murder that is relegated to the margins of the narrative. Renee Madison (Patricia Arquette) is the protagonist murdered in *Lost Highway;* Camilla Rhodes (Melissa George) in *Mulholland Dr.* Neither the murder itself, nor questions concerning the identity of the murderer and his motives (the classical "whodunit" question) form the films' narrative foci. Taking into account the obsession in which Western popular culture engages in this inquest, Lynch's choice to avoid it seems exceptional. Contrary to appearances, I argue that the "whodunit" issue is indeed raised by the Lynchian cinematic narrative: not in the sense of identifying the murderer and his motives, but rather as a philosophical question that cannot be answered in the conventional terms of narrative or mainstream cinema.

More specifically: What does the moviegoer expect to find out when asking "whodunit?" Simply speaking, when narrative cinema poses the question, the answer is likely to be the murderer's name. Looking for a murderer's name already involves philosophical premises concerning both the nature of the subject and the nature of the world. With regard to the subject, a name is assumed to stand for one's identity. That is, it posits the existence of a stable, continuous entity within the solid physical boundaries of the body; an entity acting and existing within the limits of the phenomenal, subjected to natural laws of time and space.[1]

With regard to the phenomenal world, the prominence of the murder trope in Western cinematic narratives assumes the centrality of this world as the only arena providing a valid existence. This is also the reason why the transition from "existence" to "nonexistence" is so crucial. The "whodunit" also assumes causality that can be exposed, thus conveying the notion according to which the phenomenal world operates according to a logic that may be traced. This presumed logic is subjected to a linear perception of time, as events logically lead from one to another.

Lynch is obsessed with the riddle of identity. This may hint at the "whodunit" question. However, he refuses to accept the philosophical and narrative frameworks that make the question answerable, and thereby suggests that asking the question itself is impossible. The assumption of a stable entity subjected to natural laws of time and space does not exist in these two films. Lynch's subject is fluid (i.e., unstable and ever-changing), and this fluidity is one of the most important features of his cinematic world.

Both films present protagonists whose identity is blurred or fused with other figures. *Lost Highway* blurs two male protagonists: Fred Madison (Bill Pullman) and Peter Dayton (Balthazar Getty), a musician and a car mechanic, and two female characters: Renee, Fred's wife, and Alice Wakefield, who is Peter's lover (both played by Patricia Arquette). The transition between the two male characters follows the murder that is briefly alluded to. The film follows the imprisoned Fred, tormented by headaches and insomnia. At a certain moment he abruptly disappears from the narrative succession and is replaced by Peter. Peter is younger; he is romantically and destructively involved with Alice, the paramour of an elderly Mafioso whose cars Peter maintains. Renee and Alice are both portrayed by the same actress, and the film demonstrably testifies to their identity, as the Mystery Man (Robert Blake) tells Fred, "There is no Alice. Her name is Renee. If she told you her name was Alice, she was lying."

Mulholland Dr. also jettisons the identity of its protagonists. It begins with that of the main character, Rita (Laura Elena Harring), who, at the beginning of the film, sits in a limousine driving along Mulholland Drive in Los Angeles. The drive is abruptly stopped; a gun is directed at the protagonist's head, and she is asked to get out of the limo. Wildly driven cars cause an accident that cuts the succession of planned events—apparently, the assassination of the protagonist. Her murder is never seen onscreen; however, evidence of its occurrence causes the suicide of another character who is introduced later in the film. The protagonist in the limo has a head injury, loses her memory, and from this point she is swept up in a journey that takes her to a house where she meets Betty Elms (Naomi Watts). The two, Betty and the protagonist (who calls herself Rita after glimpsing a poster of former Hollywood megastar Rita Hayworth), embark on a journey to trace the protagonist's lost identity. This search for identity becomes more and more confused and manifold. By the end of the movie, Rita is blurred with the figure of Camilla, a successful actress, and Betty is blurred with the figure of Diane Selwyn, the character who eventually commits suicide.

Both *Lost Highway* and *Mulholland Dr.* raise questions concerning the Lynchian cinematic figure. Who is he or she? What engenders the multiplicity or fluidity in it, and what is the significance of this trope? Moreover, given the fact that Renee of *Lost Highway* was murdered, how can Alice be alive? And given the fact that the protagonist of *Mulholland Dr.* is assassinated at the beginning of the film, how can she be witness to the figure of Diane lying dead on her bed? What is death in the Lynchian world? Is death possible in a world of fluid characters? Is life possible in such a world? Examining the Lynchian narrative from the normative, everyday perspective pushes the spectator into a corner where the entire familiar world, and all the presuppositions concerning the phenomenal, systematically collapse.

Rehabilitating the Lynchian Text, Restoring the Phenomenal

The distorted picture of the Lynchian world has triggered various attempts by predominant Lynch interpreters to reconstruct or rehabilitate the Lynchian text. This rehabilitation is designed to restore the lost logic, and hence make Lynch's films acceptable. Without a comprehensive reconstruction, without injecting logic into the films and making sense of the plotlines, Lynch's films would be judged as incredible and untrustworthy—that is, as ontologically invalid.[2]

How can such an order be restored? How can the cinematic text be rehabilitated? First and foremost, we can do so by sharply differentiating the scenes that are judged to be valid occurrences and those that are judged to be events that never took place. The literary theorist Tzvetan Todorov argues that incidents that could not be explained through our knowledge of the familiar world are commonly interpreted as dreams, fantasies, or illusions (i.e., as mental images that never occurred in empiric reality).[3] According to this explanation, only scenes that correlate with the premises regarding the phenomenal world can be considered as ontologically real, whereas other scenes, which notably do not correspond with them, are considered as unreal. Since the latter type of scene inhabits a central part of both _Lost Highway_ and _Mulholland Dr._—through fluid characters, nonlinear time, illogical occurrences, and incoherent space—it is commonly held that Lynch indeed does not follow an actual, real line of events, but intentionally depicts an unreal cinematic world.

If the real phenomenal world is not the Lynchian locus, what is? Lynch's interpreters turned to _depth psychology_, the psychological studies examining the unconscious aspects of human experience, and read the Lynchian world as unleashing the wild, unruly side of the human psyche. Therefore, most of the scenes may be considered as fantasies, which do not occur in the cinematic real life or real world, but in the mind of one protagonist or another. Since mental images are not perceived as ontological categories, they are not acknowledged as real events. The clear classification of certain scenes as unreal, idiosyncratic fantasies restores logic to the Lynchian scenery. Looking back at the previously raised examples, one is now able to reconstruct the Lynchian narratives and make sense of their content.

Take, for instance, the duplicity of both male and female characters in *Lost Highway*. A careful examination of facts and fantasies makes it plausible to assume, like Tim Lucas and Todd McGowan do, that it was Fred who murdered Renee, whereas Peter and Alice are nothing but fantasized extensions of these real characters. The reason for such fantasies is embedded in the psyche of its main character. As Lucas explains, Fred's fantasy proceeds from his enormous unconscious guilt following his wrongful deeds: "after realizing what he's done, Fred cannot face the overwhelming realities of the murder and his conviction, and his denial extends to the obliteration of his own identity."[4] Similarly, the fantasy of Alice provides an illusion of continuity to the dead Renee in the consciousness of the guilt-stricken Fred.[5] In short, it's all in the protagonist's mind.[6]

A similar solution has also been put forward in relation to the narrative ambiguities in *Mulholland Dr.* A reconstruction of the narrative suggests that Camilla and Diane (the real figures) were having an affair; after Camilla abandons Diane, the latter hires an assassin. Following the murder, Diane fantasizes Betty and Rita, the imagined versions of herself and Camilla, as a compensation for her failures. Lynch presents us with a brief and truncated glance into Diane's psyche. This explains the incoherent narrative as well as its nonlinear moves, which is best described by McGowan as "the a-temporal logic of desire," where chronology (or any form of consistency) is lacking since "desire does not move forward."[7]

At this point one may ask: Why is this necessary? Why is it so important for Western interpretations of the Lynchian narrative to restore it into coherence? What might be the philosophical significance of such restoration? The answer to these questions, one might argue, lies within the Western concept of a narrative. The literary theorist Michael Butor argues that narrative can be a structural distillation of ontology. Western cinematic narrative, an example of contemporary narrative, is founded on the ontological premise that the phenomenal is endowed with the highest ontological status and, as such, serves as a standard for any ontological validity.[8]

This is precisely the desired standard for which Western Lynch interpreters look in their attempts to reconstruct Lynch's narratives, as narratives that do not suit such standards are perceived as unacceptable. For example, in his interpretation of *Lost Highway*, McGowan notes that the narrative of the film "brings the logic of fantasy out into the open" and, as such, "necessarily strikes us as incongruous, as a film without any narrative at all." In other words, a narrative-less text, or a text that does not correspond with conventional narrative rules and logic, may be at risk of ontological collapse. Such a collapse can be eluded in a question posed by McGowan, who asks: "If Peter Dayton is constructed as a part of Fred Madison's fantasy, then why can everyone else see him?" This question fleshes out the Western assumption about narrative coherency and its ontological value. Western interpreters, bound by this ontological assumption, are invited to follow the belief that Fred is fantasizing, even though the filmic narrative tells us a wholly different story. [9]

The fact that we all see Peter makes it impossible to argue that he does not exist. The same is true for Alice, Betty, and Rita. All the characters are visible onscreen; no cinematic conventions (such as fade-ins, fade-outs, or dissolves) that are commonly used to differentiate between real and fantasized characters or events are employed. The existence of all the characters in the Lynchian sphere is beyond doubt: ontologically, they are all on the same level.

The question evoked by the Lynchian narrative therefore has to change. The question can no longer be, "What really exists (in the film)?" but rather, "Is our comprehension (of the film) valid or invalid?" This constitutes a shift from the ontological to the epistemological, which is exactly the fulcrum where Indian philosophy becomes especially relevant to the Lynchian context.

Snakes, Ropes, and Identities: Connecting Lynch with Indian Philosophy

In order to begin roaming within Indian thought, I shall recall the well-known proverb often used by various Indian philosophical schools. This proverb, aimed at examining the nature of knowledge, states: "This is not a snake; this is a rope."

One may imagine the situation in which this proverb was uttered. Someone walks in the wide-open spaces of the phenomenal world; at a certain point he confronts an object that elicits great existential anxiety in him. The sentence therefore defines the empirical experience as an existence constantly threatened by the notion of death. But the knowledge concerning the nature of the phenomenal object was erroneous. The argument: "this is a snake" is refuted by its counterargument, "this is a rope."

The existential anxiety was motivated by false knowledge. A correct knowledge may allay the anxiety caused by the misidentification of the empirical object. Nevertheless, the anxiety becomes redundant not because of the concrete features of the rope (a rope, when a noose, may be no less distressing) but rather because this proverb, when examined through the perspective of the Advaita-Vedānta philosophical school, is aimed at a radical change in the comprehension of the phenomenal. This radical change also relates to the status of the objects and subjects within it.

Broadly speaking, the Lynchian cinematic experience has some similarities with the use of this proverb by the Advaita-Vedānta school: both use active experience to impart knowledge (i.e., a completely different comprehension of the phenomenal world). In both cases, the point of departure is the phenomenal world: the empirical world as a locus of existence for the person who fears the snake, and the cinematic world with its mimetic abilities. This calls for the elucidation of some concepts basic to Indian thought and to two philosophical traditions: The Hindu Advaita-Vedānta and the Buddhist Mādhyamika schools.[10] Both schools assert that the common, everyday understanding of the phenomenal world is profoundly fallacious. Both promote the need for refuting the familiar, and accordingly paving the way for a new understanding.

Such an understanding can be deduced from the following story (which is told in the *Upaniṣads,* the ancient texts from which these schools draws their wisdom). In the heart of the story is a conversation between a mentoring father and his son, Śvetaketu. The topic is the nature of both the self and the phenomenal world, and it is intended to perform an upheaval in the comprehension of both natures. The father begins by asking his son to bring him a container of water and a pinch of salt. Then he asks him to put a chunk of salt in the container. The next day, the father asks his son to taste the water at the edge of the container. The son reports that the water is salty. The father then asks him to repeat this action, this time by sipping water from different parts of the container. The son obliges, and maintains that the water is still salty. Since the salt dissolved in the water, the son couldn't see it anymore. Realizing this, the father concluded: "You, of course, did not see it there, son. But it was always right there. The finest essence here, that constitutes the self in the whole world. That is the truth; that is the self (ātman); and that's how you are, Śvetaketu!"[11]

An invisible element, as expressed by the metaphor of the salt dissolved in water, is the refined essence that pervades reality as a whole. This invisible essence is the truest and the most real; it is the cornerstone of all subsistence and, furthermore, defines it. The climax of this story is that this essence, this truth, is also the self. In terms of this specific story, this essence is also the boy Śvetaketu.

This story also refers to four concepts that are widely discussed in established traditions of Indian philosophy: *brahman* and *ātman*, *māyā* and *avidyā*. *Brahman* can be defined as the transphenomenal Absolute, or the underlying Being of all beings. In puristic perspectives, it is not endowed with any phenomenal features: it is not physical in space, not personal and independent of time. It transcends the phenomenal, yet also permeates the phenomenal in that it exists at the core of any being. Here, it is termed the *ātman*. The *ātman* is thus identical to the *brahman*; it constitutes the nucleus residing within the individual, and defines its true essence.

Using these two concepts, let us return to Śvetaketu, whose true essence was metaphorically compared to the salt dissolved in the water. Śvetaketu is therefore not his physical body; nor are his own priorities, his character traits, personal history, or familial status. He is not even defined by his own name; his true essence, the *ātman* that is identical to *brahman*, is very different from all these.

Indian philosophy attempts to achieve true knowledge of the empirical through the phenomenal. This comprehension requires a prism that is utterly different from the ordinary. This perspective refutes ordinary, common knowledge (*avidyā*, also translated as "ignorance") and rejects the phenomenal as an essence of reality. In this sense, the phenomenal is a delusion. The most real of all, though interwoven in it, is not captured in any of its physical, spatial or temporal features.

The phenomenal world is therefore a delusive trick. The concept signifying this is *māyā*—an old concept whose classical definition is primarily identified with the tradition of Advaita-Vedānta. Jan Gonda's comprehensive review stresses two main ways of interpreting *māyā*: power and deceit.[12] These two attributes highlight the centrality of empirical reality in human experience and consciousness, as well as revealing it as a trap. The Advāitic contention is that that empirical reality is based upon a deluding, limited, and restraining quality, lacking a firm ontological validity. Empirical reality is often compared to a cover that should be removed. It is a delusion creating mental structures drawing on an empty reality and explains the deluded supposition that this reality indeed exists, or, as Wendy Doniger O'Flaherty puts it, "that something does exist."[13]

"*Mulholland Dr.*? I Wouldn't Know Anything about That"*

The Indian Advaita-Vedānta school promotes an understanding according to which the phenomenal is a delusion. Therefore, the correct gaze is one that exposes the world as ontologically dilapidated. From this perspective, it is not surprising that Lynch cannot know a single thing about *Mulholland Dr.* But Lynch goes further. He uses *Mulholland Dr.* as a metaphor signifying the phenomenal world, and employs it to display the idea of ontological invalidity of the phenomenal world.

What do we know about *Mulholland Dr.*? Some may begin with the knowledge that "Mulholland Drive" is the name of a well-known road in Los Angeles, curving between Hollywood's hills, which connote the dominant film industry in the West. What in fact does the Lynchian narrative reveal? Mulholland Drive is a signpost in a dark street, nothing more than a senseless name. In terms of narrative elements in the film, this is the road in which Camilla loses her identity. Is it accurate? What is Camilla's true identity?

Let us return to the story of the salt in the water and Śvetaketu's true identity. The climax of the story was the insight according to which Śvetaketu's, and every other being's true identity, is the *ātman*—that fine, invisible essence unrelated to any phenomenal aspect. The Indian path toward the understanding of the true self is directed at a paradoxical target where finding the true self equals abandoning the features of the phenomenal individual. Following this logic, is Camilla's loss of her phenomenal identity considered as a loss of identity?

I shall try to harden this rhetorical question: Camilla has perhaps lost her phenomenal identity. However, the character played by the actress Laura Elena Harring wants to trace it anew. At this stage of the film, Lynch allows the spectator to assume that the search for identity takes place in the terms of classical subjectivity. She and Naomi Watts (who portrays Betty) explore her final movements, such as the drive along Mulholland Drive, the places she might have been and people she might have communicated with, in order to trace her personal history and phenomenal figure. Retrospectively, it is possible to claim that detecting Camilla's phenomenal character is impossible, if only because of the fact that while Rita is making the journey, Camilla is already dead. This journey of Rita/Camilla is in fact an attempt

---

*A quote from David Lynch on *Mulholland Dr.*, in David Hughes, *The Complete Lynch* (London: Virgin Books, 2003), 242.

to explore the way in which one toils to constitute an identity within the world in which a phenomenal identity is not possible.

At this point, one could divide the cinematic moment in which the identity-seeking journey begins to unfold into two layers of knowledge. The first layer is the viewer's: it is driven by the common, ordinary knowledge of empirical reality (*avidyā*). It is captivated by its delusional power and refuses to be released from it. The second layer is the director's, who already knows that a phenomenal identity is not possible, and therefore the identity-seeking journey is a journey toward refuting the phenomenal. An enormous disparity obviously lies between these two layers.

This gap is depicted by the Advaitist philosopher Śankara. The following dialogue, taken from the "*Upadeśa Sāhasrī*: A Thousand Teachings of Sri Śamkarācārya," is between a teacher and a disciple who insists on identifying himself with the phenomenal subject and world (*samsāra*): "The teacher said: In spite of your being the highest *ātman* and not *samsāric*, [You hold the stand:] 'I am *samsāric*.' Despite the fact you do not act and enjoy, [you stick to your stance:] 'I act and enjoy.' In spite of the fact you do know [who you truly are, you say:] 'I don't know.' This is ignorance [*avidyā*]."[14] The student's state of *avidyā* leads him to a constant denial of his true nature. The disciple thus holds onto the phenomenal world like a drowning man clutching a plank. In this respect, his stance resembles that of the viewer who wishes to trace the identity of the dark-haired woman, and holds onto the identity defined by the phenomenal spectacle of subjectivity.

This identity is also encoded in the dialogue quoted above. By using the words "act and enjoy," the subject identifies himself as the one who acts in the world. The subject's existence in the world is defined via his actions, but not solely on this: "act and enjoy" means that the subject who acts is also the subject who enjoys the fruit of his actions. That is, the disciple perceives himself as a continuous and stable being within the dimension of time. This perception is considered erroneous, since existence in temporal dimensions (i.e., the phenomenal) is perceived as a relative existence that is ontologically shaky. When Śankara rejects the identification of the truly existent with temporal dimensions, he calls for a rupture of the temporal sequence.

The rupture of the temporal sequence is indeed the starting point for the journey seeking out Camilla's identity. A gun is pointed at her brow, and when she comes out of the limo, her phenomenal figure is already dead. Nevertheless, we see "her" acting to find "her" own identity. In another complex scene toward the end of the film, we even see "her" gazing at the figure of Diane, her ex-lover, lying dead on her bed after she shot herself several weeks after she (Diane) learned that Camilla had been murdered. The Lynchian narrative, therefore, violates temporal sequences and thus forces the spectators to witness scenes that do not adhere to the accepted Western notions of the phenomenal. Lynch rejects the customary assumptions regarding the phenomenal subject, as he does with the natural laws of time and with logical causality. In other words, he breaks with the aesthetic codes that translate the ontological superiority attributed in the West to the phenomenal. Lynch turns his back on the conventions of the realist style in film, shattering the customary view of the phenomenal.

This is also the reason why he draws his viewers into a world that lacks continuity. Take, for example, the sequence where Fred tells Renee about a nightmare he had in *Lost Highway*. Fred says: "I could not find you. . . . And there you were, lying in bed. It wasn't you; it looked like you—but it wasn't."[15] The nightmare is characterized as a split between the character's physicality and its identity. This may be a disturbing notion that shatters the familiar, but Lynch develops this further: as Fred goes on narrating, his nightmare seems to be restored in front of our eyes, when suddenly a feminine voice shrieks. Who is shrieking? That is: whose nightmare is it? A stable and coherent perception of both the subject and the world would have produced a scream in a masculine voice. Lynch crosses the subject's boundaries in both senses of physical and gendered stability. He refutes phenomenal materiality by disintegrating and deliberately repudiating it.

The inlet opened by the Advaitic stance not only attempts to disprove the phenomenal identity of the subject (Camilla, Fred) but also paves the way to exceed the subject's boundaries and breach them. By associating the Lynchian world and Indian philosophy, it can be claimed that this is enabled not only because the phenomenal is ontologically dilapidated, but also due to the broader significance of the *ātman*. Due to its a-phenomenal, absolute nature, the *ātman* cannot be different from one subject to another. Each *ātman* is distinct from any phenomenal phase; each *ātman* is identical to the *brahman*. Therefore, the true essence of any of the film's protagonists is completely identical to that of another. From this perspective, there is no ontological obstacle for the dissolution of physical/phenomenal subjectivity. Characters, like salt, can dissolve away into water. In this sense, the fluidity between the characters in both *Mulholland Dr.* and *Lost Highway*— Camilla and Rita, Diane and Betty, Fred and Peter, Renee and Alice—may be interpreted as an active presentation of the absence of essence of a subject's phenomenal definition.

From the *Dividual* to the Notion of *Anātman*

Let us momentarily return to the feminine shriek heard in the description of Fred's nightmare in *Lost Highway.* What meaning should be given to this incongruity (in Western normative terms), where the subject is engendered as male but a female voice transmits his reaction? McKim Marriott, the cultural anthropologist, coined the term *individual,* to represent the idea that the subject is not one coherent entity, but a cluster of separate elements.[16]

This idea can be better explained via the thought of early Buddhism. This thought rejected the pivotal role of the *ātman-brahman* identity and concepts, and instead formulated the idea of *conditioned origination* (*pratītya-samutpāda*). According to this idea, all phenomena are a result of mutually dependent occurrences. Everything that exists is conditioned; things arise interdependently, and reality is formed as a conditioned origination. All that exists is conditioned; therefore nothing is permanent, fixed, or absolute. There is no single stable essence, to quote a famous Buddhist philosopher who said: "Essence arising from Causes and conditions makes no sense."[17] Contrary to the concept of *ātman* as identical to *brahman,* Buddhism articulated the concept of *anātman:* the absence of essence. Nothing has an essence, or self; nothing serves as an internal uniting and stabilizing factor.

The *anātman* premise is part of a broader observation about reality. There is no permanence in anything in the world. When looking at a cloud, you should note a movement; gazing at a tree may evoke its growth, wilting, or the fact that it can become a table. The human being is part of this reality, no more and no less than a flow of events, perceptions, and sensations that engage each other and are engaged by each other. Knowledge of oneself means, to use Marriott's term, the knowledge of your actual *dividuality.*[18]

From this perspective, the Lynchian narrative may constitute the *dividuality* of its protagonists, thus confronting the viewer with this interpretation, and initiating the spectators into a reality in which knowledge of *dividuality* and the nonessentiality assumption is an active experience that takes place in a movie theater. It occurs within the experience of film viewing, imposing itself on the audience by means of characters and narrative designs.

The notion of *dividuality* may also arise from a well-known Buddhist fable, narrating a dialogue between a Greek monarch and a Buddhist monk. Like the *upaniṣadic* Śvetaketu, the king is also imprisoned by the delusion of the phenomenal world, while the teacher wishes to open his eyes to new notions regarding conditioned origination and the absence of fixed essences. The teacher asks the king how he came to meet him—on foot or in a vehicle. When the king answers he arrived by a chariot, the monk inquires: "What is the chariot? Is the pole the chariot? Or the axle, wheels, frame, reins, yoke, spokes, or goad?" The king replies that none of these things in itself is the chariot. The monk further questions: "Then all these separate parts taken together are the chariot? Or maybe the chariot is something other than the separate parts?" Following the king's negation, the monk concludes: "I can find no chariot. The chariot is a mere sound. . . . There is no chariot!"[19]

And from here, with a leap meant to respond to the structured incoherence in the Lynchian narrative, I quote the allegedly incomprehensible lines—or Buddhist fable—recited at the Club Silencio of *Mulholland Dr.*: "No hay banda! / There is no band / Il n'y a pas d'orchestre / This is all in a tape Recording / No hay banda—/ And yet—we hear a sound / If we want to hear a Clarinet / Listen—It's all recorded / No hay banda / It is all a tape / Il n'y a pas d'orchestre / It is an illusion. / Listen?" There is no band. No orchestra. No chariot. All these are illusions, or empty conventions. A single clear glance reveals that they are made from separate, constantly changing parts. There is no organizing essence. Rather, there are only transitory events, protagonists that transform into other figures. This is the Lynchian world that welcomes its spectators.

The Lynchian world thus confronts spectators with radical perceptions of reality, actively arousing a sensation of disorientation in them. From this perspective, Lynch's phenomenal world is a disventure filling the audience with a tangible sensation of uneasiness, depriving it of any terra firma. And yet, this disorientation that appears to be tormenting in the Western sense may be blessed through the prism of Indian philosophy. The new encounter with the phenomenal as ontologically dilapidated, and with the subject as unfixed and fluid, may serve as an aperture to an adventure where film viewing is a point of departure that dismantles the subject's boundaries, widens its knowledge, releasing it from the constricting boundaries of the phenomenal.

Notes

1. For a detailed discussion of classical subjectivity, see Kaja Silverman, *The Acoustic Mirror—The Female Voice in Psychoanalysis and Cinema* (Bloomington: Indiana University Press, 1988), 80.

2. At times the titles of these essays suffice: Todd McGowan's essay is entitled "Finding Ourselves on a 'Lost Highway'"; the title of Paul A. Woods' chapter analyzing this film in his book is "*Lost Highway*—the Highway Back." They suggest that we have to "find" ourselves, restore order, and "remediate" the Lynchian incoherent world (see Todd McGowan, "Lost on Mulholland Dr.: Navigating David Lynch's Panegyric to Hollywood," *Cinema Journal* 43, no. 2 [Winter 2004]: 67–89; and Todd McGowan "Finding Ourselves on a 'Lost Highway': David Lynch's Lesson in Fantasy," *Cinema Journal* 39, no. 2 [Winter 2000]: 51–73).

3. Tzvetan Todorov, *The Fantastic: A Structural Approach to a Literary Genre*, trans. Richard Howard (Ithaca: Cornell University Press, 1987), 25, 91.

4. Tim Lucas, "Kiss Me Doubly: Notes on David Lynch's Lost Highway," *Video Watch-dog 43* (1998): 31, cited in McGowan, "Finding Ourselves on a 'Lost Highway,'" 60.

5. McGowan, "Lost on Mulholland Dr.," 67–89; McGowan "Finding Ourselves on a 'Lost Highway,'" 51–73.

6. As David Hughes notes: "Fred constructs an alternate reality for himself . . . an amnesiac/schizoid state from which he may not return" (see Hughes, *The Complete Lynch*, 206).

7. McGowan, "Lost on Mulholland Dr.," 73.

8. David Smith, "Construction and Deconstruction, Narrative and Anti-Narrative: The Representation of Reality in the Hindu Court Epic," in *The Indian Narrative*, ed. Christopher Schackle and Rupert Snell (Wiesbaden: Otto Harassowitz, 1992), 33.

9. McGowan, "Finding Ourselves on a 'Lost Highway,'" 51, 70 n. 9). McGowan, as well as Michel Chion, were involved in a debate on the question of whether Lynch differentiates between the realistic and the fantastic layers, and they also discussed the meaning of this differentiation as regards the normality of the subject constituted in his films. I disagree with the argument regarding the Lynchian differentiation between the layers of reality/fantasy/desire (see Michel Chion, *David Lynch*, trans. Robert Julian [London: BFI, 1995], 136). From another angle, it is possible to attest to the precedence of the phenomenal world in McGowan's phrasing: "By combining sense with the texture of fantasy, Lynch uses the first part of *Mulholland Dr.* to explore the role that fantasy has in rendering experience coherent and meaningful" (McGowan, "Lost on Mulholland Dr.," 67).

10. These schools do differ in pivotal aspects. The reason for employing them both is twofold: first, these traditions are related and have influenced each other. The second reason is the eclectic nature of the Lynchian text, which is not obliged to adhere to the premises of a single school.

11. P. Olivelle, trans., *Upaniṣads* (Oxford and New York: Oxford University Press, 1996), 154–55.

12. Jan Gonda, quoted in Thomas O'Neil, *Māyā in Śankara: Measuring the Immeasurable* (Delhi, Varanasi, and Patna: Motilal Banarsidass, 1980), 33.

13. Wendy Doniger O'Flaherty, *Dreams, Illusions and Other Realities* (Chicago and London: University of Chicago Press, 1984), 114.

14. Swāmī Jagadānanda, *Upadeśa Sāhasrī: A Thousand Teachings of Śrī Śamkarācārya* (Mylapore, Madras, India: Sri Ramakrishna Math, 2003), 35. All the notes in parentheses are mine. I am deeply grateful to my friend and colleague Daniel Raveh for his help in translating and interpreting this dialogue.

15. I am deliberately ignoring the image of the old woman that glimmers for a moment on the screen. This image may indeed explain the nightmare as the vision of Renee in her old age, and therefore as the vision of the dismantling of the human body as signified by the female body. However, in the same scene, the young Renee is presented as a figure Fred fails to recognize. The interpretation I favor here refers therefore to the dread aroused by the split between the question of identity and the physical entity, in other words, the notion of the subject as unstable and fluid.

16. Andre Certel, *Categories of Self: Louis Dumont's Theory of the Individual* (New York: Berghahn Books, 2005), 61.

17. Jay L. Garfield, *The Fundamental Wisdom of the Middle Way: Nāgārjuna's Mūlamadhyamakārikā* (New York: Oxford University Press, 1995), 39–40.

18. Contrary to the common perception that tends to see a human being in a physical body as stable and continuous, Buddhism proposes an alternative explanatory model. According to this model, a person is a psycho-physical unit composed of five clusters (*Skandhas*): matter, sensations or emotions, perceptions and cognitions, voluntary tendencies leading to action, and consciousness. These powers frequently join and change, and they form an explanatory model (*Skandhas* are not ontological categories) for understanding a human being as this ontologically empty convention.

19. Ainslee T. Embree, ed., *Sources of Indian Tradition*, vol. 1 (New York: Columbia University Press, 1988), 105–6.

Part 2

SELFHOOD AND SUBJECTIVITY: THE EXISTENTIAL DRIVE TOWARD SELF-UNDERSTANDING

ALL ROADS LEAD TO THE SELF

Zen Buddhism and David Lynch's *Lost Highway*

Mark Walling

In 1929, Arthur O. Lovejoy observed that, for future historians of philosophy, the twentieth century would prove to be the "Age of the Great Revolt against Dualism." As a theological concept, *dualism* points to a belief in an existence formed by two fundamental entities, such as God and Satan as equal forces, and contrasts with monism and pluralism. However, philosophers utilize the term to refer to any system of thought that describes human existence as comprised of two fundamental yet separate elements. Much of Western philosophy may be categorized, in one form or another, as dualistic. For Plato (427–347 BCE), the body imprisons the soul, which informs the mind of its immaterial nature and encourages it to seek a return to the eternal and universal form that inspired it. For René Descartes (1596–1650), mind and body are separate entities yet both formed of substance. Descartes is often described as a *substance dualist*. In his view, the mind influences the body through a physical relationship. Other philosophers have offered a wealth of views describing the nature of a dualistic existence. Yet Lovejoy perceived a reaction against the overall concept of philosophical dualism, and, while the accuracy of his prediction remains debatable, it is true that throughout the twentieth century, numerous philosophers conducted inquiries into the nature of consciousness and the problems presented by Cartesian (i.e., Descartes' version) dualism.[1] In addition to questions raised by Western thinkers, Zen Buddhism, which was introduced to the United States in the late nineteenth century, also encouraged intellectuals and practitioners alike to recognize the ontological trouble presented by dualistic systems of thought. "If you have been in the habit of thinking logically according to the rules of dualism," writes D. T. Suzuki, a man who was instrumental in the spread of Zen Buddhism in America, "rid yourself of it."[2]

The specific degree of influence of twentieth-century philosophy on American filmmakers is difficult to pinpoint; nevertheless, Lovejoy's observation of a "revolt" against philosophical dualism is born out repeatedly in the work of significant film directors. Stanley Kubrick, Sam Peckinpah, and Martin Scorsese explicitly broach concerns of duality throughout their respective careers, typically challenging an inherited concept before coming to an uneasy compromise with reality's dual nature. However, for David Lynch, such compromise is not as easily accepted. Confirming observations offered by Zen Buddhists, Lynch's work persistently reveals the destructive consequences of a dualistic worldview. But in *Lost Highway* (1997), he espouses a Zen Buddhist vision most fully, arguing that a person must "rid" him- or herself of dualism in order to contact the true nature of reality, which, for Zen as well as for Lynch, is one with the nature of the self. In Zen philosophy, a divided self cannot find contentment. It will, as a result of its split nature, be unable to apprehend the unity of existence. In *Lost Highway,* Lynch demonstrates the destructive personal consequences of such a philosophical view, arguing that people trapped in a dualistic world are "lost" because they believe unity can only be attained through the pursuit and acquisition of a fundamental yet missing element.

Zen Buddhism and the Illusion of Two

Confronting the concept of dualism may appear as problematic as posing a challenge to the universe itself. In Western philosophy, the view of an intrinsic linked pairing as the basis of reality is so pervasive that refutations of dualism often become dualistic through repeated efforts to demonstrate what is not there, which is a dilemma recognized by Zen Buddhism.[3] "When a thing is denied," Suzuki asserts, "the very denial involves something not denied. The same can be said of affirmation. This is inevitable in logic. Zen wants to rise above logic. Zen wants to find a higher affirmation where there are no antitheses."[4]

From a Zen perspective, Western concepts of reality typically focus on a dualistic foundation that is formulated by placing the conscious ego as a fundamental reference point, creating a dichotomy between subject and object. The perceiving "I" (the subject) becomes a discrete, self-contained entity that forms a relationship with the perceived "it" (the object) through the power of consciousness. Awareness of objects that exist outside our bodies is often called space-consciousness because we are aware of objects in the space around us. Time-consciousness exists when we turn our attention inward, gaining awareness of objects, including projections of the self, through contemplation, memory, or imagination. Even though an awareness of time may not exist in this type of perception, the term allows us to separate inner and outer objects of perception. In both cases, the word *consciousness* simply refers to an act of perception. These terms do not imply an awareness of the act of consciousness itself.

Yet, for a Zen Buddhist, when we attempt to utilize these dualistic Western concepts to conduct an analysis of self-consciousness, and thereby understand the nature of the self and its relationship to reality, we encounter problems. If a distinct conscious ego is always present during each act of perception, we should be able to identify and describe this perceiving subject. However, as T. P. Kasulis observes in *Zen Action, Zen Person,* "when we are self-conscious, the *agent* of that self-consciousness is not reflected upon. There must always remain the unself-conscious entity having the self-consciousness; any attempt to capture the self is directed toward the self that *was*, not the self that is." Thus, while we may believe we are engaging in acts of self-consciousness when we conduct inner contemplation, we are actually regarding an object of the self that is separate from the source of perception. Zen Buddhism does not deny that we are able to reflect on ourselves, reviewing past actions or projecting the consequences of future decisions on our lives. However, Zen insists that if we claim that a fundamental aspect of existence is a perceiving self, yet we can never see or describe that self during the act of perception, we are clinging to a false and illusory view of reality. For Zen, such a perspective increases the distance that the self-reflection intends to diminish, spawning the common Western complaints of angst and alienation.[5]

For a Zen Buddhist, this complaint is just the beginning of the problem. If the self that conducts perception is comprised of two fundamental parts, it follows that visions of a bifurcated existence will be the natural result. A self consisting of a perceiving subject and a perceived object will, in turn, identify similar fundamental pairings, leading to an assortment of other significant, universal dualistic perceptions: mind-body, self-society, self-nature, love-hate, good-evil. Zen Buddhism sees this type of division as an illusion. In this context, illusion does not mean that the inner and outer worlds fail to exist. Rather, for the Zen Buddhist, illusion means that the concept is not permanent or eternal and cannot substitute as a representation of reality. "Although the world itself is not illusory," Kasulis notes, "our *characterizations* of the world are fundamentally self-contradictory, relative, and tentative. Without the insight of *prajna* we run the risk of becoming attached to our characterizations, of thinking of them as absolutes, rather than as names convenient for a given purpose." Knowledge of an object's distinct individual characteristics is useful as long as such knowledge is not substituted for an understanding of the entirety of the object. Prajna— interpreted as wisdom or enlightenment—is mindfulness of an object's context and relationships, in addition to its salient features. A dualistic mind may become "attached" to its "characterizations" by virtue of its focus on subject-object perceptions, limiting its attention to the object's relationship to the observer or to its opposite. Shaped by the fundamental concept of a linked pairing, such minds frequently endorse one aspect of a perceived object at the expense of the other. For example, the mind-body dichotomy in Western philosophy commonly consists of arguments identifying one aspect as possessing greater truth than the other. According to Kasulis, "Any assertion or distinction only highlights one aspect of a situation and, in so doing, casts into shadows an equally important, though incompatible, aspect." For Zen, this dualistic perspective commits a logical error by favoring one existence over another, which it must reduce in order to subjugate. "In analyzing any conceptual dichotomy," Kasulis explains, "we fluctuate between two contradictory models . . . which depend on each other for their definition." Such thinking removes the observer further from reality, secluded in a singular position that deems itself authentic by virtue of its superior attachment to a defeated object. If the dual pairing is not placed in a confrontational context, the very act of perception can, nevertheless, convey a sense of control to the subject (the perceiver) over the object (the perceived). This sense of control through perception is one source of anxiety for many Westerners and may explain why so many people continue to register high levels of surprise when confronted with the unexpected.[6]

In practice, the ego-conscious participant will apply the same dichotomy to individual and social problems alike. The dualistic framework insists that the subject locate an object to which it may form an attachment (a love interest, a social group). Once an attachment is made, the perceiving self will seek to become one with the object; at times, the self will even attempt to locate a personal identity through this association. "Without being aware of it," Shunryu Suzuki explains, "we try to change something other than ourselves." However, a dualistic approach demands that the object remain "other" in order for the perceiving self to maintain its function. Therefore, in an attempt to force the unity it seeks, the self must either submit to the will of the other (allowing the love interest complete domination; submitting to the demands of the social group without question) or assume dominion over the attached. In either case, the regarded "object" with which the "subject" seeks unity must remain oppositional.[7]

Zen sees this pursuit as an expression of the individual's natural search for unity. However, for Zen, such unity is inherent. To exist is to be unified with all things that exist. To live in such awareness is to be enlightened, an occurrence that is not attained as much as it is acknowledged. Shunryu Suzuki downplayed the concept of *satori,* which in the Japanese tradition of Zen is a moment of sudden awareness, fearing it would encourage beginning practitioners to become obsessed with its pursuit. He maintains that "Buddha nature is our original nature; we have it before we practice zazen [seated meditation] and before we acknowledge it in terms of consciousness. . . . If you want to understand it, true understanding is always there. . . . This is how we attain enlightenment." It is the discriminating mind that disrupts natural unity and alienates humanity from existence. Zen insists that such an approach to existence is at best arbitrary, at worst, illusory.[8]

Lynch's Trip down a Lost Highway

Such attachment may also become destructive, as is demonstrated by Lynch's *Lost Highway.* All of Lynch's work explores philosophical concerns, but he is particularly intrigued by the role of duality. Prior to the release of *Lost Highway,* Lynch revealed a curiosity about duality in the films *The Elephant Man* (1980), *Blue Velvet* (1986), and *Wild at Heart* (1990), as well as the TV series *Twin Peaks* (1990–1991). In these works, Lynch focuses on the disparity between appearance and reality, particularly the deceptive nature of physical forms. In *The Elephant Man,* physical disfigurement masks an intelligent, sensitive human being. In subsequent works, Lynch shifted his concerns with duality into a neo-noir environment. Characters leading double lives, unleashing darker desires and secrets lurking beneath a pleasing façade, form Lynch's artistic signature during this phase of his career.[9]

But with *Lost Highway,* Lynch intensified his exploration of this thematic landscape by plunging the focus within the world of the self. As with many of its predecessors, *Lost Highway* evokes a noir locale, with criminal intrigue prowling in the shadows of a manicured suburban neighborhood, and makes effective use of paired characterizations. Yet in this film, Lynch places the darkest heart in his main character, a man with sketchy motivation and no memory of his criminal act. While injury-induced amnesia is a common noir trope, Lynch locates the problem within a character who simply cannot remember the crime of which he is accused and whose source of trouble appears to be the human condition. In addition, *Lost Highway* utilizes doppelgangers (another noir trademark) with such loose physical connections that their significance to one another becomes a matter of contemplation more than fear. While noir films traditionally seek to unsettle the audience, developments in *Lost Highway* disrupt the plot with sufficient force to leave most audience members perplexed on a first viewing, too confused to be disturbed. As we will see, such befuddlement serves Lynch's philosophical intent: to force the audience to question not only the logic of the world they have witnessed but also the stability of an existence formed by a dualistic perception. In so doing, Lynch reveals the same distrust of duality that forms the foundation of Zen Buddhist theory.

The story reveals the degradation of one, or perhaps two, main characters. Fred Madison (Bill Pullman), a jazz saxophonist, is suspicious of his wife Renee's (Patricia Arquette) fidelity. Packages left on the couple's doorstep contain videotapes depicting exterior shots of their home and interior shots of the couple asleep in bed. The tapes fuel Madison's suspicions. Dreams and memory fuse with his waking reality, resulting in a scene in which he inserts a new tape and discovers himself as the murderer of his wife, an act he denies to the police and cannot remember committing.

In prison, Madison continues to experience strange and confusing visions, which culminate in what could be equally described as a fit, seizure, or breakdown on the cell floor. The subsequent scene depicts a prison guard discovering a stranger in Madison's cell. Madison has disappeared. In his place is Pete Dayton (Balthazar Getty), a much younger man. Baffled, the authorities discover that Dayton is an auto mechanic who lives with his parents. He has no previous association with Madison. Like Madison, he has no memory of recent actions, and his dream and waking states seem to be merging. Since he has committed no crime, he is released from prison.

Soon after, Dayton meets Alice Wakefield (also played by Patricia Arquette), the blond mistress of a local crime figure, Mr. Eddy (Robert Loggia). Wakefield is a stranger to Dayton, but not to the audience. It is clear that she is played by the same actress who plays Renee, Madison's wife. Except for hair style and color, no visual attempt is made by the film to separate the two characters. The audience knows some mysterious link exists between the two female characters, just as one exists between the two male characters. The binding of these uncertain pairs is further tightened once Dayton and Wakefield begin an affair. Although Dayton knows Wakefield is involved with Mr. Eddy, he becomes jealous of her connection to other men. As with Madison, Dayton's suspicions lead to intensified desire and anger. In each instance, desire to control the object of their attachment cannot be accomplished, resulting in a crisis of the self for both characters.

Desire as a source of suffering is one of Indian Buddhism's Four Noble Truths. In *Buddha* (2001), Karen Armstrong explains that "mindfulness also made Gotama [the Buddha] highly sensitive to the prevalence of the desire or craving that is the cause of this suffering."[10] Though many Buddhist notions did not appeal to thinkers in the Far East, both Taoists and Zen Buddhists accepted the idea that satori could be located only through a cessation of desire.[11] In the grip of desire, "we almost never see things as they are in themselves, but our vision is colored by whether we want them or not. . . . Our vision of the world is, therefore, distorted by our greed."[12] For Zen Buddhism, the problem of desire does not emerge through sinful acts inspired by physical want. Rather, desire places the subject in search of an object it mistakenly believes it must have in order to survive. Such an approach imprisons the self in a dualistic mind-set, wherein reality is only represented by the subject and object of desire. "If your mind is related to something outside itself," Shunryu Suzuki states, "that mind is a small mind, a limited mind. If your mind is not related to anything else, then there is no dualistic understanding in the activity of your mind."[13] The pursuit of desire not only robs the self of its inherent freedom, it dooms the self to a course of dissatisfaction from lack, if the object of desire is not attained, or to satiety, if it is apprehended. "On the one hand, desire makes us 'grab' or 'cling' to things that can never give lasting satisfaction," Armstrong notes. "On the other, it makes us constantly discontented with our present circumstances."[14] Shunryu Suzuki concurs: "Even though you try to put people under some control, it is impossible."[15] Ultimately, the individual turns once more to desire in order to find reality, resuming the cycle of suffering. Satori, which is not the denial of desire but rather the cessation of it, cannot be located by an individual on this path because enlightenment is recognition of universal connection.

Lost Highway creates uncertainty from the beginning. The film opens on Madison, who appears tired and perplexed. Prompted by a buzzer, he walks to his front door. Through the intercom he hears an unidentified voice state, "Dick Laurent is dead." Car tires and a police siren can be heard, but Madison fails to gain a glimpse of the visitor through the window. A deep bass soundtrack signals suspicion and underscores the intrigue. A fade-out draws the visual curtain on the scene, but when new scenes refuse to reveal the source of the voice or Laurent's relationship to Madison, who makes no inquiries, takes no action, and fails to mention the apparently important incident to his wife, the audience is placed in the position of wanting something they cannot identify. In this way, Lynch creates the state of mind in the audience that often plagues a person in the grip of a dualistic struggle, frustrated by its insufficiency, isolated by its own desire. For a Zen Buddhist, such entrapment is inevitable for a self bound by desire of an unattainable object. The suffering that results cannot be alleviated by attainment of the desire; rather, one must recognize the problematic nature of the desire itself.

Within this setting, which is visually suburban and conventional but thematically strange and unsettling, Lynch depicts Madison as a man succumbing to the obsessive grip of his own desire as he struggles to cope with doubts about his wife. Before Madison articulates his fears to the audience, Renee reveals an awareness of his concerns by asking if it is okay with him if she doesn't go to the club, where he performs professionally, because she wants to stay home and read. His skepticism is gentle and good-natured but present nonetheless. He questions her explanation, asking, "Read? Read what?" She laughs with him, telling him he can wake her up when he gets home. But before he drives home following his act, he calls from a pay phone, his face and arms bathed in a red light. There is no answer. Upon his return, he discovers Renee asleep in bed. Later, Madison lies in bed viewing scenes in his memory that contain Renee at the club, searching for evidence that will confirm his suspicions. Throughout the sequence, Lynch returns to shots of Madison's face to maintain awareness that Madison is the subject seeking an object he desires in the form of Renee's infidelity. In this mind-set, his past becomes an object to be examined, focused on the "self that *was,* not the self that is."[16]

Through Madison, Lynch shows how quickly curiosity can become an obsession. Madison becomes convinced by his own suspicions that he must find an answer to questions he is generating in order to ease his agitated mind and return to a peaceful and loving state. Attachment conveys negative connotations for a Zen Buddhist for precisely these reasons. A person who decides he must possess the object of his desire believes he can not be whole until he attains the object of his fascination. As a result of this dualistic obsession, Madison becomes increasingly detached from his own experience. The touch of Renee's hand on his back startles Madison while they make love, further marking her as a distanced other. Subsequently, he tells her of a dream in which she is inside the house, calling his name, but he cannot find her. His search through the home is visually intercut by images of a blazing fire in the fireplace, flames swept upward by a draft that seems too powerful for the size of the chute, and roiling smoke, images that are understood to be the products of a dream but clearly indicative of raging desire disproportionate to the vessel meant to contain it. Further in the dream, when Madison finds her in bed, he says, "It wasn't you. It looked like you. But it wasn't." The audience can see Renee is lying in bed, and we are required to conclude that Madison wrongfully identifies the figure. His detachment has now produced confusion of the familiar, a central component of alienation, which is an indicator of suffering from a Zen Buddhist perspective. Visually, Lynch establishes that Renee has not changed. Throughout, her dominant demeanor is placid and stable. It is the narrowing of Madison's dualistic focus that becomes the vehicle of his trouble. Zen Buddhism does not deny that a human can divide himself into twin parts. The problem emerges when the same human defines the self as the sum of this division and insists that unity can only take place through a forced merger of subject and object.

Madison's confusion results in an inability to discern dream and waking states. In effect, larger common dual concepts of reality fold in on top of Madison's obsession with his own polarity, further alienating him. As the dream, which he is narrating, concludes, Madison awakens, as if the story may have been conducted within a dream. Startled, Renee sits up, concerned. When Madison looks, her body remains the same, but her face has changed to one that is gray and unfamiliar. Frightened, Madison switches on a lamp, but the light reveals Renee's normal face.

The videotapes, which have been mysteriously and anonymously delivered to Madison's home, are also not what they seem. In a conventional film noir, the appearance of tapes left on a doorstep from an unidentified source would provide clues to the Dick Laurent mystery generated by the opening scene, building a bridge between this important plot point and the thematic concerns of Madison's jealousy. But in *Lost Highway,* Lynch's intent is to "dive within" the existence of his main character. Such links form solely as conduits for the film's philosophical vision.[17]

The first tape reveals a simple slow pan of the exterior of the Madison home. When the second does the same but then enters the home, revealing the Madisons in bed asleep, two detectives are notified. Yet their investigation only serves to perpetuate audience frustration and confirm their confusion. The detectives are as baffled as the audience, discovering that the Madisons do not own a video camera because Fred "hates them." He tells the police he likes to remember things his own way, "How I remember them. Not necessarily the way they happened." Voiced at this juncture of the film, Madison's admission does not assist the development of the plot but does work on a thematic level, a further clue that his perception creates faulty representations because, as Zen Buddhism asserts, a split mind cannot apprehend the entirety of reality.

The viewing of the third tape is preceded by Madison's slow walk down a dark hall in his home. He encounters his own image, but it is not clear if he is gazing at himself in a mirror or has located another "Fred" within the home. In either case, the divisive effects of his obsessions are made manifest. Standing at the edge of the same dark hallway, Renee asks, "Fred, where are you?" Her voice is small and unacknowledged, but within this philosophical context, her question echoes the film's primary concern. The subsequent image is a pair of shadows ghosting across a bedroom wall. Madison appears from out of the dark hallway. The tape he removes from an envelope conducts the same slow pan of the home before entering, as before, but this recording leads to Madison in the bedroom kneeling over the bloody body of Renee on the floor. The grainy black-and-white imagery of the taped scene is intercut with color shots of the same scene, blending the strange, dual perceptions. Even though Madison does not remember the act, he is sentenced to die in the electric chair. By showing only the aftermath of the murder, and not the act itself, Lynch distances the audience from Madison. The intended effect is a detachment of the audience, similar to the detachment Madison is experiencing from his own existence.

More important, the tapes serve to show that while Madison remains a subject searching for one object, he has reduced reality to a singular act of perception that does not allow him to see the entire landscape of existence. In spite of the intensity of his focus, he fails to see himself because of his perspective. His dualistic obsession ultimately splits him into both subject and object, resulting in alienation and destruction. The tapes reveal the divisive nature of Madison's desire. In the tapes he becomes the object viewed by an unidentified subject. This second act of perception does not allow the unity Madison hopes to attain through his jealous fixation. But, through the use of the videotapes, Lynch asserts that a mind trapped in a dualistic view of reality cannot see the truth because the subject is also the object of another's perception. The final tape offers a broader view of the character's actions, but we still cannot see the entire truth of Fred Madison. The film's first act concludes with Madison in a prison cell, a visual trope of the confinement he has chosen for himself through his view of existence. From a Zen Buddhist perspective, Madison has fashioned the arbitrary parameters of existence that now isolate him from reality.

Pete Dayton's character is another element that baffles the audience, spawning a variety of explanations. He could be a distinct character trapped by the same desire as Madison, paralleling his obsessive difficulties. Because his appearance and disappearance from the film involve both the apparent psychic disintegration of Madison in the prison cell and his reemergence in the desert, Dayton can also be viewed as a younger incarnation of Madison. Statements made by Renee and Alice, who visually appear to be the same character, suggest that their lives coincide and that Alice might be Renee at an earlier phase in her life. Lynch, who remains averse to explicit discussions of his films' themes, has revealed that the notion of a "psychogenic fugue" was openly discussed during the making of the film: "The person suffering from it creates in their mind a completely new identity, new friends, new home, new everything—they forget their past identity."[18]

In any case, Dayton suffers from the same desirous obsession as Madison. When Alice tells him of the sexual acts Mr. Eddy forced her to perform at gunpoint, instead of showing concern for her suffering, Dayton's response is dictated by his desire to own her as an object, controlling her emotions, desires, and past actions: "Why didn't you just leave? You liked it, huh?" Alice, who later made pornographic films for Mr. Eddy and was complicit in the jobs, informs Dayton that she can leave him alone, yet in spite of his polarized emotions, Dayton says, "I don't want you to go away." Kissing her, he says he loves her, even though he was decidedly disgusted moments before. A range of conflicting human emotion can be provoked by an array of factors, but within the dualistic context that Lynch has meticulously staged, Dayton appears to be suffering from a split nature produced by his worldview.

Another parallel between Dayton and Madison is the murderous acts both men commit as a result of their obsessive desires. But instead of killing Alice out of a jealous rage, Dayton ambushes Andy (Michael Massee), the man who led Alice to Mr. Eddy and the pornographic jobs. The purpose of killing Andy is to steal his cash so Alice and Dayton can escape the clutches of Mr. Eddy. Dayton successfully murders Andy, but while he does so, a film projector beams a pornographic scene of Alice onto a large screen, visually reinforcing the futility of Dayton's need to possess the object of his desire. This notion is made more apparent when Dayton sees a photo of Renee and Alice. He does not know Renee, but the visual similarities between the two women stun him. Alice identifies herself in the photo, but the image of the two Alices is a mirror of the split world that Dayton is experiencing. Seeing the photo, Dayton suffers an intense headache and bloody nose. Such consequences seem to stem from internal confusion rather than an external, physical blow and are congruent with the head pain Madison suffers in the prison cell prior to his breakdown. Madison's pain appears to be caused by an internal realization as well. The scenes, and their thematic concerns, are further linked by the fact that Madison's confusion in the prison cell led to the mysterious appearance of Dayton in the same cell.

After Dayton and Alice kill and rob Andy, they drive to the desert to locate a fence Alice knows who will pay them for the stolen property. They find his cabin empty. Waiting, they make love on the desert floor, illuminated by the headlights of a car they stole from Andy but that appears to be the same 1965 Ford Mustang owned by Madison. Naked, focused entirely on Alice, Dayton repeats the Western mantra of desire: "I want you." Alice's reply articulates Lynch's thematic vision: "You will never have me." As she returns to the cabin, a naked male body stands in the headlights, but it is Fred Madison, not Dayton. In terms of narrative logic and character development, the move is surprising and baffling. But on a philosophical level, the unification makes sense: both men are naked in the desert (the landscape of heat), perpetually isolated and persistently yearning, cut off from the wholeness of themselves by virtue of their approach to reality, a result predicted by Zen Buddhism. "When your mind becomes demanding, when you long for something," Shunryu Suzuki warns, "you will end up violating your own precepts."[19]

The character identified in the credits as Mystery Man (Robert Blake) also features prominently in the realization of the film's vision, serving as a catalyst for other characters' confrontations with reality. The character, serving a role similar to one played by the homeless man in Lynch's *Mulholland Dr.* (2001), has human shape yet possesses inexplicable powers. His cryptic greeting of Madison at a party—"we've met before . . . at your house . . . you invited me . . . it is not my custom to go where I'm not wanted"—combines with his ability to speak with Madison in person and simultaneously on a phone within Madison's home to form the illusion of a professional magic trick. His physical appearance contributes to this initial impression. His face is coated in white makeup and is bereft of hair, including eyebrows.

However, the audience realizes before Madison does that the Mystery Man's face is the startling form that appeared on Renee's head following Madison's recounting of his strange dream. As with other developments in the film, the Mystery Man defies logical apprehension, but in a film focused on exploiting the destructive elements of a philosophical mind-set, the character becomes a harbinger of trouble for characters split in half by their dualistic tendencies. In addition to his encounter with Madison, the Mystery Man appears with Mr. Eddy—whose divided nature is revealed by his destructive actions and use of two names, Mr. Eddy and Dick Laurent—during a phone conversation with Dayton after he begins his affair with Alice. The Mystery Man's conversation with Dayton directly parallels his dialogue with Madison at the party. "We've met before, haven't we . . . at your house?" Yet with Dayton, the Mystery Man not only presents mysterious comments that point to the ontological trouble within the main characters, suggesting that he is the only character not bound by the restraints of subject-object perception, he also offers a narrative that provides a signal of Lynch's Eastern tendencies. According to the Mystery Man, in the Far East when a man is sentenced to death, he waits in a room where he does not know the date or means of execution. At an unannounced time, the convict is shot in the back of the head. In keeping with the Mystery Man's statements and actions, the story's relevance to the film's plot and character relationships is difficult to discern. Yet, thematically, the narrative calls attention—albeit in a cryptic and violent way—to the problems of duality. The convicted man is granted a moment before his life's conclusion wherein searching ahead through time or space is impossible, rendering the ineffectuality of the subject-object approach, an approach that, in this film's view, would have likely caused the crime in the first place. For a Zen Buddhist, the split dilemma caused by the subject-object approach to life is crime enough.

After Madison returns to the film in the desert, he is greeted by the Mystery Man inside the cabin's garage. Pointing a video camera at Madison, a signifier of reality in *Lost Highway,* he asks, "Who the fuck are you?" By this point in the story, the audience wonders the same thing, which may be the reason Lynch intentionally distorts the relationship between Madison and Dayton. Yet the statement clearly punctuates the film's central question, one it has been exploring thematically throughout. Madison never answers the question. He flees the garage, pursued by the Mystery Man, who continues to point the video camera at him, suggesting, as many Zen Buddhists observe, that reality cannot be escaped, no matter how far or fast an individual runs. Reality includes the perceptions of the self. Thus, a person who seeks to escape reality seeks to escape the self, which is an impossibility.

In the Mustang, Madison returns to the highway, the same highway depicted behind the opening credits and that will become the film's concluding image, the visual trope of the film's "lost highway" theme. Still lost and desperate on this road, Madison pulls into the parking lot of the Lost Highway Hotel. The blatant symbolic importance of the hotel continues to herald the film's overriding philosophical concerns and serves as the meeting place for the story's "lost" characters, all of whom, except for the Mystery Man, have acquired two identities. The audience witnesses Renee in bed with Dick Laurent. She leaves the hotel before Madison breaks into Laurent's room, assaulting him and taking him hostage in the trunk of the Mustang. The Mystery Man watches from a hotel window.

In the desert, Madison and Laurent fight. The Mystery Man hands Madison a knife with which he cuts Laurent's throat. The literal link in the story line between Madison and Laurent is so sketchy that the violent act becomes another puzzling occurrence in a film that for many has become an impenetrable riddle. Yet thematically, the unifying purpose is clear. Laurent, like Madison, is a man who has divided himself in two as a result of his philosophies, which have, in turn, allowed desire to become his master, a problematic result predicted by Zen Buddhism. The Mystery Man hands Laurent a portable, hand-held television, which shows Laurent at home with Renee, watching pornographic films that depict scenes combining acts of eroticism and violence. Buddhism, in all of its various manifestations and practices, recognizes the deep relationship of human emotions born from longing: "Desire and hatred, its concomitant, are thus the joint cause of much of the misery and evil in the world."[20] Throat cut, chest and neck soiled with blood, Laurent tells Madison, "You and me, Mister. We can really out-ugly them sumbitches."

The Mystery Man kills Laurent with two shots from a handgun. Whether Lynch utilizes violence and other noir elements to entertain Western audiences while he instructs them or because his philosophical vision insists that a departure from the problems of duality requires a radical act is debatable. Nevertheless, the film reveals that a bifurcated man, under the control of his desires, requires the help of a unified guide in order to recognize the nature of his philosophical dilemma. Zen Buddhism repeatedly endorses the need for a split self to recognize that it cannot find the unity it seeks until it relinquishes a dualistic worldview.

Finally, the trope of the lost highway signals a wrongful departure from the right path, philosophically speaking. The film concludes with Madison, pursued by police, driving down the same highway that appeared during the opening credit sequence, suggesting that in spite of the assistance he has received from the Mystery Man, he has only begun to find himself. Final shots of Madison depict him experiencing a breakdown or seizure similar to the one he endures in the prison cell. Such a conclusion promotes a variety of possible interpretations.[21] The blurred, flashing light could signal an execution, implying that we have been watching the fantasy of a condemned man during the second half of the film. Yet one might also argue, in keeping with a Zen Buddhist approach, that Lynch is depicting the annihilation of the self, a requirement for a person who seeks satori, a mindfulness beyond discernment, "a state of consciousness in which the dichotomy between subject and object, experience and experienced, is overcome."[22] In any case, the ending remains equally obscure and prevents a settled interpretation, which may have been Lynch's intent. In a film that explores the ontological trauma invoked by a dualistic philosophy, an outcome described specifically by Zen Buddhism, an indeterminate conclusion in a film that defies Western conventions of storytelling throughout might be Lynch's final indicator of his Zen Buddhist vision. Often described as opaque and indiscernible by Western critics, Zen Buddhism baffles many logical minds with the use of illogical koans, which are questions that do not have a rational answer and are designed to reveal to the student the limits of reason, and descriptions of reality as arising from "a source that cannot be described as either Being or Nonbeing, form or no form."[23] Yet the method to this madness stems from the conviction that truth does not reside in an abstract world apart from particularized experience. Satori, as a concept, cannot be discussed or analyzed. It must be recognized by an awakened mind.

In keeping with this approach, Lynch does not allow his characters to engage in a separated, abstract debate about duality. His concerns with dualism and the problems they exact on his characters are embodied in the framework of the film, through the paired characterizations, the inexplicable plot developments, and the illogical appearances of a character known only as the Mystery Man. In addition to these elements, the very structure of the film points to the Zen notion that an insight derived from analysis will not solve the problems of these characters. In fact, the traditional patterns of Western storytelling, with emphasis on conflict, complication, and resolution, are ill-suited for the rendering of Zen truth. As D. T. Suzuki observes, Zen's "paradoxical statements are not artificialities contrived to hide themselves behind a screen of obscurity; but simply because the human tongue is not an adequate organ for expressing the deepest truths of Zen, the latter cannot be made the subject of logical exposition." While *Lost Highway* has not greatly influenced American filmmaking, it does offer a unique philosophical counterpoint to problems that continue to plague individuals and society, teaching bewildered audiences that "by returning to the indeterminate, one finds oneself again in the world of the determinate."[24]

Notes

1. See Arthur O. Lovejoy, *The Revolt Against Dualism: An Inquiry Concerning the Existence of Ideas* (1929; La Salle, Ill.: Open Court, 1955), 1. For a detailed categorization and description of the types of duality, see ibid.; and Rich Shusterman, *Practicing Philosophy: Pragmatism and the Philosophical Life* (New York: Routledge, 1997). For brief introductions to duality, see *Stanford Encyclopedia of Philosophy*, http://plato .stanford.edu/. See also *Dictionary of Philosophy of Mind*, http://philosophy.uwaterloo .ca/MindDict/index.html. Philosophers such as William James, John Dewey, and Richard Rorty express concerns with the influence of dualism. James's 1904 essay "Does Consciousness Exist?" is often identified as the initial work in the reaction against dualism described by Lovejoy. See also John Dewey, *Experience and Nature* (Chicago: Open Court, 1925); and Richard Rorty, *Philosophy and the Mirror of Nature* (Princeton, N.J.: Princeton University Press, 1979).

2. D. T. Suzuki, *An Introduction to Zen Buddhism* (New York: Grove Weidenfeld, 1991), 88. Carl Jung, Huston Smith, and many others recognize D. T. Suzuki's cultural introduction of Zen Buddhism to the West. See Jung's foreword to Suzuki's *An Introduction to Zen Buddhism*. See also Huston Smith's preface to Shunryu Suzuki's *Zen Mind, Beginner's Mind* (New York: Weatherhill, 1985), 9–13. Smith asserts that D. T. Suzuki "brought Zen to the West single-handed."

3. While an existentialist such as Jean-Paul Sartre (1905–1980), for example, continuously asserted that existence precedes essence, his desire to locate a self through analysis of past actions, and thus locate meaning or authenticity to life, can be seen as similar to the quest of a metaphysical dualist who seeks a divine source or of a substance dualist who seeks a material source. Both approaches involve an individual consciousness seeking an "other" in order to locate a sense of unity and authority.

4. D. T. Suzuki, *An Introduction to Zen Buddhism*, 39.

5. T. P. Kasulis, *Zen Action, Zen Person* (Honolulu: University of Hawaii Press, 1981), 63.

6. Kasulis, *Zen Action, Zen Person,* 25, 22, 24.

7. S. Suzuki, *Zen Mind, Beginner's Mind,* 27. Shunryu Suzuki, no relation to D. T. Suzuki, was also responsible for the spread of Zen Buddhism in the West, though he came to the United States fifty years after D. T. Suzuki. According to Huston Smith, D. T. Suzuki, who was criticized by some for his broad nationalistic comments, described a Zen that was "dramatic," with strong emphasis on satori, whereas Shunryu Suzuki's teachings were "ordinary," never mentioning satori (see Smith, preface to S. Suzuki, *Zen Mind, Beginner's Mind,* 9).

8. S. Suzuki, *Zen Mind, Beginner's Mind,* 131–32.

9. Lynch's concern with dualism is not surprising given his interest in Transcendental Meditation. A devoted practitioner, Lynch established the David Lynch Foundation for Consciousness-Based Education and Peace (www.davidlynchfoundation.org) to promote understanding and practice of TM. The foundation provides funding and other resources to students, schools, and research institutions in order to reduce student stress and depression, enhance critical thinking and creative ability, and to explore the effects of TM on intelligence, brain functioning, and academic performance, as well as its impact on psychological disorders and substance abuse. The foundation is not affiliated with a particular religious group or philosophical bias.

10. Karen Armstrong, *Buddha* (New York: Lipper/Viking, 2001), 74.

11. S. Suzuki, *Zen Mind, Beginner's Mind,* 21–25; Kasulis, *Zen Action, Zen Person,* 48; D. T. Suzuki, *An Introduction to Zen Buddhism,* 46–47.

12. Armstrong, *Buddha,* 74.

13. S. Suzuki, *Zen Mind, Beginner's Mind,* 35.

14. Armstrong, *Buddha,* 74.

15. S. Suzuki, *Zen Mind, Beginner's Mind,* 32.

16. Kasulis, *Zen Action, Zen Person,* 63.

17. According to Lynch's Foundation for Consciousness-Based Education and Peace Web site, to "dive within" is the goal of Transcendental Meditation. It also appears to be a goal of Lynch's films.

18. Stuart Swezey, "911—David Lynch, Phone Home," *Filmmaker* (Winter 1997). Available through David Lynch's personal Web site at www.lynchnet.com/lh/lhfm.html.

19. S. Suzuki, *Zen Mind, Beginner's Mind,* 22.

20. Armstrong, *Buddha,* 74.

21. For critical responses that attempt to grapple with the film and its conclusion instead of simply dismissing it, as many professional reviewers did, see Tom O'Connor, "The Pitfalls of Media 'Representations': David Lynch's *Lost Highway,*" *Journal of Film & Video* 57, no. 3 (2005): 4–30; Terrence Rafferty, "Mistaken Identity," *New Yorker* 73, no. 3 (1997): 98; Todd McGowan, "Finding Ourselves on a *Lost Highway*: David Lynch's Lesson in Fantasy," *Cinema Journal,* 39, no. 2 (2000): 51–73.

22. Kasulis, *Zen Action, Zen Person,* 25.

23. See Jung's foreword to D. T. Suzuki, *An Introduction to Zen Buddhism,* 9; and

D. T. Suzuki, *An Introduction to Zen Buddhism,* 33. While Jung appreciated the integrity and rigor of Zen Buddhism, he saw it as "more or less unassimilable by the average Western understanding." Suzuki acknowledged that a person who approaches Zen "conceptually" would "consider Zen utterly absurd and ludicrous, or deliberately making itself unintelligible in order to guard its apparent profundity against outside criticism." See also Kasulis, *Zen Action, Zen Person,* 14.

24. D. T. Suzuki, *An Introduction to Zen Buddhism,* 33; Kasulis, *Zen Action, Zen Person,* 48.

CITY OF DREAMS

Bad Faith in *Mulholland Dr.*

Jennifer McMahon

While it commands its audience's attention with the allure of familiar forms, David Lynch's *Mulholland Dr.* (2001) simultaneously subverts multiple cinematic conventions. Though Lynch employs archetypal elements of film noir (e.g., the presence of a femme fatale and a whodunit plot), he also confounds his audience's expectations by incorporating surrealist imagery and vignettes that disrupt the continuity of the narrative. Effortlessly synthesizing iconic elements from the golden age of Hollywood film and postmodern features that introduce a profoundly cynical air, Lynch's *Mulholland Dr.* simultaneously deconstructs and celebrates the essence of noir film. Though the link between Lynch and noir is itself worthy of examination, this essay goes in a different direction. It offers an analysis of *Mulholland Dr.* that links Lynch's fascination with noir to prominent existential themes including absurdity, authenticity, and bad faith. In particular, this essay focuses on the theme of illusion as it is made evident in the film.[1] Drawing primarily from the works of Friedrich Nietzsche (1844–1900), Jean-Paul Sartre (1905–1980), and Albert Camus (1913–1960), it argues that *Mulholland Dr.* illustrates that, when confronted with unsavory aspects of existence, individuals often opt to disguise these truths by creating self-consoling, but also self-deceptive narratives. These narratives are the lies we tell to make existence "bearable for us." *Mulholland Dr.* reveals the human tendency to create such fictions as well as what follows from their fragility.[2]

Though most of us would not want to admit it, the German philosopher Friedrich Nietzsche asserts that dishonesty is a standard response to existence. In fact, he states, "delusion and error are conditions of human knowledge and sensation."[3] According to Nietzsche, people "[have] to deceive themselves"[4] because "untruth is a condition of life."[5] Rather than being a rare and detrimental activity, Nietzsche sees lying, particularly self-deception, as commonplace and frequently productive. He and other existentialists agree that individuals often lie to themselves in order to try and disguise undesirable truths. Nietzsche argues that "untruth [has] constantly proved to be useful" because "man has to believe, to know, from time to time why he exists; his race would not flourish without . . . trust in life—without faith in reason in life."[6] In Nietzsche's estimation, self-deception is useful because it provides the illusion of reason in a world that lacks it.

Though they are not as emphatic about its efficacy, Nietzsche's existentialist successors concur with him regarding the prevalence of self-deception and its cause. Prominent twentieth-century existentialists like Albert Camus and Jean-Paul Sartre also devote significant attention to the phenomenon of "[lying] to oneself."[7] Where Nietzsche calls it "the will to . . . untruth,"[8] Camus deems the phenomenon "philosophical suicide"[9] and Sartre calls it "bad faith."[10] Regardless of the term used, they all agree that humans "are accustomed to lying."[11] They also agree that lying and self-deception are pervasive because individuals resist honest acknowledgment of the human condition. Camus argues that "living . . . is never easy" because the facts of existence are hard to bear. Lying is commonplace because "the true is not . . . what is desirable."[12]

According to the existentialists, the principal truth that humans seek to avoid is absurdity. According to Nietzsche, "the total character of the world . . . is in all eternity chaos—in the sense not of a lack of necessity but of a lack of order, arrangement, [and] form."[13] He argues that individuals have a deep-seated "fear of [this] truth,"[14] and to combat it "we have arranged for ourselves a world in which we can live—by positing bodies, lines, planes, causes and effects, motion and rest, form and content." Nietzsche argues, "without these articles of faith nobody could now endure life. But that does not prove them. Life is no argument." Life, it would seem, compels us to lie.[15]

Sartre offers analogous insights regarding absurdity in both his philosophic and literary works. His most powerful treatment of the subject is found in his novel *Nausea*, where his protagonist, Roquentin, reluctantly confronts the truth of absurdity. At the root of the chestnut tree, the scales fall from Roquentin's eyes as he discovers the nature of existence. He cries: "existence suddenly unveiled itself. It had lost the harmless look of an abstract category . . . the diversity of things, their individuality, were only an appearance, a veneer. That veneer had melted, leaving soft monstrous masses, all in disorder."[16] Following his horrifying epiphany, Roquentin asserts, "I understood I had found the key to Existence . . . Absurdity." This discovery "shakes [Roquentin] from top to bottom." He registers his discontent, screaming vehemently: "I hated this ignoble mess . . . I knew it was the World, the naked World suddenly revealing itself, and I choked with rage at this gross, absurd being."[17]

Albert Camus offers a less dramatic but equally compelling account of absurdity in his essay *An Absurd Reasoning*. There he outlines an "equation" for absurdity. For Camus, absurdity is a "feeling" born of the "confrontation between the human need [for reason] and the unreasonable silence of the world." Camus argues that "absurdity springs from a comparison," or more accurately from a "confrontation" between the "irrational [world] and the wild longing for clarity whose call echoes in the human heart." As Camus makes clear, the absurd "depends as much on man as on the world." Without a human consciousness to contemplate "the absence of any profound reason for living," the world simply is. However, for beings that possess a "longing . . . for reason"[18] in an environment they perceive as "indifferen[t],"[19] the world evokes the feeling of absurdity or, more properly, angst.

Camus argues that when absurdity reveals itself and existence is robbed of the illusion of meaning, humans feel "alien, [like] stranger[s]." Camus argues that the feeling of absurdity can be inspired by any number of sources, including cognizance of one's mortality, the hostility of nature, the mechanical repetition of life, and the often inexplicable behavior of others. Regardless of the cause, Camus argues that the confrontation with absurdity compels profound anxiety, anxiety so unbearable that it commonly elicits a "longing for death." It initiates an "odd state of the soul . . . in which the chain of daily gestures is broken [and] . . . the heart vainly seeks the link that will connect it again." Camus argues that the encounter with absurdity ends in either "suicide or recovery."[20] Sartre and Nietzsche agree. Nietzsche states, "honesty [can] lead to nausea and suicide."[21] Sartre concurs that honesty could lead to "hundreds of suicides."[22] Existentialists agree that suicide is one "solution" to the absurd.[23] If human consciousness, particularly the human desire for reason, is a prerequisite for absurdity, then the eradication of the human eliminates the absurd.

Though they admit that suicide eliminates the absurd, the existentialists do not recommend it. The price of suicide's solution is too steep: the extermination of the subject. Suicide offers no relief for the individual save that of annihilation. To the extent that existentialists, particularly the atheistic existentialists upon whom we are focused, deny the existence of an afterlife where the individual could enjoy her escape from the absurd and place an unwavering emphasis on existence, the forfeiture of existence represented by suicide is a tragic mistake.

In addition to being undesirable, existentialists agree that suicide is not a common occurrence. Camus asserts that humans do not normally act on the suicidal impulse that absurdity evokes because their bodies "shrin[k] from annihilation."[24] Because of their visceral attachment to life, individuals normally resolve the problem of absurdity through less extreme means than suicide: they lie. They lie to themselves, and they lie to others. They construct elaborate webs of deception designed to screen them from all the commonplace things that whisper of the absurd.

Not surprisingly, the lies that people tell are as varied as people are themselves. What they share is that they introduce meaning and purpose. Our lies typically suppress our awareness of absurdity through a combination of delusion and diversion. First, we convince ourselves—or let ourselves be convinced—that something is intrinsically meaningful, that it possesses a clear and unequivocal significance. Then we single-mindedly pursue that something on the assumption that by obtaining it, or subscribing to it, we will have meaning as well. Nietzsche, Sartre, and Camus agree that religion and romance are common means that individuals use to deceive themselves and conjure the illusion of personal significance, necessity, and incommensurability. Regardless of the means employed, humans not only find satisfaction in our lies, we also find consolation in the activities our lies so often involve. We enjoy these activities because constant action represents a sort of talisman against the absurd. The existentialists agree that activity reduces the opportunity for conscious reflection on the nature of existence. As such, it represents a diversion from the sort of reflection that could at any time disclose the "monstrous" truth of absurdity.[25]

David Lynch's *Mulholland Dr.* not only illustrates the tendency that humans have to lie to themselves, it shows that our illusions are simultaneously tenuous and of tremendous consequence. It reveals that our lives depend on the webs that we weave. *Mulholland Dr.* focuses on the mysterious and alluring amnesiac Rita (Laura Elena Harring) and her unexpected ally and aspiring actress, Betty Elms (Naomi Watts). Set in Los Angeles, the city of angels and dreams, the film opens violently with the attempted murder of Rita in a car by unnamed individuals, a car crash in which Rita's assailants die, and Rita's escape onto Mulholland Drive. Traumatized by the preceding events and fearing further persecution, Rita finds her way into an apartment complex, indeed into Betty's aunt's apartment, where she is discovered by Betty when Betty returns home from an audition. Betty cares for Rita and discovers that her guest suffers from amnesia. Rita doesn't know who she is or why the men were trying to kill her. She does not even know her own name. She identifies herself as Rita because she sees a picture of Rita Hayworth on the wall when Betty discovers her in the shower. Rita's personal effects offer no clue to her identity either. Instead, they compound the mystery. In Rita's purse, Betty and Rita find a strange blue key and a large sum of money, both of which hint at illicit activities and suspicious interpersonal associations. Intrigued by Rita and also attracted to her, Betty takes on the role of amateur detective, vowing to harbor her unexpected guest until she can discern her true identity. The film then follows the two women as they strive to unravel the mystery of Rita's identity, a journey that leads them to encounters with unsavory characters and places where nothing is at it seems. One of Betty and Rita's most disturbing discoveries is that of the badly decomposed corpse of a woman, Diane Selwyn, which is found inside what appears to be a charming and perfectly innocuous garden apartment.

Importantly, Betty and Rita's story is interrupted by the abrupt insertion of vignettes that disrupt the narrative and introduce characters that are unrelated to the dominant plot regarding Rita and Betty. Because these vignettes seem to have nothing to do with the main plot and involve enigmatic and often disturbing characters who have little formal development, they serve to confuse the audience and undermine their ability to apprehend the logic of the narrative. In this way, the vignettes heighten dramatic tension. Though they eventually achieve some internal coherence, the relevance of these vignettes to the dominant plot remains a mystery until the film's denouement. As the film winds down, subtle clues in the vignettes allow audiences to draw psychologically disturbing, but aesthetically satisfying inferences regarding the relevance of the vignettes to the dominant story line. Wonderfully, the inferences command an epiphany of ontological reversal as audiences are compelled to conclude that the initial plot involving Betty and Rita is simply an illusion conjured by the character Diane moments before her suicide. The plot that audiences assumed was the "real story" is instead discovered to be a tragic dream.

As discussed previously, individuals can be driven to suicide by the confrontation with absurdity. Though they typically opt for some form of psychological denial, if these veils of illusion are not sufficient to assuage their anxiety and despair, suicide can follow. Existentialists like Nietzsche,

Sartre, and Camus suggest that humans cannot view existence in its raw form without risking their very being. Nietzsche states, "Indeed, it might be a basic character of existence that those who would know it completely would perish, in which case the strength of a spirit should be measured according to how much of the 'truth' one could still barely endure . . . to what degree one would require it to be thinned down, shrouded, sweetened, blunted [and] falsified." As Nietzsche's comment suggests, people create fictions to preserve themselves. They tell lies to make life livable. The degree of deception needed is proportionate to the individual's ability to withstand the disclosure of the absurd.[26]

As the vignettes in *Mulholland Dr.* slowly disclose, the character Diane tells herself lies in an effort to combat the overwhelming despair she experiences at the discovery that her professional and personal lives are bankrupt. Through the vignettes, viewers learn that despite her idealistic aspirations, Diane is not going to rise quickly to stardom. Instead, she seems destined to enter the ranks of the thousands of actresses who labor in terminal anonymity inside the city of dreams. In addition, we learn that Diane's lover, Camilla Rhodes, has opportunistically abandoned her for the affections of a lover more capable of advancing her career. Rather than tell Diane's real story, the dominant plot of *Mulholland Dr.* represents the delicate web of self-deception that Diane creates to shield herself from her own obscurity and loss of romantic centrality. However, as the existentialists warn and Lynch illustrates, the harsh realities of our lives cannot be denied. Diane's illusion does not immunize her. Instead, the brutal facts of her life break through the architecture of her illusion, and Diane's beautiful lie—and ultimately Diane herself—succumb to the pressure of absurdity.

Once the dominant plot is seen as an illusion born of Diane's existential despair, one can interpret its contents from a psychological perspective. One can see how various features of the illusion serve the function of self-consolation and how others, in a predictable return of the repressed, allude to the reality that lurks beneath the lie. For example, when one analyzes Rita, one sees that she serves as a substitute for Diane's lover, Camilla, and possesses all the appeal of her real counterpart. Characteristic of a jilted lover, Diane retains her passion for Camilla. Diane's unrequited passion is what compels her despair. However, the love that is denied in life is fulfilled in dreams. Diane restores her relationship to Camilla in her imagination. In the context of Diane's illusion, Camilla's substitute, Rita, both arouses and satisfyingly reciprocates the affections of Betty—Diane's psychological surrogate.

The amnesia that affects Rita is also significant. Though it is a convention of the noir genre designed to created suspense, amnesia also has special psychological significance in *Mulholland Dr.* Clearly, it works to reinforce the message that humans repress traumatic truths of their existence. It also serves an important function in the context of Diane's illusion. Keeping in mind that Camilla is simultaneously the object of Diane's affection and the cause of her pain, one can read Rita's amnesia as a psychologically satisfying solution unconsciously crafted by Diane's subconscious to overcome the problem of her romantic abandonment. Specifically, if Camilla's decision to end the relationship with Diane can be attributed—in the context of the illusion—to a problem in Rita (Camilla), as opposed to a lack in Diane, Diane's self-concept can remain intact. The breakup with Camilla can be read as an unfortunate consequence of the fact that she has literally forgotten who she is and what is important to her, rather than a consequence of the fact that Diane is no longer of interest or use to her.

Rita's donning of a blond wig is also expressive of Diane's deep-seated desire to reunite with her beloved. Midway through the film, Rita playfully simulates Betty's appearance by putting on a cropped blond wig. Lynch furthers the impression of doubling through quick edits and diminished focus. Rita's identity blurs with that of Betty. In *Being and Nothingness,* Sartre offers a close analysis of romantic love and suggests that individuals seek to "appropriate" the objects of their desire. The visual assimilation into self that Rita's game of dress-up represents is expressive of Diane's desire to "possess" Rita, more specifically, Camilla. Interestingly, the visual collapse of Rita's identity that is facilitated by the charade also alludes to the fact that the dominant plot is an illusion emanating from one character: Diane.[27]

Like Rita, Betty too fulfills Diane's psychological needs. Presented in unequivocally positive terms, Betty represents Diane's ideal self. Rather than be delegated to the periphery as Diane is, Betty is center stage in a life-and-death drama. She is the female lead in a compelling Hollywood tale. She captivates producers with her acting talent, and rather than suffer love lost, Betty commands the affections of her dark and deeply alluring costar, affections that Diane was unable to control in life. In short, Betty is the converse of Rita. She is the buoyant golden girl who embodies innocence, enthusiasm, charity, and loyalty. Unlike Diane and Rita, Betty is clear-headed and unaffected by any psychological weakness. She possesses all the talent that Diane lacks. Her savvy and self-possession are qualities Diane desperately wants.

Rather than serve the purposes of self-consolation, other features of Diane's illusion serve as psychic substitutes for the truths that Diane seeks to suppress. As mentioned previously, Rita's adoption of Betty's appearance serves to suggest that the dominant plot is a dream stamped with Diane's identity. In addition, Rita's portrayal as the dark mistress not only aligns her with the femme fatale of noir, it also works in the context of Diane's illusion to express Diane's ambivalence toward Camilla. Camilla is Diane's beloved, but she is also her betrayer. As such, Diane both loves and loathes her. Rita's dark portrayal and the suspicion and uncertainty that surround her character effectively articulate the ambivalence Diane harbors toward Rita's real correlate: Camilla. As a psychological reading of the first scene of Rita's attempted murder suggests, Camilla is the one that Diane wants—but loves too much—to kill.

Another significant feature of the vignettes is the horrifying figure of the homeless man who appears repeatedly. No harmless tramp, this character is menacing, even monstrous. He inspires anxiety in the audience not only by virtue of his grotesque appearance, but also because he compels horror in other characters. As the vignette in the diner illustrates, the homeless man is the creature who haunts people's dreams and whose presence is sufficient to rob them of consciousness. This latter fact is of particular interest when one reads the homeless man in symbolic terms. Clearly, insofar as his appearance is disheveled and his presence random, he both embodies the absurd and represents its effects. He is both representative of the absurd and the man made a stranger by absurdity, the individual who is no longer at "home" in the world. As the diner incident reveals, the homeless man is who we want to avoid lest we too become infected. He carries the germ of truth against which we attempt to inoculate ourselves with lies.[28]

When one considers Diane's illusion, the homeless man is also representative of mortality. He is a fearful character because he is representative of a fearful truth. As death, the homeless man robs individuals of consciousness, as he does the dark-haired man in Winkie's diner. Supporting the notion that the homeless man represents death is the fact that he is synonymous in appearance to the decaying corpse that Betty and Rita discover. The earthen tones and decay of the two figures are analogous and contrast sharply to the pristine Technicolor in which Betty and Rita are usually presented. The visual association between the two entities is also significant because it allows one to read the corpse that Betty and Rita discover as an unconscious representation of Diane's suicidal impulse. While Betty represents Diane's ideal self, the corpse—who is in fact identified as Diane—represents the destiny that awaits her outside the dream. It is the memento mori that weaves its way into the fabric of Diane's illusion.

Mulholland Dr. reinforces the inference that the dominant plot regarding Betty and Rita is an illusion as well as the insight that humans employ illusion to disguise unpalatable facts in other important ways. Strange dialogue, surrealist imagery, and discontinuous narrative all introduce a dreamlike quality and serve to call the dominant plot into question. Additionally, Lynch's thematic emphasis on dreams and illusions is of particular relevance. In *Mulholland Dr.*, Lynch repeatedly takes his audience, and his characters, to the Club Silencio, a captivating, yet ominous theater where illusionists transfix the audience while a woman sings a Spanish version of Roy Orbison's "In Dreams." Through their incorporation of illusion and references to dreams, the scenes in the club not only further the impression that the dominant plot is an illusion, they can be read in the context of Diane's illusion as subconscious indications of her self-deception. In the context of Diane's illusion, Orbison's lyrics are suppressed by translation into Spanish. However, they are easily recalled by the audience and allude clearly to Diane's romantic loss and dream of reunion. As the lyrics indicate:

In dreams I walk with you.
In dreams I talk to you
In dreams you're mine, all of the time . . .
It's too bad that all these things can only happen in my dreams
Only in dreams, in beautiful dreams.[29]

The homeless man, the illusionists in the Club Silencio, the name Silencio, and the incorporation of Orbison's "In Dreams" all serve to remind Diane (and the audience) that she is in a dream of her own making, a dream that she uses to try to silence undesirable truths.

Interestingly, the Club Silencio also serves a self-referential function for Lynch. With it, Lynch invites the audience to consider their own tendency to escape into illusions, in this case to escape into the dark and satisfying world of cinema. During the scenes in the club, viewers observe Betty and Diane in positions analogous to their own, namely seated in a theater transfixed by what they see. By visually identifying the audience with his protagonists, and then disrupting that identification with new vignettes, Lynch pushes the audience to consider their own fascination with illusion. Thus, as much as Lynch represents the tendency to employ illusion, he reproduces it, and undercuts it, and in doing so encourages audiences to approach truth through the vehicle of dreams.

Ultimately Lynch's utilization of the noir style in *Mulholland Dr.*—and elsewhere—is consistent with the existential insight that humans typically employ illusion to disguise unwanted truths. Though debate persists regarding the definition of noir, theorists of the genre agree that it focuses on phenomena that most people would prefer not to encounter in real life. It is characteristic of works produced in the noir style to speak of murder and corruption, and of strange perils that lurk around familiar corners.

Arguably, the noir style derives much of its appeal from the fact that it packages unpalatable truths in the ever-satisfying security of fiction, in alluring settings and seductive characters. Interestingly, Lynch's works, particularly *Mulholland Dr.*, operate like the screens to which Nietzsche refers, the screens that individuals use to shield themselves from potentially fatal truths.[30] As Nietzsche indicates, such fictions command audience interest through the "attraction of illusion." At the same time, on the assumption that the truth cannot be denied, works crafted in the noir style usually push their audiences to disconcerting discoveries. In *Mulholland Dr.*, Lynch capitalizes on the appeal of escape into a story about glamorous characters who are enmeshed in an intriguing plot. Then, Lynch urges the discovery of a disturbing web of dreams that only the audience sustains. The dominant plot becomes a dream, and the reality beneath that dream is denied as well. Lynch gives no indication that Diane will survive. Instead, it appears that the dominant plot is the dream that passes through Diane's mind moments before her suicide, as ephemeral as the images audiences observe on the screen.[31]

Indeed, by pushing the audience to recall their own participation in illusion, Lynch spurs them to remember that in the theater, it's all dreams. Diane too is an imaginative figure; she exists only onscreen. Lynch conjures a compelling world only to steal it away. Of course, this is what the existentialists argue we must be prepared for. Though our lies can transform "man into so much art, surface, play of colors, graciousness that his sight [of himself] no longer makes [him] suffer,"[32] the absurd awaits around "[any] streetcorner"[33] and the nausea "will come back again."[34]

Of course, if the truths lying beneath our lies cannot be repressed, it begs the question whether self-deception is as productive as Nietzsche contends. If our illusions encourage us to want more from existence than it could ever deliver, then our lies are self-fulfilling prophecies of disappointment that compound anxiety, not things that deliver us from it. In *Mulholland Dr.*, it could be that Diane's dream is what shatters her psyche as opposed to what placates it. Insofar as its intrigue stands in diametrical opposition to Diane's actual obscurity, the dream might ultimately confirm Diane's self-loathing by showing her what she can never have. Arguably, it is this potential for our lies to backfire that precludes the existentialists from endorsing wholesale self-deceit. Though Nietzsche says that we need to lie, he also makes it clear that he values honesty when he indicates that strong individuals can survive the encounter with the absurd. Similarly, he supports honesty when he asserts that lying is frequently born of weakness and resentment. Throughout his corpus, Nietzsche sings the praises of strength and suggests that the ideal toward which we should aspire is that of needing only illusions that buffer, but do not obliterate, the absurd. Similarly, Sartre and Camus both encourage authenticity, or honesty, not its opposite. Though it might seem that the existentialists are inconsistent on the issue of lying, first saying it is necessary and then deriding it, one can make sense of their divergent statements if one recognizes that the existentialists distinguish between necessary and unnecessary fictions, namely lies we need to function and ones we don't.

As Nietzsche, Sartre, and Camus agree, the world unmitigated is—in the words of William James—"a blooming, buzzing confusion" that individuals simply cannot navigate.[35] In order to survive in the world, we need to make sense of it. We need to distinguish things from one another. According to the existentialists, lying is the process we use to carve out reality from chaos by "positing bodies [and] lines"[36] and numerous other entities. The process is lying because the ontological distinctions that most of us assume are absolute are distinctions that humans create rather than discover. Though they are manufactured, these distinctions are absolutely essential for our individual and collective survival. They are the pragmatic, provisional truths that make action and knowledge possible.

Other lies are equally understandable, but less necessary. For atheistic existentialists like Nietzsche, Sartre, and Camus, these unnecessary beliefs include belief in a heavenly realm, immortality, and intrinsic meaning. While the existentialists admit that it is natural for humans to want to have a purpose, fear death, and desire that existence continue in an ideal realm, they do not regard such beliefs as justified or necessary. Without empirical evidence for these entities, they are illusions. Moreover, the existentialists express deep concern about the personal and social consequences of indulging these illusions to the extent they can exacerbate existential despair and promote social conflict. The existentialists agree that there are distinct advantages that follow from cultivating the strength to view truth, even truth viewed through the subtle screens of necessary lies. For example, if one accepts one's mortality, one is unlikely to take time for granted. Instead, one will likely display poignant appreciation of each moment. Similarly, if one accepts that existence has no intrinsic purpose, then one will recognize that things are not determined. As Sartre indicates, though this discovery is daunting, it is also liberating. Without inherent purpose, the course of our individual and collective destiny is open to our own making. It is a destiny that demands immediate action, not one that awards passivity and awaits us in the hereafter. When it comes down to it, the existentialists advocate honesty while simultaneously recognizing the psychological basis and practical necessity for some deceit. Knowing that we will have to sometimes close them for respite, they nonetheless urge us to open our eyes and see as much as we can of the world. Though Camus suggests that he prefers deceit to death when he says, "the point is to live," his empowering portrait of the man of revolt reminds us "a determined soul [can] always manage." Whereas he argues that "killing yourself amounts to confessing . . . that life is too much for you" and constitutes a tragic surrender to the absurd, he states that in contrast "there is no finer sight than that of an intelligence at grips with a reality that transcends it[s] [comprehension]." For Camus, though illusions assuage anxiety, they "debilitate [us] at the same time . . . [by] reliev[ing] [us] of the weight of [our] own life." Like Camus, Sartre suggests that ordinary people can survive absurdity given that his Everyman, Roquentin, makes peace with reality and finds a way to live with a minimum of lies. Sadly, survival is not implied in *Mulholland Dr.* Rather, it illustrates "the fatal game that leads from lucidity in the face of existence to flight from light."[37] Not only does it depict the tendency that individuals have to insulate themselves with illusions, it shows what can happen when our fragile dreams are subject to existential pressure. As David Lynch teaches us through the character of Diane, not only truths, but also lies, can be fatal.

Notes

1. The noir style is an appropriate one in which to explore existential themes not only because existential concepts like absurdity strike many as disturbing or *dark*, but also because illusion and deception are prominent themes in the noir genre itself. To the extent that works crafted in the noir style often center on the unraveling of a mystery, a

process that usually involves discriminating reality from appearance, the noir genre is a perfect one in which to examine illusion from a philosophical perspective.

2. Friedrich Nietzsche, *The Gay Science,* trans. Walter Kaufmann (New York: Random House, 1974), 163.

3. Ibid.

4. Ibid., 170.

5. Friedrich Nietzsche, *Beyond Good and Evil,* trans. Walter Kaufmann (New York: Random House, 1966), 12.

6. Nietzsche, *The Gay Science,* 281, 75.

7. Ibid., 325.

8. Nietzsche, *Beyond Good and Evil,* 71.

9. Albert Camus, "An Absurd Reasoning," in *The Myth of Sisyphus and Other Essays,* trans. Justin O'Brien (New York: Vintage Press, 1991), 28.

10. Jean-Paul Sartre, *Being and Nothingness,* trans. Hazel Barnes (New York: Washington Square Press, 1956), 86.

11. Nietzsche, *Beyond Good and Evil,* 105.

12. Camus, "An Absurd Reasoning," 5, 41.

13. Nietzsche, *The Gay Science,* 175.

14. Nietzsche, *Beyond Good and Evil,* 71.

15. Nietzsche, *The Gay Science,* 177.

16. Jean-Paul Sartre, *Nausea,* trans. Lloyd Alexander (New York: New Directions, 1964), 127.

17. Ibid., 129, 122, 134.

18. Camus, "An Absurd Reasoning," 50, 6, 28, 30, 21, 21, 21, 5, 28.

19. Albert Camus, *The Stranger,* trans. Matthew Ward (New York: Vintage Press, 1989), 122.

20. Camus, "An Absurd Reasoning," 6, 14, 6, 12, 13.

21. Nietzsche, *The Gay Science,* 163.

22. Sartre, *Nausea,* 159.

23. Camus, "An Absurd Reasoning," 6.

24. Ibid., 8.

25. Sartre, *Nausea,* 127.

26. Nietzsche, *Beyond Good and Evil,* 49.

27. Sartre, *Being and Nothingness,* 776, 478.

28. Camus, "An Absurd Reasoning," 6.

29. Roy Orbison, "In Dreams," *In Dreams,* compact disc, Legacy Records, 2006, ASIN: B000005C17.

30. Nietzsche, *Beyond Good and Evil,* 49.

31. Nietzsche, *The Gay Science,* 134.

32. Nietzsche, *Beyond Good and Evil,* 71.

33. Camus, "An Absurd Reasoning," 12.

34. Sartre, *Nausea,* 157.

35. William James, *The Principles of Psychology* (Cambridge: Harvard University Press, 1981), 462.

36. Nietzsche, *The Gay Science,* 177.

37. Camus, "An Absurd Reasoning," 65, 41, 5, 55, 55, 5.

CONSTELLATIONS OF THE FLESH

The Embodied Self in *The Straight Story* and *The Elephant Man*

Tal Correm

The Straight Story (1999) opens with a peaceful set of a lazy sunny after-noon in a typical suburban yard that is suddenly interrupted by a sound of a fall. Only after a while the backyard neighbors who break into the house find that the sound was caused by Alvin Straight (Richard Farnsworth), a seventy-three-year-old man whose weary body has betrayed him, and who now cannot get to his feet without help. After this incident, Straight, because of a promise to his daughter Rose (Sissy Spacek), begrudgingly visits the doctor. After a thorough physical examination, Dr. Gibbons (Dan Flannery) severely warns Straight that he should make serious changes in his lifestyle to improve his physical health. Straight, however, cynically responds to the warning by smoking a cigar back at his house and comforts Rose by telling her that the doctor predicted a long life for him. A late-night phone call soon after urges Straight to go on an almost impossible journey to visit his sick brother, Lyle (Harry Dean Stanton), whom he has not seen or spoken with for ten years due to an old quarrel between them. This journey seems hopeless, not merely because of its long distance (Lyle lives a few hundred miles away) or Straight's health but also because Straight's chosen method of transportation is an old lawnmower. Nevertheless, Straight decides to transcend his physical constraints and illness and go on this journey to meet with his brother one last time. The film develops from this point on, following Straight in his long, slow journey through struggles and hardships of the road and his encounters with various people along his way. Often this film has been understood as depicting the story of a man who goes on a journey in which he succeeds in going beyond his own limitations. But does Straight transcend his limits, or do these limits structure his journey? Is this Straight's real drive for starting this journey, or is it something else?

A similar task, constructed in a different setting, also motivates Lynch's *The Elephant Man* (1980), which delineates the journey of a man who attempts to transcend his limitations. This is the journey of John Merrick (John Hurt) from the fringes of society—the gutter of a circus freak show—to the heart of the Victorian high society of London. Merrick is labeled the Elephant Man because of his deformed physical appearance. His face and body are distorted by tumors that cause his lameness and other physiological deformities. He is a young man who has lived most of his life under the supervision of Mr. Bytes (Freddie Jones), a cruel manager who exploits him in his circus freak show. A young surgeon and lecturer on anatomy at the London Hospital, Frederick Treves (Anthony Hopkins) discovers Merrick when the circus arrives in town. He takes an interest in Merrick and brings him to the hospital in order to examine his deformed anatomy. Merrick, who in the beginning could barely talk, gradually acquires social and artistic skills and assimilates into London society. The society elite seek his company: he befriends a glorious theater actress, and even the queen bestows her grace on him. However, is this integration complete? Merrick rarely goes out since, as he tells his esteemed guests, "people find my appearance disturbing," and his relations with high society are put into question by Mrs. Mothershead (Wendy Hiller), the head nurse. Moreover, Merrick's nights are brutally interrupted by the night porter (Michael Elphick), who also brings the crowd that pays money to catch a glimpse of Merrick. Thus, Merrick remains an object of voyeurism and exploitation.

Alvin Straight and John Merrick experience the world through their points of view, which are contingent on their specific bodily conditions. Thus, these films tell not only the story of the voyages of individuals through their confrontations and hardships, but also how their embodiment paths their journey. I argue that, through these films, Lynch illuminates the way in which the body shapes and structures our experience. Through discussion of these protagonists' sense of themselves, the way they communicate their will, emotions, and aims, and how other people react to these intentions and perceive them, I reveal how their experience of the world, their relations with other people, and their self-understanding are largely shaped by their embodiment. Lynch's treatment of embodiment, I will show, also has ethical implications: understanding the centrality of embodiment in our experience leads to the realization of our nonseparateness from our body, the world, and other people, which requires responsibility and empathy. His work also reveals the unavoidable destructive consequences of violence, abuse, and exploitation that follow when these reciprocal relations are transgressed.

The Corporeal Subject: Objective Body and Lived Body

In order to understand the role that Merrick's or Straight's body plays in shaping their experience, their relations with other people, and their self-comprehension, I turn to the distinction between the *objective body* and the *lived body* that is found in *phenomenology*. Phenomenology is a philosophical movement that was founded by the German philosopher Edmund Husserl (1859–1938), and that includes some of the prominent European philosophers of the twentieth century, among them Martin Heidegger (1889–1976), Jean-Paul Sartre (1905–1980), and Maurice Merleau-Ponty (1908–1961). Phenomenology is a philosophical approach rather than a philosophical theory. It is the study and description of how things appear to us (*phenomena*), rather than what they are. As such, all presuppositions of the ontological status of the appearances (that is, whether they refer to existing things in the world or not) are suspended or bracketed, remaining out of consideration. In order to investigate the appearances as they manifest, all other theoretical assumptions, such as those of the sciences or psychology, are also suspended. For Husserl, phenomenology aims to provide a ground for all the sciences. It goes beyond the epistemology (the theory of knowledge) of modern philosophy because it denies that knowledge consists of representations of the world in inner mental states, and it attempts to go beyond the traditional dichotomies of modern philosophy, such as that of subject and object or body and mind. Followers of Husserl extended the phenomenological investigations and descriptions to domains such as the social sciences, art, history, and politics.[1]

According to Husserl, the methodological suspension, or, as he calls it, the *epoché*, leads to the investigation of the basic structures or the essential features of human experiences and their correlate objects. One of these fundamental structures is intentionality. Consciousness, according to the phenomenological account, is always *directed to, about,* or *of* something. We think about something or somebody, we remember a past event, we listen to a melody, we aspire to a successful life, and so on. Every conscious act is intended or directed toward an object. When we watch a film, for instance, our perception is of the images on the screen; we think of the character in front of us; we empathize with her or are scared by her; we imagine the forthcoming events; and so on. Another basic structure of experience is temporality. For example, when we watch a film, part of it is being perceived in the present, part has already been perceived, and part is yet to be perceived. Thus, the act of watching a film requires not only perception of its present moment, but also awareness of its previous phases, as well as of those that are about to emerge. The complexity of our perception allows each moment of the film to be anchored within a unity of succession together with the rest of the phases, the ones that just have elapsed and the ones that are about to emerge.

The phenomenological analysis of experience reveals our body not as an appearance of object among other objects in the world, but as the center, or *zero point of orientation,* of our actions and perceptions. Merleau-Ponty elaborates on this phenomenological description of the body through his investigation of perception. When we perceive some object, we always perceive it from a certain perspective, and thus we perceive only a certain part of it and not its entirety. According to the phenomenological description, there is no objective overarching point of view from which we can see things. Our perception is perspectival, finite, and partial. This reveals that our body is always situated in a certain location in space and time (as well as in a certain culture, society, and history). However, we assume the other parts of the perceived object and that we can move and perceive them. From our past experiences, we have an expectation that the objects we encounter will have a bottom, a back, or other sides, and we will be surprised if the case is otherwise. Our body usually has the ability of movement, and it can adjust its capacities according to the circumstances of its situation.[2]

Accordingly, the phenomenological analysis makes a distinction between the objective body (*Körper*) and the lived body (*Leib*). The objective body is the body as observed in everyday situations, or as perceived from a scientific point of view. This is the body as a psychophysical complex system that consists of organs, sense perceptions, and movements and has certain functions and abilities. The body in this sense can be an object of study for the scientists in fields such as biology, psychology, or cognitive science or our body as is seen in the mirror. The phenomenological description rediscovered the body also as a lived body. It is the body as we experience it from within, or the body of other people, that is distinct from any other physical things in the world, for it is of course physical, but its physicality is of a living being. What does it mean to feel our body from within? We always feel our body even if pre-reflectively: we feel whether we are standing, sitting, or walking, where we are located, whether we are in pain or feel lively and refreshed.[3]

This phenomenological distinction does not refer to two different bodies. It refers to the same body from two different points of view. On the one hand, the objective body is analyzed and understood through the third-person point of view, where the body is known objectively qua object. On the other hand, the lived body is analyzed and understood through the first-person point of view (or the second-person point of view), where the body is known qua subject. The body in this sense is seeing and being seen, perceiving and being perceived, touching and being touched. Having now fleshed out the phenomenological distinction between the lived body and the objective body, we can use this distinction to shed light on the way both Straight and Merrick experience their world.

The Embodied Life of Alvin Straight

We should return first to the opening scenes of *The Straight Story*. After Straight's fall, he is forced to see a physician and undergo a medical checkup. During this medical encounter, Straight's body is subjected to the physician's perception. In other words, Straight's body is perceived as an objective body by his physician. This is evident because, as a physician, his interest is to examine and diagnose the problems of Straight's body and to look for a way to improve its condition and prevent future deterioration. What about Straight himself? It seems that, in the way he ignores his body's aches and demands and in trying to resume his normal life despite the doctor's warnings, Straight alienates his body and thus treats it as the objective body as well.

However, I argue that the movie actually deals with Straight's lived body and shows how his body structures his experience. How is it possible to show in cinematic language the way one perceives his body from within or the way one perceives the world from his bodily perspective? One way is to use first-person point-of-view shots through which we can follow how the world is seen and experienced from the perspective of the protagonist. However, Lynch does not provide many first-person point-of-view shots in this film. We can see how he nevertheless uses the cinematic apparatus to structure the film at Straight's pace and thus provides us with the sense of Straight's experiencing of the world. For example, the long shots of the landscape enable us to experience the journey as Straight experiences it. In particular, there is the narrative decision to use a lawnmower as the means of transportation for Straight's long journey. Like Straight's aching and exhausted body, his lawnmower is old, drained of energy, and moves spasmodically. Like his aging body, the mower betrays him and forces him to turn back after a short while on the road. Straight reacts to this in a violent act of alienation, setting it on fire with a shot from his shotgun. Even when he replaces it with a newer model John Deere mower, he continues to suffer mechanical troubles and has to stop and get help to fix it along his way. When he is alone in the woods just a few feet away from Lyle's house, his final destination, the mower almost breaks down. Straight stops on the side of the dusty pathway and waits patiently. To a random passerby, he says that the mower is just tired, and after another attempt he successfully starts it and continues his drive.

The phenomenological description explains the lived body as a practical center of abilities, or "I can." Our bodily capacities can be extended and expressed by the tools and devices we use. They become an extension of our body. The classical example is the blind person's cane that becomes part of his or her practical lived body. Similar to the way in which the two walking sticks become Straight's means of walking, the mower becomes an extension of his bodily capacities, his ability to move from place to place and to reach Lyle. The mower is adequate to his bodily abilities, and it sets the pace of the film. The film advances patiently and steadily and enables us to see the world as it is experienced and conditioned by Straight's embodiment.[4]

The phenomenological description emphasizes how our sense of the space we are in, or our physical surroundings, is influenced by our lived body and at the same time affects it. For instance, we walk one way when we are alone in an empty street at midnight and in a different way when we cross a crowded street at rush hour. Similarly, when we are depressed the world seems dark, and when we are thrilled it looks bright and promising. As Straight tells Rose, his is a lone journey: "I got to go see Lyle. I got to make this trip on my own." The wide-open midwestern landscapes during the harvest season highlight the lone road that Straight is on. The long, solitary, and laborious road echoes his body's long life and his sense of aloneness. His gauged movements, his heavy breath, and his pensive, reflective gaze shape the way he absorbs the landscape. Straight's point of view is embedded in his situation and shaped by his embodiment. Lynch uses long, slow camera movements accompanied by the soundtrack's melodies to express this idea.

Another cinematic way to express one's point of view is through dialogues. The literal communication can reveal what seem to be hidden and internal mental states, feelings, moods, or emotions. Straight's various encounters on his journey indeed shed more light on his personality, biography, and state of mind. But I want to focus less on the literal contents of these dialogues and more on the way the communication, even through language, is first of all a bodily expression. Phenomenology rejects the sharp distinction between a hidden psyche and an external body or the claim that we can infer internal mental states from external behavior. Instead, it regards the body and the mind as a unified whole. Every action or bodily event can be interpreted in various ways; for instance, a sensation of pain can be explained physiologically, psychologically, or culturally. Each way illuminates the others but does not absorb the others. In this way, dialogue and communication are not merely explained according to their literal contents. Moreover, language itself is understood as an expression that carries through bodily gestures. The intonation, rhythm, tone, and volume of our voice are controlled and influenced by our body. The lived body, according to phenomenologists, is always already meaningful and communicative. Facial or bodily gestures express meanings. They show intentions. An expression in the phenomenological sense is "more than simply a bridge supposed to close the gap between inner mental states and external bodily behavior"; it is "a direct manifestation of the subjective life of the mind."[5]

Straight does not talk much, but nevertheless his emotions and moods—pain, concern, fear, relief, embarrassment, care, or empathy—are expressed throughout the film in his eyes, with his facial gestures, in his labored breathing. Whether it is tight, smiling, doubtful, or nodding in understanding, his face communicates. Throughout the film, the camera stays for long moments on his face and emphasizes these details.

Straight's drive and motivation is to see his brother, Lyle, is what initiates his journey in the first place. A talk on the phone is not sufficient; he wants to be in Lyle's presence, and he longs for the physical proximity. When they finally meet one another, they do not say much, but their bodies in their shared presence nevertheless communicate. The men sit in silence, tired and weary. They look at each other, their eyes move, their chins shiver, tears run down their cheeks, their noses sniffle, they smile, and, through such communication, they are brought closer together.

Lynch, in *The Straight Story* and *The Elephant Man*, in a similar way that is suggestive of the phenomenological approach, draws our attention to the centrality of our body in our experience. He shows something that we all experience but that is usually unnoticed. Straight's and Merrick's confrontations with the world, other people, and themselves are shaped by their embodiment. Merrick suffers rare anatomical deformation, and Straight struggles with the pain and illness that aging brings. But what is the significance of their stories? It seems that any illustrations that examine human experience or social situations can illuminate how embodiment shapes our experience of ourselves, the world, and others since embodiment is something that we all share and is a constitutive feature of human beings (as well as of animals). However, this constitutive feature often remains silent; we are not aware of the pervasive role of our embodiment, and we take it for granted. It is only in moments of crisis or extreme situations such as physical injury or disease, as well as, from different perspectives, in physical attraction or embarrassment, that we become aware of our embodiment. Or sometimes, when we are looking at a photo of ourselves that was taken a while ago, we become aware of our aging and the transformation that our body undergoes through the years.

One of the ways in which Merleau-Ponty's phenomenological analysis reveals the features of bodily experience that we take for granted is through investigation of pathological phenomena. For instance, he turns to the study of the case of Schneider, a brain-injured patient of the German psychologists Adhémar Gelb and Kurt Goldstein in the 1920s. Schneider cannot touch different organs of his face upon request, but, nevertheless, when a mosquito stings his forehead, he immediately recognizes the location and scratches it. This shows, according to Merleau-Ponty, that prior to any conceptualization or use of language, there is a meaning to our intentional actions. They are oriented toward a purpose even if this directness or purpose is not deliberate and cannot be expressed in language. This analysis reveals the basic structures of experience that remain unnoticed in everyday experiences. Thus, both Lynch and the phenomenologists, through investigation of pathological or extraordinary cases, open a way for us to notice our body, its function and importance, which we ordinarily take for granted.[6]

The Embodied Life of John Merrick

In John Merrick's world, the shift between the two points of view of the body, as objective body and as lived body, is more evident and motivates the plot itself—the transformation and assimilation of Merrick into society. This dialectic of points of view also carries an ethical significance: in *The Elephant Man*, Lynch reveals the cruelty, abuse, and exploitation to which a perception of one's body as objective body can lead, as I discuss below. At the beginning of the film, Merrick is presented as an object of spectacle even before his body is actually seen onscreen. He is the main attraction of Bytes's freak show—"The Elephant Man." The curious people want to see with their own eyes the phenomenon of his deformed body. Mr. Bytes calls him "my treasure," but not because Merrick is dear to him. These cynical words only point to the fact that Bytes makes his living at Merrick's expense. He brutalizes Merrick and treats him worse than an animal. With Treves, the young doctor, Merrick has a more ambivalent relationship. On the one hand, Merrick is an object of study for Treves. The doctor indeed takes care of him and saves him from the grip of Bytes, but only to examine his bodily deformity. Treves presents Merrick's body and enumerates its abnormal phenomena and diseases before the Pathological Society of London. He makes a name for himself as a researcher and a doctor at Merrick's expense. On the other hand, Treves also reflects on his use of Merrick's body. In the middle of the film, he expresses his moral dilemma to his wife and compares himself with Bytes, asking whether he is "a good man" or "a bad man." However, although his relations with Merrick are developed gradually throughout the film, their asymmetrical relationship is preserved almost until the end. Through most of the social encounters, people perceive Merrick's body as an object of desire. Whether they belong to the drunken mob or to high society, people desire to see him for his deformed figure. Even at the theater, in one of the culminating scenes after his social status is well established, when the audience applauds him, he remains the deformed and shattered "Elephant Man" for them. The camera perpetuates these asymmetrical relations and presents Merrick's body as an object of torture and oppression, an object of study and curiosity, or an object of desire: the camera is looking down, framing his body from above, and thus objectifying it.[7]

At this point, however, we may ask: How does Merrick treat his body, and how is his sense of himself affected by the perception of his body by other people? How does his body structure the way he experiences himself, the world, and other people? And how is this shown through Lynch's cinematic means? Merrick is aware of his body and of the reaction it causes. He understands this reaction. However, he seems alienated from his own body. The absence of a mirror and the head nurse's explicit direction not to hang a mirror in his room under any circumstances strengthen this alienation. When he is forced to look at his face in the mirror, as an adult by the night porter or as a child as his dream reveals, the extreme close-ups reveal it as a traumatic experience for him. It seems that he would rather prefer to immerse himself in manners, social rituals, and art.

However, Merrick's sense of subjectivity—his self-understanding as a person who is an autonomous agent in the world, carries out projects, has intentions and purposes, controls his actions, and takes responsibility for his decisions—develops in the film and is shaped by his embodiment. One of the central indications of his individuality is his preoccupation with art. Merrick constructs a model of a cathedral. The top of a cathedral seen from his window inspires him to construct this miniature replica. Because he never leaves the hospital, he relies on his imagination to complete the missing parts. His creativity and sense of design distinguish him from his past as a spectacle that was presented as half-human and half-animal. When he completes the model just prior to his (supposed) death, he adds his signature. The signature is an evident sign of agency and a testimony left for the future. He has gained his name; that is, he has gained his selfhood. However, this delicate handiwork cannot be performed without a skilled body as the camera that patiently follows Merrick's only functioning hand emphasizes. This is the way his body creatively expresses itself through artistic means.[8]

Merrick's body also enables him to fulfill his subjectivity in a stronger sense. Tragically, what marks his refined sense of subjectivity is his decision to take responsibility for his life. At the end of the film, after the dramatic climax at the theater and after he signs his model, he decides to go to sleep lying on his back like any other human being, a decision that, regrettably and intentionally, leads to his demise.

Merrick's sense of subjectivity is developed gradually through his social relations. According to phenomenology, *intersubjectivity*, or the relations between people in a shared world, requires and presupposes embodiment. The perception of other people as subjects starts with the recognition that the other body is perceived as a lived body, that is, as a center of activity and intentionality, and it is different from other physical things we perceive in the world. It means that we do not perceive another person through ordinary cognitive perception. We do not perceive another person in the same way we perceive objects in the world, but through what phenomenologists call *empathy*. Empathy is an intentional experience in which we are directed to one's lived experiences and we perceive the other's subjectivity from a second-person point of view. According to phenomenology, we do not perceive someone's external behavior and then infer that person's inner mental states, moods, or feelings; instead, we perceive them as already expressive.

Through empathy, we understand the behavior of other people as an expression of their feeling. As the German philosopher Edith Stein (1891–1942) argues: "For him who is cheerful, the world is baptized in a rosy glow; for him who is depressed in black. And all this is co-given with acts of feeling as belonging to them. It is primarily appearances of expression that grant access to these experiences . . . the mind 'become visible' in the living body."[9]

Thus, the phenomenological analysis reveals the body as always already expressive and communicative. It is social, intersubjective, in the world among other people. The communication between people is even prior to its formulation in language, as Straight and his brother communicate without words when they finally meet again. Language carries the embodied communication further. When Treves takes Merrick to the hospital, he has some sense that Merrick is trying to communicate with him. But even though Treves is occupied with Merrick's body, he fails to see its communication because he perceives it as an objective body. The camera captures Merrick's body from above, leaving his face in the dark, expressing Treves's point of view of Merrick's body. Thus, he urges Merrick to speak; as if only Merrick's speaking could convince Treves that he is truly human. Treves begs him: "I can't help you unless you help me, unless I know what you are feeling. . . . I believe there's something back there, there's something you want to say, but I've got to understand you. . . . You are going to talk to me!" This pressure forces Merrick to express himself in words. In the beginning, it is a great effort for him, and his words come out fragmented. The mask on John Hurt's head is still and frozen, but his shriveled eyes and broken voice attest to his evident effort. Still, Merrick's talking here is an imitation and not authentic speech. He mouths the words Treves taught him. Mr. Carr-Gomm (John Gielgud), the hospital chairman, recognizes this and tells Treves that talking is one thing, but understanding is another. However, Merrick does understand. When he realizes that Mr. Carr-Gomm is refusing to host him in the hospital, he loudly recites a biblical passage that Treves never taught him; hearing him from downstairs, Treves and Carr-Gomm hurry back up to his room in surprise. They discover that not only he can speak, but he also knows how to read. Merrick's speaking and reading establish him as a civilized person in their eyes. Only then can they recognize him as a fellow human being.

The situation is different with the head nurse. Although she perceives him in the beginning as a lost cause and says to Treves that she cannot see how he can help Merrick, she treats him with professional care: she cleans his body and feeds and dresses him. As she says later to Treves, she shows loving-kindness through care of his body. The high angle is replaced by frontal medium shots that place the two on the same level and show Merrick's body through her perspective as equal. Another example is Merrick's meeting with Treves's wife, Anne (Hannah Gordon), which brings Merrick to tears. He is excited by the way she treats him. He says that he is not used to being treated so well by a beautiful woman. When he reveals his memories of his mother, he brings Mrs. Treves to tears. The intimate relation between the two is established by the alternating close-ups of their expressive faces. Though this encounter is emotional, it is hindered because Mrs. Treves is still deterred by Merrick's appearance; she turns her head in discomfort and finds it difficult to directly address him.

The encounter with Mrs. Kendal (Anne Bancroft), a famous actress, enables Merrick to fully realize his subjectivity. She is the only one who truly turns to him with empathy. She read about him in the newspaper and becomes curious to meet "this gentleman." Unlike Mrs. Treves, when she talks with Merrick, her look is direct and trustful. A straight-on angle takes the dialogue shots on the same level and structures their mutuality. Unlike Mrs. Treves, she does not avoid making eye contact. They read *Romeo and Juliet* together. She tells him, "you are not an elephant man," and he responds with wonder. From her perspective, he is Romeo, and she kisses him on the cheek. She kneels in front of his bed. Her point of view is expressed through flattering soft lighting and a low angle looking up to him, showing his greatness in her eyes. Merrick's sense of subjectivity is affirmed by her recognition. She calls him "my very dear friend" and addresses him from a second-person point of view as a Thou. Their relationship offers friendship, mutual respect, and love. Merrick says later to Treves that he has gained himself and that his life is full because he knows that he is loved.

It seems that Merrick reaches this kind of mutual relationship with Treves. However, it appears to be more superficial, or at least more one-sided. In the beginning, there is an asymmetrical relationship between them. Treves is interested in Merrick's body as an object of study. Whenever Treves addresses him, Merrick's body is presented from a high angle, looking down on him and isolating his body as an object for scrutiny. Though Treves approaches Merrick and tries to stimulate him to speak, Merrick's speech in the beginning is imitative and unauthentic. The men remain distanced from each other. Merrick's body is presented in these scenes as bent and submissive, not looking directly at his interlocutor, and speaking hesitantly. Gradually, the two become closer, and we witness their growing friendship onscreen as reflected in their bodily expressions. Merrick is invited to be a guest in Treves's home and meet his wife, although Treves keeps his own children away. Merrick is dressed up in his new suit, and his posture is stable and relaxed. We see the two men smiling to one other, and, although Treves's bodily gestures remain distanced and reserved, he politely encourages Merrick to feel comfortable at his home. It is a very emotional experience for Merrick, but he doesn't share it with Treves; instead, he shares it with Anne, his wife. The camera maintains the asymmetrical relation between them. While using close-ups to highlight the growing proximity between Merrick and Anne, it keeps Mr. Treves himself in the distance with medium-long shots.

Toward the end of the film, when the policemen safely bring Merrick back after the traumatic kidnapping by Bytes, the two men hug heartily. In one of their last conversations, they stand close to each other, and Treves helps Merrick with his suit and tie. The camera establishes them as peers when they are shot from the same height and distance. Merrick calls Treves "my friend" and thanks Treves for his efforts to help him. Treves at this moment gets affirmation that seems to address his earlier moral puzzlement about the ethics of his relationship with Merrick, and he responds that Merrick has helped him too. It seems, yet, that there is no real conciliation, for Treves in his reserved gestures feels rather uncomfortable and quickly changes the subject.

Merrick gains his sense of subjectivity through these reciprocal relations. He feels loved and accepted. Care and empathy also give him a home. The sympathy for him and his popularity convinced the hospital Governing Committee to vote unanimously to provide him permanent housing in the hospital. He finally has a home, and it seems that he has fulfilled his subjectivity. The embodied self needs habitation, a place to dwell. However, right after this dramatic climax Lynch reverses the point of view. We see Merrick in his room delighted with the dressing case he received as a present for his new home. The scene is alternately cut to the bar where the night porter gathers a crowd to watch the Elephant Man. We see that Merrick enjoys himself with the delicate gift that expresses good taste and refinement. But immediately afterward, we return to the enthusiastic crowd paying money to see the show. Merrick looks at his well-dressed figure with satisfaction, brushes his hair, and sprinkles eau de cologne on his neck in the calm and softly lit room. The peaceful scene of a man alone with himself is brutally cut short when the night porter breaks into his room. A frightened look on Merrick's face predicts the turmoil that will follow. The reversal of points of view from the lived body to the body as an object is apparent in the way Lynch presents Merrick in these scenes: When Merrick is alone in his room dressed in a fine suit, his body is upright and confident. When the night porter enters, Merrick's body suddenly loses its balance and is drained of his energy, becoming a puppet in the cruel hands of the night porter, who drags Merrick and controls his gestures. In this transition, Merrick loses all sense of subjectivity, and in the following scenes his condition deteriorates further. A crowd of people, with Bytes among them, enters after the night porter and causes destruction everywhere. The carnival loses all constraints. They force a woman to kiss him and pour alcohol in his mouth. They break his fragile cathedral model and cause disorder and damage. The horrible event culminates when Bytes kidnaps Merrick. In this horrified turmoil, Merrick's body is perceived as an objective body, as an object of voyeurism, abuse, and mockery. Lynch discloses the ethical significance that recognition of the body as a lived body illuminates and the horrible implications that can follow when the body is perceived only as an objective body. I end the phenomenological account of the embodied self in *The Elephant Man* and *The Straight Story* with a discussion of these ethical implications.

Embodied Subjectivity as a Basis for Ethical Relations

In *The Straight Story* and *The Elephant Man*, Lynch shows that the possibility of ethical relations arises with the understanding of the centrality of our body in our experience; he also depicts the horrible consequences when the body as a lived body is ignored. Empathy is a necessary condition for reciprocal relations between people because it discloses both persons as subjects. As the contemporary American philosopher Judy Miles argues, following Stein and the French philosopher Simone de Beauvoir (1908–1986): "Empathizing is the process of putting oneself in another's mental place; of bringing before one's consciousness the experience of the Other. This is the possibility Beauvoir was describing when she said we could see the Other as other-subject. The mere recognition that one can see the Other as other-subject makes reciprocity theoretically possible." Only when a body is perceived as a lived body, as a communicative and expressive body, can ethical relations be established.[10]

The body's initial communication, openness, uniqueness, and sensitivity require responsibility, reciprocity, and mutual recognition. This understanding illuminates *The Elephant Man:* so long as his body is objectified and alienated, or, in other words, is being seen merely as objective body, Merrick suffers abuse and torture. This is seen throughout the film in the manner in which Bytes and the night porter treat him, and in the abusive chaos toward the end. In contrast to the objectified body, the lived body communicates and requires empathic response. Ethical relations are established through the exchange of address and response. The vulnerability of the body demands responsibility and reciprocity, without which destructive consequences follow.

Straight's journey in *The Straight Story* is a journey of a man by himself, but his motivation for the drive is ethical: to see his brother in person, to be with him. His journey also develops from one personal encounter to another. These dialogical encounters share memories, emotions, and pensive reflections. Lynch emphasizes the ethical significance of embodiment in his works in the sense in which *The Elephant Man* and *The Straight Story* suggest the possibility of transcending violence and power relations and motivating ethical relations of mutual respect and empathy. He also shows that the reciprocal relations between human beings are not separated from their relations with the world at large. He ends both films by panning up to the open starry sky so that viewers inwardly enter an infinite space, continually moving toward the constellations.

Notes

1. For a further discussion of phenomenology, its aims and methods, see Edmund Husserl, *Cartesian Meditations: An Introduction to Phenomenology*, trans. Dorion Cairns (Dordrecht: Kluwer, 1993); Maurice Merleau-Ponty, *Phenomenology of Perception*, trans. Colin Smith (London: Routledge; Atlantic Highlands, N.J.: Humanities Press, 1962), vii–xxiv; Martin Heidegger, "My Way to Phenomenology," in *The Phenomenology Reader*, ed. Dermot Moran and Timothy Mooney (London and New York: Routledge, 2002), 251–56; Shaun Gallagher and Dan Zahavi, *The Phenomenological Mind: An Introduction to Philosophy of Mind and Cognitive Science* (London and New York: Routledge, 2008), 1–10; Evan Thompson and Dan Zahavi, "Philosophical Issues: Phenomenology," in *The Cambridge Handbook of Consciousness*, ed. Philip David Zelazo, Morris Moscovitch, and Evan Thompson (New York: Cambridge University Press, 2007), 67–87; Hubert L. Dreyfus and Mark A. Wrathall, eds., *A Companion to Phenomenology and Existentialism* (Malden, Mass.: Blackwell, 2005), 1–3; Dan Zahavi, "Phenomenology," in *The Routledge Companion to Twentieth-Century Philosophy*, ed. Dermot Moran (London: Routledge, 2008), 661–92; and Dermot Moran, introduction to *The Phenomenology Reader*, ed. Dermot Moran and Timothy Mooney (London and New York: Routledge, 2002), 1–26.

2. Merleau-Ponty, *Phenomenology of Perception*, 73–89. See also Edmund Husserl, *Ideas Pertaining to a Pure Phenomenology and to a Phenomenological Philosophy*, Second Book, trans. R. Rojcewicz and A. Schuwer (Dordrecht: Kluwer, 1989).

3. Gallagher and Zahavi, *The Phenomenological Mind*, 129–51; Dorothy Leland, "Embodiment," *Cambridge Dictionary of Philosophy*, ed. Robert Audi (Cambridge: Cambridge University Press, 1999), 258.

4. Gallagher and Zahavi, *The Phenomenological Mind*, 139, 147; Thompson and Zahavi, "Philosophical Issues: Phenomenology," 79.

5. Thompson and Zahavi, "Philosophical Issues: Phenomenology," 82.

6. Schneider is a patient in Gelb and Goldstein's neurological study, a veteran who suffers from brain lesions due to an injury in his military service in World War I. Merleau-Ponty, *Phenomenology of Perception*, 98–107; Kim Atkins, *Self and Subjectivity* (Malden, Mass.: Blackwell, 2005), 101–5.

7. For Lacanian analysis of John Merrick in Lynch's film as an object of desire, see Todd McGowan, "The Integration of the Impossible Object in *The Elephant Man*," in *The Impossible David Lynch* (New York: Columbia University Press, 2007), 51, 62.

8. For a phenomenological analysis of artistic expression, see Maurice Merleau-Ponty, "Cézanne's Doubt," in *Sense and Non-Sense*, trans. Hubert L. Dreyfus and Patricia Allen Dreyfus (Evanston, Ill.: Northwestern University Press, 1964), 9–25.

9. Edith Stein, *On the Problem of Empathy*, trans. Waltraut Stein (The Hague: Martinus Nijhoff, 1965), 83–84. For a discussion of empathy, see also Thompson and Zahavi, "Philosophical Issues: Phenomenology," 82; Husserl, *Ideas Pertaining to a Pure Phenomenology*; Dan Zahavi, *Subjectivity and Selfhood: Investigating the First-Person Perspective* (Cambridge: MIT Press, 2005), 148–62.

10. Judy Miles, "Simone De Beauvoir's Feminism," in *Phenomenology World-Wide: Foundations, Expanding Dynamics, Life-Engagements: A Guide for Research and Study*, ed. Anna-Teresa Tymienieck (Dordrecht: Kluwer, 2002), 577. For further discussion of the ethical implications of embodiment in Merleau-Ponty's phenomenology, see David Michael Levin, "Justice in the Flesh," in *Ontology and Alterity in Merleau-Ponty*, ed. Galen A. Johnson and Michael B. Smith (Evanston, Ill.: Northwestern University Press, 1990), 35–44.

David Lynch's Road Films

Individuality and Personal Freedom?

Richard Gaughran

The history of narrative has often been dominated by a character or characters on a quest. Homer's *Odyssey*, to begin at the beginning, establishes a pattern: the central character desires to return home, but the long journey is fraught with dangers and unexpected obstacles. In more recent examples, the quest narrative often functions to satirize the surrounding culture and its values, as the protagonist stands apart as an outside witness. Such is the case, for instance, with Cervantes' *Don Quixote* (1615), or, to move the examples still closer to the present and onto the American landscape, Mark Twain's *Adventures of Huckleberry Finn* (1884), in which the title character and Jim, a runaway slave, engage in a journey that "becomes a penetrating commentary on the society they travel past and through, revealing corruption, moral decay, and intellectual impoverishment."[1]

The outside observers in these and other tales can serve as moral registers because life on the road loosens the ties that bind them to the dominant culture and its manifestations. When they do stop along the way and find circumstances beginning to threaten or confine them, they presumably can simply move on, erasing the memory. Such characters, whether in print or onscreen, possess a kind of freedom that allows the distance necessary for cultural critique.

Yet, the road also tests the individual's character, and the success or failure of the journey depends largely upon the traveler's personal qualities, what the ancient Greeks called *arête*, meaning virtue or excellence, the degree to which the individual lives up to his or her potential. The culture might indeed be corrupt, but how immune to this corruption is the rebel on the move? As David Laderman says of certain road films, the journey is sometimes essentially internal, "'rebellion' thus becoming an amorphous anxiety about self." Or, as Kenneth C. Kaleta succinctly puts it, "A road film presents a rite of passage resolved through a journey." To put it still another way, the road can become a testing ground for freedom. By placing themselves on the road, the characters, whether they say so or not, are declaring themselves free. The road then forces these characters to give a meaning to this freedom.[2]

Freedom and the Open Road

American history, as many have noted, has been characterized by movement across space, by the investigation and eventual settling of frontiers. Many Western films, as a result, mythologize the vast American landscape, and many are in effect road films. The advent of the automobile, especially as it gained a central place not only in the American economy but also in the American imagination, has given rise to road movies with a different look, with the car and endless miles of paved highway replacing the horse and dusty trail. In a real sense, Jack Kerouac's novel *On the Road* (1957) provides a kind of template for postwar road films. The words of Sal Paradise, the novel's narrator, could come from any number of film protagonists: "There was nothing to talk about any more. The only thing to do was go."[3]

The road figures so prominently in the American imagination that it is hard to think of a major American director who has not made a road film. David Lynch is no exception. Some of his films directly refer to the road in their titles, notably *Lost Highway* (1997) and *Mulholland Dr.* (2001). The difficult *Lost Highway* is hardly a typical road movie, however, if it can be called one at all. It is, as Laderman says, "a 'road movie' of the psyche."[4] And though, as we shall see, Lynch's concern throughout is with the individual psyche, two of his films, *Wild at Heart* (1990) and *The Straight Story* (1999), directly draw upon the tradition of the road movie.[5] In fact, *Wild at Heart* overtly appropriates an earlier road film, Victor Fleming's *The Wizard of Oz* (1939), as it follows its protagonists not along a yellow-brick road per se but along asphalt marked by yellow lines. Lynch's allusions to this iconic film suggest that his protagonists, like Dorothy in *The Wizard of Oz*, are searching for a condition, if not a physical space, that they can call home.

Lynch's two road films seem wildly dissimilar at a glance, with *Wild at Heart* containing some of the director's most violent and grotesque images and scenes, while the gentle *Straight Story* contains nothing more violent than a car's hitting a deer on the road, the film garnering an uncharacteristic

"G" rating. Yet the films deserve comparison, in spite of the differences in tone and the psychological orientations of the major characters. Both films feature protagonists who—like Homer's Odysseus and *Oz's* Dorothy—desire to get "home," though in these cases the home in question is not a physical place but a reunion, the settling into harmony with another. In fact, in both films the protagonists paradoxically travel away from their physical homes in an attempt to realize this state of connectedness.[6]

Most significantly, as mentioned earlier, both films use the road as a testing ground for character, especially in measuring the degree to which the characters, particularly *Wild at Heart's* Sailor Ripley (Nicholas Cage) and *The Straight Story's* Alvin Straight (Richard Farnsworth), possess authentic individuality and genuine freedom. The earlier film announces the theme very early, as Lula Fortune (Laura Dern) meets Sailor outside Pee Dee Correctional Facility, where he has been doing time for manslaughter. Lula surprises Sailor with his prized snakeskin jacket. Seeing it, he exclaims, "Did I ever tell you that this here jacket represents a symbol of my individuality and my belief in personal freedom?"

Free Will or a Unified Field?

On its face, Sailor's declaration is striking for a couple of reasons. For one thing, he redundantly says the jacket *represents* a symbol, not that it is directly symbolic. He also refers to his *belief* in personal freedom, which could be taken as meaning that he believes in the abstract principle behind the term but doesn't actually possess the quality to which he refers. In other words, viewers are immediately suspicious that Sailor's individuality and freedom are both complicated and compromised. The simple fact that he has just been released from prison and is bound by the terms of his parole puts his freedom in question. In short, Sailor's boastfulness constitutes wishful thinking, a conclusion supported by Lula's reply to his question: she says he's told her about the jacket's significance "about fifty thousand times."

Existentialist philosophers have much to say on the subjects of identity and freedom. Jean-Paul Sartre (1905–1980), perhaps the spokesperson who has done the most to popularize existentialist views, uses the formula "existence precedes essence" in explaining his view of individual identity. Humans are not presented with a how-to manual when they enter the world. True, throughout history, humans have argued for what they claim are a priori values, that is, a ground of meaning that exists outside of human existence, one that exists before the individual appears on the scene. Such believers proselytize, and they impose these systems of belief on others. But Sartre, like Friedrich Nietzsche (1844–1900) before him and his own contemporary Albert Camus (1913–1960), does not assume the existence of a God or of a realm of absolutes: "If existence really does precede essence, there is no explaining things away by reference to a fixed and given human nature. In other words, there is no determinism, man is free, man is freedom. On the other hand, if God does not exist, we find no values or commands to turn to which legitimize our conduct. So, in the bright realm of values, we have no excuses behind us, nor justification before us. We are alone, with no excuses." We cannot claim essentially to *be* something until we bring that identity into being through an act of will. For this reason, existentialists generally prefer to speak not of "human nature" but of the human condition. We have not been deeded an identity or a ground of meaning. We are free to create these for ourselves. As Sartre explains, "If man, as the existentialist conceives him, is indefinable, it is because at first he is nothing. Only afterward will he be something, and he himself will have made what he will be. . . . Man is nothing else but what he makes of himself."[7]

The character dynamics in *Wild at Heart* involve Sailor's forging of an identity and the discovery of the meaning of freedom. His boast and his donning of a snakeskin jacket do not suffice. On the road he must come to the awareness of which Sartre speaks: "Man is responsible for what he is. Thus, existentialism's first move is to make every man aware of what he is and to make the full responsibility of his existence rest on him."[8] However, the degree to which Sailor succeeds in securing his freedom remains in doubt. As we shall see, Sailor consistently evades taking responsibility for himself. He has an excuse, claiming more than once, "I didn't have much parental guidance." In fact, even his epiphany at the end of the film—in which he makes a stand on behalf of love (for Lula and their son, Pace [Glenn Walker Harris Jr.])—depends on outside assistance and intervention. The film's stance on freedom remains ambiguous to the end, with Sailor throughout clinging to notions and patterns that precede him, primarily pop-culture models such as *The Wizard of Oz* and the performances of Elvis Presley.

In fact, Sailor and Lula's rebellion is not even genuine. They act as though they are in revolt against an absurd world, trying to forge meanings for themselves. In reality, they're running in fear of the deadly designs and influences of Lula's mother, Marietta (Diane Ladd), merely posing as rebels against the establishment. Including *Wild at Heart* in his discussion of other films of the era featuring a "killer couple," Jack Sargeant rightly notes that these films "play with images of alienation and angst, but always resolve the protagonists' dilemmas with a return to the conservatism of 'being' (be it via the mechanisms of an arrival at the destination, or the destruction of the killer). The potentialities of chaos remain ungrasped. Rebellion is rendered merely as a pastiche of previous rebellious icons."[9]

Lynch himself seems to see the resolution of *Wild at Heart* differently, as a success story for Sailor. It is noteworthy, however, that Lynch admits to changing Barry Gifford's original story in order to realize the happy ending. The novel ends with Sailor's walking away from Lula. The film includes that scene, but then, as Sailor lies on the asphalt after receiving a beating in a fight he initiated, a guardian angel appears in the form of the Good Witch (Sheryl Lee) from *The Wizard of Oz*, squeaking out banal platitudes about love. After this encounter, Sailor rushes back to Lula and again reveals his penchant for imitation as he sings Elvis Presley's "Love Me Tender" to her. As Lynch says, "Sailor and Lula had to be together: the problem was figuring out how they could be together and still have the scene where they part. In the end that problem was helped by *The Wizard of Oz*."[10]

Of course, Lynch, as a creative artist, has the right to craft filmic resolutions that match his vision. His inclusion of this deus ex machina in *Wild at Heart*, however, exemplifies ways in which his own philosophy departs from, or confuses, the philosophies of freedom mentioned earlier. The individual's identity, as Sartre says, derives from an act of will: "Not only is man what he conceives himself to be, but he is also only what he wills himself to be after this thrust toward existence."[11]

On the contrary, Lynch's stated philosophy, one that he expresses openly in print and in interviews—and that emerges also in his films—recommends passivity and surrender to an a priori internal force or field of meaning that has a mystic correspondence in the wider universe. It finally does not matter, then, whether Sailor's Good Witch is simply a manifestation of Sailor's desires or an individualized entity. Lynch has spoken openly about the zone of nourishment to which the witch refers, which in her speech she calls "love": "The nourishment is the 'unified field.' Modern science has discovered the unified field. They say it's there. It's known by many different names of course—'the absolute,' 'the unmanifest,' 'pure bliss consciousness,' 'transcendental consciousness'—many names. It is unity. It's the thing that never had a beginning, and will never have an end. It's knowingness. It's pure creative intelligence. It is the one and only thing. It's the universe and it's all of us, and it permeates all manifestation. That's the nourishment."[12]

In *Catching the Big Fish* (2006), his short text on the relationship of Transcendental Meditation to filmmaking, among other topics, Lynch includes an extremely brief chapter called "Identity," here quoted in its entirety: "The thing about meditation is: You become more and more you." The formulation can be construed as saying "essence precedes existence," precisely the opposite of Sartre's motto. In fact, the phrase "wild at heart," which Lula applies to the world at large and Sailor to himself, suggests a predetermined nature, contrary to the existentialist understanding as articulated by Sartre and others. For Sartre, "there is no human nature, since there is no God to conceive it." Human identity derives from the individual's act of self-creation; it is not predetermined. In short, Lynch's own views of identity and freedom, though in many particulars compatible with philosophies of freedom that derive from assuming a universe without intrinsic meaning, ultimately rest on a belief in a ground of preexisting value.[13]

This confusion manifests itself throughout *Wild at Heart,* which often implies that Sailor, in particular, must shake himself out of passivity, stop making excuses, and claim his own identity and freedom. To be sure, his many troubles derive from passive submission: he was the unwitting driver of the getaway car when Lula's father was murdered according to Marietta's plan. Because Marietta thinks he knows more than he does, she is bent on eliminating him. Similarly, he goes along with Bobby Peru's (Willem Dafoe) robbery scheme when confronted with the conventional view that a man with a pregnant woman on his hands could use a little extra cash. Far from being a rebel or a free spirit, Sailor submits to numerous conventions and conventional stances.

But if passive submission is Sailor's problem, it's also his salvation according to the Lynchian vision. He's flat on his back when the Good Witch visits him, and, as he earlier vowed to himself and Lula, at his moment of triumph he resorts to the most maudlin of Elvis Presley's lyrics in order to express himself. He is not Camus' rebel, admitting his absurd condition and finding his values in rebellion. Considering the way the film resolves his dilemma, Sailor does not support his existence through rebellion against his absurd condition, nor does he find value in that rebellion and, to paraphrase Camus, fight to uphold that value unceasingly. The Good Witch instructs him, "If you're truly wild at heart, you'll fight for your dreams." But Sailor has been and still is a faux rebel, in the end opting for the most conventional existence, one derived not from individuality and personal freedom but from a preexisting set of values, and very conventional ones at that. As the nay-saying Lynch critic Jeff Johnson points out, because Sailor never actually chooses his life, it is inauthentic: "Sailor lives in a world of simulation, imitating Elvis, always in costume, posing and playing roles, ever on stage."[14]

It bears noting that Lula, likewise, clings to very conventional values. In fact, her subservience to her diabolical mother demonstrates ignorance, stupidity, or both. Surely she knows that Marietta is bent on separating her from Sailor, and she must at least suspect that her mother is responsible for her father's death. But as Sailor does prison time in the wake of the disastrous heist in Lobo, she returns, even if reluctantly, to the safety of home and the domain of dear old mom. Admittedly, she defies her mother in going to meet Sailor upon his release—and she dramatically tosses a glass of water on a photograph of her mother, in imitation of Dorothy's melting of the Wicked Witch in *Oz*. However, it's not unreasonable to wonder what took her so long. Perhaps the best we can say of Lula is that she is insecure and afraid. But that hardly demonstrates her rebellion or her freedom.

In short, *Wild at Heart* presents us with a philosophical inconsistency. On one hand, the film suggests that the characters must define themselves, ending their reliance on others or excuses that refer to one's environment or upbringing. However, the film implies something like the opposite—that Sailor, in particular, must surrender his will to a ground of meaning outside himself, whether this meaning goes by the name "Love" or "Unified Field."

Making the Trip Alone

In contrast to Sailor, *The Straight Story*'s Alvin Straight resolves, even before embarking on his trip, that he will take full responsibility for himself. Rather than posing as a rugged individualist or declaring himself one, he acts like one. Rather than making grandiose declarations about his freedom, he quietly says, "I've gotta make this trip on my own." It's tempting to suggest that whereas most Lynch films, including *Wild at Heart,* depend on Lynch as a writer or cowriter, this film, based on an actual incident and transformed into a screenplay by John Roach and Mary Sweeney, possesses a logical consistency lacking elsewhere in Lynch.

In any case, this later Lynchian road film often appears to revise or comment upon the earlier one. Watching the two films in quick succession, in fact, gives a viewer the sensation that the later film, *The Straight Story,* mirrors and comments upon the earlier road film. The two films present similar patterns and images, though *The Straight Story* always revises the earlier film so as to showcase a character who possesses genuine individuality and personal freedom, not one merely playing at rebellion. Alvin Straight has a complicated past, as the film gradually reveals, and his journey represents his conscious effort to rectify a particular past failing, namely the estrangement from his brother Lyle (Harry Dean Stanton). The journey's success is underscored by the film's understated ending scene, with the two brothers exchanging glances that mean more than their words; finally, both men lift their heads skyward to view the stars, an image that signals the restoration of harmony.

Taking these two road films as companion pieces, a first, very obvious contrast presents itself, namely the different physical conditions of the two main characters. The contrast is ironic, of course, serving to demonstrate that the individual's freedom to shape an identity need not be constrained by physical circumstances. Sailor is in top condition, as he demonstrates in *Wild at Heart*'s opening scene, when he brutally kills a hired assailant. Furthermore, his style of dancing, with its rapid-fire flailing of limbs, requires considerable agility. On the contrary, when we first see Alvin Straight, he is flat on his back, recalling Sailor's prone position as he takes a beating at the end of the earlier film and then hears the Good Witch's message. But Alvin Straight, though unable to move without assistance, is not about to surrender his will to another's. His doctor later instructs him to use a walker, but he refuses, settling on a second cane. His chosen method of travel, a riding lawnmower, is comically slow, able to accelerate to about five miles an hour. In contrast, Lula and Sailor's car zooms down the highway, and almost all their actions—driving, dancing, sex—occur at a fast pace. Ironically, Alvin's mode of transport gets him to Mt. Zion, his stated destination, whereas *Wild at Heart*'s wild ride goes in a circle, with the film almost ending where it began, with Lula again picking up Sailor as he is released from prison for a second time.

As mentioned earlier, Sailor and Lula's journey mimics the road trips that derive from popular culture's collective memory. In keeping with the paradigm, they travel from east to west. Alvin, on the other hand, trying to reach his estranged ailing brother, travels his straight line from Iowa to Wisconsin, a very atypical northeasterly direction.

Besides these general observations, the two films present some very precise images that underscore the different views of individual freedom.

For instance, in *Wild at Heart,* as Sailor and Lula first hit the open road, the camera zooms in on the yellow line in the center of the highway. It then briefly tilts from side to side, moving the yellow line off center as the car veers slightly. The camera then pulls back and shows us the two passengers. The camera similarly zooms in on the yellow line when Alvin first takes to the open road in his lawnmower.

The yellow line in *Wild at Heart* refers also of course to the yellow brick road in *The Wizard of Oz.* As mentioned before, Lynch alludes to this film in paralleling the hopes and fears of the two travelers through a world that Lula says is "wild at heart and weird on top." *The Straight Story* lacks the obvious *Oz* references, but comparing the camera's tight shots of the yellow lines in the two films reveals differences that openly point to the characters behind the wheel in each case. In *Wild at Heart,* Sailor's driving lane is marked by a solid yellow line, meaning that he is technically in a no-passing zone, and he briefly violates the solid line. The tight shot of the yellow line in *The Straight Story,* on the other hand, reveals that Alvin is gliding along in a passing zone, the broken line on his side of the two-lane road. The contrast implies that Sailor is driving with less freedom than is the septuagenarian invalid.

Freedom and Responsibility

These two drivers' different relationships to the yellow lines might subtly signal a further meaning. Specifically, Sailor's driving tendency suggests that he thinks freedom means release from any restraint, the lack of limitations of any kind—nihilism, the belief that since there is no preexisting ground of value, all things are permissible. On the other hand, Alvin stays near the shoulder on the right side of the road, reluctant to venture near the yellow line, much less cross it. He expresses awareness that freedom is never total, even though we dwell in a world without absolutes.

Camus writes at some length about the paradoxical relationship of freedom and responsibility, distinguishing between the rebel's awareness of his absurd condition and the nihilist's destructiveness. In *The Rebel,* he writes, "Rebellion is in no way the demand for total freedom. On the contrary, rebellion puts total freedom up for trial." The nature of rebellion, as Camus explains, is a revolt against death, even though death is ultimately certain. But this embrace of our absurd condition, this revolt against death, cannot accept the potential death of another: "The rebel undoubtedly demands a certain degree of freedom for himself; but in no case, if he is consistent, does he demand the right to destroy the existence and the freedom of others. He humiliates no one. The freedom he claims, he claims for all."[15]

Similarly, Sartre frequently mentions our "being condemned to be free," by which he means that individual freedom bears with it a profound responsibility: "And when we say that a man is responsible for himself, we do not only mean that he is responsible for his own individuality, but that he is responsible for all men. . . . In fact, in creating the man that we want to be, there is not a single one of our acts which does not at the same time create an image of man as we think he ought to be." Thus, Alvin Straight implicitly understands the meaning of individual freedom, and he bears the full weight of the concomitant responsibility. Sailor and Lula, on the other hand, posing as free rebels, act without this profound sense of responsibility.[16]

The two films underscore this distinction most compellingly in their references to fire. *Wild at Heart*'s fire images are more obvious than those in *The Straight Story*, but only because the film itself is far more frantic in its pace and, even more important, because the characters attempt to live without restraint, consuming, like fire, everyone and everything in their paths. Marietta's plot against Sailor, in fact, which propels the road trip in *Wild at Heart*, derives from her arranging to have her husband burned to death. She also organized the death by fiery crash of Uncle Pooch (Marvin Kaplan). Even the film's opening credits appear against the image of intense, consuming flames, probably the same flames that took the life of Lula's father.

Throughout the film, the lighting of a match, filmed in close-up, punctuates Sailor and Lula's frantic sex. And at one point, as they share a postcoital smoke, they talk in detail about their history of smoking, with Sailor claiming that he started smoking at age four, sometime *after* his mother died of lung cancer. Again, he evidently does not think there are consequences to his own excessive consumption, and the frequent lighting up continually underscores his and Lula's recklessness. In another reference to fire, Lula even imagines that because the ozone layer is disappearing the earth will soon burn: "One of these mornings the sun is going to come up and burn a hole clear through the planet like an electrical x-ray." Even seemingly minor vignettes develop the image, as, for example, when the camera cuts to a lounge where the singer Koko Taylor, playing the role of what's commonly called a "torch singer," sings the Lynch-penned song "Up in Flames," with the refrain "Now my love's gone up in flames." Todd McGowan, referring to *Wild at Heart,* rightly remarks, "Each time that we see fire, characters are enjoying themselves, even—or especially—when another character burns to death."[17]

In *The Straight Story,* on the other hand, images of fire and references to its destructive potential occur almost as frequently as in the earlier film, but in this case fire is treated with a cautious respect. The most overt reference to fire's destructiveness comes as Alvin sits around his campfire at night, talking to the hitchhiking young pregnant woman who has wandered in to join him. Again, they are staring into a fire, a controlled one, on which they are roasting Alvin's wieners. Then Alvin relates the history of his daughter, Rose (Sissy Spacek), and how she lost custody of her four children: One night when the children were being minded by someone else, as Alvin says, "There was a fire. Her second boy got burned real bad." Because Rose appears "slow," the state deemed her unfit for motherhood and took her children from her. This story parallels *Wild at Heart*'s references to the burning of Lula's family members, but the tone is far different, as are the characters' attitudes toward consuming fire and its consequences. Alvin's story also explains why Rose, in an earlier scene, gazes wistfully at a boy playing with a ball outside her house. As Alvin says, "Not a day passes she doesn't pine for those kids."

In *Wild at Heart,* the characters never express much regret over the results of fire's destructiveness. Marietta, of course, uses it to kill. When Lula first tells Sailor the story of her father's death—believing her mother's lie that he set fire to himself—Sailor hesitates, and his expression suggests that he is considering his own involvement in the incident. But instead of saying anything or pursuing the thought, he sloughs it off and initiates sex with Lula. Sailor is not willing to accept the responsibility for his actions, precisely because he is unwilling to accept the full meaning of freedom. Or, to return to Sartre's language, he has made a free choice: He has participated in the murder of Lula's father. But he is being dishonest: "If we have defined man's situation as a free choice, with no excuses and no recourse, every man who takes refuge behind the excuse of his passions, every man who sets up a determinism, is a dishonest man."[18]

Later, Sailor does tell Lula of his driving for Marcelles Santos (J. E. Freeman) on the night of the decisive fire, but he answers her shocked reaction by merely saying, "We all got a secret side, baby." Again, coming close to accepting responsibility, he veers away and hides behind a pose. Still dishonest, he refuses to embrace "the complete freedom of involvement."[19]

Alvin's daughter, Rose, on the other hand, had no choice in the fire that burned her child, nor did she have a say in the removal of her children. As she gazes at children at play, pining for her own loss, she is experiencing what Sartre refers to as the existentialist's despair: In exercising our own will, we cannot count on the cooperation of the world. We must "confine ourselves to reckoning only with what depends upon our will." Likewise, when Alvin tells Verlyn Heller (Wiley Harker) about his accidental shooting of an American scout in World War II—"I fired," he says—he is in despair, trying to determine the extent to which that death resulted from his own will or from mere bad luck.[20]

Another notable fiery scene in *The Straight Story* further contrasts the fires of excess in *Wild at Heart*. As Alvin approaches Clermont, Iowa, about to descend a steep hill that will damage his riding mower, the film cuts to a close-up of a house on fire, with violent flames and smoke that recall the house afire in *Wild at Heart*. But then the camera pulls back and we see a group of people—Danny Riordan (James Cada) and others—sitting on lawn chairs, watching firefighters as they hone their skills on a controlled blaze. "Well, they sure picked the right place to practice a burn on," Riordan says, and the tension subsides. This is a community of people exercising their free choice to prepare for contingencies, and the spectators find pleasure in fire, knowing that in these conditions it poses no threat. Curiously, however, this potentially destructive fire also serves as a backdrop to the scene in which Alvin jeopardizes his well-being by careening down a hill without brakes on his trailer, suggesting that as free individuals we live on a tightrope over an abyss, with death very real.

Besides these contrasts between the two films featuring images of fire—which, to reiterate, show reckless disregard among the characters in the earlier film and a responsible embrace of the implications of freedom in the other—*The Straight Story* echoes *Wild at Heart* in other, less noticeable ways. I have already mentioned the conversation in which Alvin and Verlyn talk with deep regret about their war experiences. Bobby Peru in *Wild at Heart* also mentions his time in war, as a marine in Vietnam, where he seems to have been involved in a massacre. But this memory, unlike the one at the Clermont bar with Alvin and Verlyn, is never developed past the point of evasion by Peru and those who listen, including Sailor and Lula.

There are other minor echoes of *Wild at Heart* in *The Straight Story*. Both films include women inconvenienced, at least initially, by a pregnancy. And the road trips in both films show the main characters coming upon accidents. In *Wild at Heart*, these are deadly and gruesome, in keeping with the film's over-the-top style, and they have little effect on the main characters except to shock them and compel them to keep moving. Sailor's later advice to his son, Pace, expresses his and Lula's overall attitude toward unpleasantness. He says, "If ever somethin' don't feel right to you, remember what Pancho said to the Cisco Kid: Let's went, before we're dancin' at the end of a rope, without music." In *The Straight Story*, except for the barely averted accident as Alvin descends the hill into Clermont, Alvin witnesses one ultimately comic accident—the hitting of a deer by a woman (Barbara Robertson) who claims to have hit thirteen deer in seven weeks. He offers assistance but then merely listens patiently as the woman delivers a tirade expressing her frustration with a world that presents obstacles—here randomly appearing deer—that she cannot conquer. In the next scene, however, we see that Alvin has made the best of the situation: he roasts deer meat on his campfire that evening and decorates his trailer with antlers.

The Triumphant Stargazer

Alvin Straight, unlike Sailor Ripley, is an authentic rebel. He remains true to his vision, insisting throughout, "I wanna finish this one my own way." And because he accepts the responsibilities of freedom, he achieves heroic status, becoming a wise sage to those he encounters, whether an unwed pregnant runaway, a group of arrogant bicyclists, a pair of bickering twin brothers, or a fellow veteran. He refuses to succumb to nihilism, nor does he adopt preordained poses in the manner of Sailor Ripley. He's seen all that life has to dish out, as he says, and he knows that though he may not be able to account for the world's contingencies, he can account for himself. He is the man Camus describes near the end of *The Rebel:* "Man can master in himself everything that should be mastered. He should rectify in creation everything that can be rectified."[21]

In some ways, *The Straight Story* invites an allegorical reading, the action beginning in midsummer and moving toward deep autumn, with Alvin spending his final night camped in a cemetery, before he ascends to Mt. Zion, the city of God. Rather than taking the religious allusions literally, however, it makes more sense to understand that they signal the progress of a meaningful life lived in the face of an intrinsically meaningless universe. At the end, Alvin need not leap across cars and burst into song. He and brother Lyle need not say anything; they can gaze together at a sky full of stars, knowing they have created authentic meaning out of a void.

Notes

1. David Laderman, *Driving Visions: Exploring the Road Movie* (Austin: University of Texas Press, 2002), 8. Laderman's study considers many road films, but he rightly begins by noting the genre's sources in literature, and his opening chapter includes many more examples.

2. Ibid., 83. Laderman specifically refers to road movies of the early 1970s, but his remark can be more broadly applied, specifically to the Lynch films under consideration here, which appeared a couple of decades later (Kenneth C. Kaleta, *David Lynch* [New York: Twayne, 1993], 160).

3. A full list of American road movies would be virtually endless. Laderman's book has numerous examples, as does Katie Mills's useful *The Road Story and the Rebel: Moving through Film, Fiction, and Television* (Carbondale: Southern Illinois Press, 2006). Jack Kerouac, *On the Road* (1957; New York: Penguin,1976), 109. Both Laderman and Mills cite the influence of Kerouac's novel on contemporary road movies, with Mills in particular discussing the novel at length, especially in her second chapter, "Before the Road Genre: The Beats and *On the Road,*" 35–63.

4. Laderman, *Driving Visions,* 236.

5. In her generally compelling and thorough study of Lynch, Martha P. Nochimson briefly, and somewhat inexplicably, insists that *Wild at Heart* should not be classified a "road picture," saying the film is "closer to the genre of the maternal melodrama" (see Nochimson, *The Passion of David Lynch: Wild at Heart in Hollywood* [Austin: University of Texas Press, 1997], 48). Lynch himself has said, "*Wild at Heart* is a road picture, a love story, a psychological drama and a violent comedy. A strange blend of all those things" (see Chris Rodley, ed., *Lynch on Lynch* [New York: Faber and Faber, 2005], 193).

6. Todd McGowan, in his Lacanian study of Lynch's work, correctly identifies these films as "companion pieces," and though he analyzes the films in separate chapters, he briefly contrasts the two at the end of his discussion of *The Straight Story* (191–93), rightly noting that the protagonists do differ markedly in their attitudes (see McGowan, *The Impossible David Lynch* [New York: Columbia University Press, 2007]).

7. Jean-Paul Sartre, *Existentialism and Human Emotions,* trans. Bernard Frechtman (New York: Philosophical Library, 1957), 22–23, 15.

8. Ibid., 16.

9. Jack Sargeant, "Killer Couples: From Nebraska to Route 666," in *Lost Highways: An Illustrated History of Road Movies,* ed. Jack Sargeant and Stephanie Watson (London: Creation Books, 2000), 167.

10. Rodley, *Lynch on Lynch,* 198.

11. Sartre, *Existentialism and Human Emotions,* 15.

12. Rodley, *Lynch on Lynch,* 261.

13. David Lynch, *Catching the Big Fish: Meditation, Consciousness, and Creativity*

(New York: Jeremy P. Tarcher/Penguin, 2006), 57; Sartre, *Existentialism and Human Emotions*, 15.

14. Albert Camus, *The Rebel: An Essay on Man in Revolt*, trans. Anthony Bower (New York: Vintage, 1991), 285; Jeff Johnson, *Pervert in the Pulpit: Morality in the Works of David Lynch* (Jefferson, N.C., 2004), 104.

15. Camus, *The Rebel*, 284.

16. Sartre, *Existentialism and Human Emotions*, 16–17.

17. McGowan, *The Impossible David Lynch*, 113.

18. Sartre, *Existentialism and Human Emotions*, 44–45.

19. Ibid., 45.

20. Ibid., 29.

21. Camus, *The Rebel*, 303.

LYNCH'S ZARATHUSTRA

The Straight Story

Shai Frogel

David Lynch's *The Straight Story* (1999) centers on a seventy-three-year-old World War II veteran, Alvin Straight (Richard Farnsworth), who lives in the farmlands of Laurence, Iowa, with his daughter, Rose (Sissy Spacek). On a thunderous night, as if being struck by lightning, Alvin learns that his brother, Lyle (Harry Dean Stanton), recently suffered a stroke. Alvin and Lyle have been estranged for a decade. Straight decides that he must see his brother and make amends with him before it is too late, and therefore goes on a journey to Mt. Zion, Wisconsin. Once reunited, they look again, just as they did together in their childhood, at the stars on a cold and clear night.

This, in brief, is the story line of David Lynch's *The Straight Story*. We can take the meaning of Lynch's title in several ways. First, we can take the straight story to mean that it is, simply put, the story of the protagonist, Alvin Straight (i.e., it is Alvin Straight's story). Second, we can take the straight story to mean that it is consistently true or accurate, in the sense that it depicts the events that occurred in the real life of Alvin Straight during the summer of 1994. But we can also see that Lynch is treating the title in a different way. Not only is this a story about Alvin Straight, which reflects true events about a journey taken in the real world; this is also a story about the journey of true self-discovery and self-overcoming.

In order to see how Lynch's tale captures this third meaning, let us turn to another famous journey, which echoes Straight's journey toward self-discovery and self-overcoming: the story of the character Zarathustra in *Thus Spoke Zarathustra,* a philosophical work by Friedrich Nietzsche (1844–1900). Although there are many famous tales of journeys in the history of Western culture (from Homer's *Odyssey* to L. Frank Baum's *The Wonderful Wizard of Oz*), Nietzsche's Zarathustra most clearly captures the individual existential journey upon which Alvin Straight embarks. In this essay, I follow Alvin Straight from Iowa to Wisconsin, using Nietzsche's Zarathustra and Carl Jung's (1875–1961) seminar on Nietzsche's work to help serve as our guides. As we take up this journey, we will move from Nietzsche's idea of self-overcoming in *Thus Spoke Zarathustra* to Jung's interpretation of Zarathustra as an expression of the old wise man's archetype, in order to present Straight as an American Zarathustra.

Zarathustra's Journey: From Man to Overman

Much like that of Alvin Straight, the story of Nietzsche's Zarathustra begins with a sense of estrangement—though Alvin is estranged from his brother, Zarathustra is estranged from society. Named after Zoroaster, the ancient forefather of the Western dualism between good and evil, Zarathustra has lived in the mountains for a decade, enjoying his spirit and solitude. Now, however, Zarathustra experiences a change of heart and realizes that he has a gift to bestow upon humanity. As a result, he descends the mountains, returns to society, and begins a journey of self-discovery, encountering along the way a most diverse crowd, which includes such characters as a dwarf, a serpent, an eagle, a tightrope walker, a jester, a spirit of gravity, and a leech. The end of this journey, at which he arrives after suffering existential nausea and then convalescing, is the cathartic self-revelation, which can be summed up with the idea of the *overman* (*Übermensch*).

The overman is Zarathustra's ultimate gift to humanity. It is the ideal for human beings to aim in the process of overcoming, or freeing themselves from, their humanity as a decayed nature. Zarathustra refers to this process of freeing oneself from the shackles, or stagnation, of being, as *self-overcoming* (*Selbst-Überwindung*). In order to properly explicate this gift that Zarathustra gives humanity, we must turn to two further Nietzschean concepts: the *will to truth* and the *will to power*. For Nietzsche, life is an ongoing activity; it is a dynamic process of becoming—an eternal struggle of wills and assertions he calls the will to power. This battle of wills reflects various motivations and attitudes, one of which is the will to truth. The philosopher's will to truth, claims Zarathustra, is the will to make everything thinkable. A thing can be considered as truth in philosophy if and only if it can be conceived by thought. This process is not a process of representation, as it might be understood, but a process in which human thought coins its forms in existence. In other words, Zarathustra states that human thought does not discover the world but always creates worlds in human forms and images. Thus, the higher one's ability to think, the higher his ability to coin his own forms, or images, in reality becomes. This is the reason why the philosopher's ideas are received by common people as truths, especially as moral truths, and are considered with seriousness that belongs only to truths. Common people, argues Zarathustra, wrongly conceive these ideas not as human inventions but as a part of the world's structure.

Zarathustra's wish is to reveal this illusion, which determines, in many respects, the human's attitude toward his or her own existence: "Your will and your values you set on the river of becoming; what the people believe to be good and evil reveals to me an ancient will to power." Common people, argues Zarathustra, unconsciously obey the will to power that forms their concepts of good and evil, since they will the power embodied in these concepts. Therefore, the only thing that might threaten common concepts of good and evil is not truer concepts but a stronger will to power; only a stronger will might overcome them.[1]

Zarathustra argues that life (i.e., the world of living beings) is an expression of the will to power since life is a process of becoming. In this process, each particular moment of being should be overcome for the purpose of becoming. Hence, from the perspective of life, the idea of an unchangeable truth is a lie. This explains why it is hard, and indeed wrong, to live according to unchangeable concepts of good and evil. Not only do these concepts reflect nothing more than their creators' mode of existence, but, worse than that, their static character stands in opposition to the logic of life.

In order to explain this idea, which is the logic of the will to power, Zarathustra presents his view concerning the nature of life and living beings. First, he contends that each living being obeys. Second, if it does not obey to itself, it obeys to others. Third, "commanding is harder than obeying." Living beings, according to this idea, necessarily obey and only rarely command. Commanding is rarer and harder than obeying, since one who commands takes upon oneself not only the responsibility of his- or herself, but of others as well. "It must become," claims Zarathustra, "the judge and avenger and victim of its own law." For that reason, human beings prefer obeying to commanding.[2]

This brings us to the true meaning of the will to power. It is not a will to control others, as the term might initially suggest, but a will to be more powerful. The weaker creatures, according to this logic, are willing to give themselves to stronger creatures (that is, to obey) in order to enjoy the latter's power. As such, the will to power explains the act of obeying rather than the act of commanding. Every living being searches for a stronger being and willingly obeys this being, since it serves its will to power. Thus, the will to power, in opposition to its connotations, reveals the weakness of living beings, their need to obey others, rather than a secret desire to command other beings. Zarathustra's ethical goal is to make people question this need, not to say this desire, to put their lives in the hands of others. Yet, the will to power is not the nature of life but only its result: "And this secret life itself spoke to me: 'Behold,' it said, 'I am that which must always overcome itself.'"[3]

Life, therefore, is not a will to power but a process of self-overcoming. Hence, when this process ends, one finds degeneration or death. This is, Zarathustra argues, not only a biological fact but also, and more important, an existential and ethical demand. Since life is an act of self-overcoming, one who is not involved in this process is actually in a process of degeneration.[4]

This account of self-overcoming explains Zarathustra's ethical message to humanity: "Truly, I say to you: good and evil that would be everlasting—there is no such thing! They must overcome themselves from out of themselves again and again." Ethical life is vital only for one who accepts that the concepts of good and evil are not, and could not be, eternal. The notion of the eternal stands in opposition to the logic of life and therefore could not be conceived, from the perspective of life, as good. Ethical life should be actualized by overcoming common concepts of good and evil. This process is indeed dangerous, since it brings one into conflict with common values, yet it prevents ethical degeneration. According to Zarathustra, the wise person who creates values has a strong feeling of vitality, since she or he overcomes her or his values. This is the meaning of self-overcoming in human ethical existence. Therefore, one could do it if and only if one finds in oneself the power and the courage to command and not only to obey.[5]

Zarathustra's new ethical message, then, is that the concepts of good and evil are no more than human inventions, products of the will to power and not eternal or divine truths. To be wise, from this perspective, is to find the power of self-overcoming, which means the power to reevaluate one's own values. One who is able to overcome himself is an overman; he is aware of the contingent status of human existence and values, and finds the power to live in accordance with this awareness. As such, the overman is similar to a rope-dancer. Like the rope-dancer, the overman must display acute balance as he takes the journey across life, acknowledging that dangers, including death, await him with only one false move. The overman, as such, is one who overcomes man's common will to certainty and stability, thereby defeating the degeneration of humanity.

The Complexity of Zarathustra's Journey: Between Inferiority and Megalomania

Although, biologically, Nietzsche's Zarathustra is not an old man (he begins his descent when he is forty), his journey and character have inspired the Swiss psychiatrist Carl Gustav Jung (1875–1961), who saw him as the perfect manifestation of the "old wise man" archetype. Jung's theory of archetypes relates to his idea of the *collective unconscious,* which can be understood in contrast to the idea of the *personal unconscious.* In general, the idea of the unconscious, which was first presented by Nietzsche but is more publicly known through Freud's psychoanalysis, claims that our consciousness is only a distorted surface of our psychic life. This life is mostly determined by different things that do not appear in our conscious and therefore are not under our control. When Nietzsche, and then Freud, presented this idea, both spoke about the personal unconscious. The personal unconscious is made up of one's personal history. It contains results of one's interactions with the world of which one has been unaware, or has kept repressed. In contrast, the collective unconscious belongs to the collective aspect of one's psychic life. Thus, it does not reflect one's personal history but one's belonging to human culture and history. The content of the collective unconscious, according to Jung, is made up essentially of *archetypes.* The concept of the archetype, which is an indispensable correlate of the idea of the collective unconscious, indicates the existence of definite forms in the psyche that seem to be present always and everywhere in human existence.[6]

Jung analyzes Nietzsche's book from this perspective. What Nietzsche presents through Zarathustra as a new insight, Jung presents as an old archetype. Jung claims that Zarathustra and his new recognitions actually reflect Nietzsche's psychological state at the time of writing this book. His basic claim is that Nietzsche's claim that "God is dead," an atheistic proclamation about the end of Western religion, leads him to existential disorientation.[7] In this psychological situation, Jung claims, the archetype of the old wise man from the collective unconsciousness affects one's consciousness. That is to say, Nietzsche did not create a new idea, but rather an archetype from the collective unconsciousness captured his consciousness and gave birth to his Zarathustra. At a time of existential and ethical confusion, the father of all prophets, Zarathustra, comes to give a new meaning to life.[8]

Zarathustra, therefore, should be understood as a symptom of a psychological state in which one's self is captured by an archetype of the collective unconsciousness. In this state, one is not able to distinguish between one's personal self and one's non-personal self. Zarathustra is for Nietzsche an immediate perception of individuation, his self; yet Zarathustra actually expresses the old wise man archetype from the collective unconsciousness. There is no contradiction in this claim since the self is a concept of totality that includes collective archetypes and the individual's consciousness at the same time.

The archetype of the old wise man is the persona of the great teacher who appears in the self for a time as a vision or intuition. From this respect, Zarathustra is not different from God, since both are manifestations of the old wise man archetype. Nietzsche, Jung claims, wrongly thinks that God is a human invention, whereas it is really, like Nietzsche's Zarathustra, a psychological experience that reflects a human desire for metaphysical meaning (meaning of the totality). In other words, Nietzsche's notion of the death of God led him to the very same experience that we usually name God. Jung agrees with Nietzsche that the origin of God is in human psychology, yet he does not believe that this experience could die, per se.[9]

Jung's argument about the psychological relation between Nietzsche and Zarathustra may be explained on the basis of Jung's distinction between the ego and the self. Whereas the concept of the self stands for the totality of one's psychological facts, the ego stands only for the conscious part of the self. The ego, one may say, is the visible part of the self, where only spatio-temporal material could appear. This means that many archaic materials, which are not spatio-temporal in nature, could not appear in the ego (for example, metaphysical entities, such as spirits or God). Yet, they are part of the self and affect psychological experience.[10] According to this conceptualization, Jung suggests that Nietzsche is the ego while Zarathustra is the self. Zarathustra expresses the way in which the archetype of the old wise man affects Nietzsche. That is to say, it is Nietzsche who is unconsciously captured by the archetype and not Zarathustra, who is Nietzsche's puppet.

Jung's analysis endows Zarathustra with an autonomic existence in Nietzsche's psychology. The persona of Zarathustra overcomes other aspects in Nietzsche's psychology, which may explain why Nietzsche perceives him as a great prophet. This persona reflects Nietzsche's need to cope with his own psychological complexity: a man with a feeling of inferiority, on the one hand, and with great obsessions to power on the other—a very sick and weak man who projects his complex of power on everything.[11] In fact, Jung's interpretation of the psychological origin of Nietzsche's philosophy settles well with Nietzsche's own claim about the great philosophers: "Gradually it has become clear to me what every great philosophy so far has been: namely, the personal confession of its author."[12]

Thus, according to Jung, Zarathustra is not a symbol of self-overcoming but an expression of an old archetype: the archetype of the old wise man. This archetype breaks into one's consciousness from the collective unconscious at a time of existential disorientation. It is a very powerful psychological experience that we usually name God. This psychological experience brings together feelings of inferiority and megalomania: the feeling of inferiority is an expression of existential anxiety; the feeling of megalomania grows from a desire for a moral teacher. At times of existential crisis, most people search for a moral teacher outside themselves, but few find him or her in themselves. Nietzsche, according to Jung, belongs, of course, to the second group. Zarathustra is the moral teacher that grows in Nietzsche's psyche as a result of his existential anxiety at the time of writing this book. It is a manifestation of the archetype of the old wise man from the collective unconsciousness that captured Nietzsche's consciousness.

Now that we have examined Nietzsche's Zarathustra and Jung's analysis of Zarathustra, we can ask ourselves: How should we understand Lynch's Alvin Straight from this perspective? Should we perceive him as a person who overcomes himself or as a marionette in the hands of the collective unconscious?

The Straight Story of Overcoming the Stupidity of Youth

The analysis of the persona of Zarathustra could help us to understand the persona of Alvin Straight. Both Straight and Zarathustra embark on a journey of self-overcoming. Though Zarathustra is not an old man, Jung's interpretation of him by the archetype of the "old wise man" opens the way to analyze the story of old Straight from the perspective of our discussion concerning Zarathustra. Thus, Straight's story is befitting of Nietzsche's idea of self-overcoming and Jung's archetype of the old wise man.

In his first appearance in the film, Straight is lying on the floor—an old man with a strong body and a nice white beard—after having a stroke in his little home. From this low existential starting point, Straight goes on a long journey to salvation, whose aim is to overcome the stupidity of his youth. He takes a long ride on a riding mower in order to reconcile with his brother, who suffered a stroke on the same day. They will forget their terrible history by looking silently, as in their childhood, at the stars on a cold and clear night. The distant stars help them achieve a better perspective on life and make their conflicts and fights look ridiculous.

From the very moment that Straight decides to go on this journey, it is clear to him that he should do it on his own. He leaves behind his miserable daughter and his worried friends, since he has a strong feeling that he has to do it alone and in his own way. The idea of "doing it my way" explains all his deeds: from the preparation for the journey, to the choice of transportation, to the journey itself, and until his arrival at his brother's. My suggestion is that he feels that he should do it on his own, and in his own way, since it is an existential test for him. This journey should prove for Straight that he could overcome himself, overcome his old angers and fears and also his old body.

Straight does not go to the mountains, like Zarathustra, but to the wide roads of America. He is not a philosopher with a new message concerning human existence, but an old man who feels that he should correct his mistakes before his death. Yet, Straight's journey is full of reflections on the human condition from the perspective of an old wise man. This brings together Zarathustra and Straight through the mediation of Jung. Whereas Zarathustra is not an old man but an expression of the old wise man archetype in Jung's interpretation, Straight is indeed an old man with a wisdom of an old man.

Straight has several meetings during his journey. The first is with a young hitchhiker who is running away from home because of her pregnancy. Straight gives her a lesson about the importance of family by telling her about his daughter's trauma and the fable of the bundle of sticks: it is easy to break one stick but very hard to break sticks that are tied together. The lesson is that the family together is always stronger than any of its members singly. The second meeting is with the bicycle riders, with whom he talks about aging. The worst thing when you are old, he tells them, is to remember your youth. In his later meeting with an old man at the bar after his accident, he confesses about his drinking problem and his evil behavior after he came back from the war, illustrating the merging of collective and individual history.

Straight's last conversation, not coincidentally, is with a priest. This conversation is formed as a confession in which he tells the story of his family and about his quarrel with his brother. He expresses, during this confession, his desire to reconcile with his brother:

> STRAIGHT: Lyle and I grew up as close as brothers could be. We were raised on a farm in Moorhead, Minnesota. We worked hard. My mom and dad darn dam killed themselves trying to make that farm work. And me and Lyle we made games out of our chores. We'd make up different races and wages. Do anything to keep our mind off the cold. Lord, it was cold. . . . We talked about the stars and whether there might be somebody else like us out in space, places we wanted to go and it made our trials seems smaller . . .
>
> PRIEST: Well, . . . whatever happened between you two?
>
> STRAIGHT: Well that's a story old as the Bible . . . Cain and Abel . . . anger . . . vanity . . . mix those things up with liquor and you get two brothers not talkin' for ten years. . . . [W]hatever it was made me and Lyle so mad doesn't matter to me now . . . I want to make peace . . . I want to sit with him again and look up at all the stars.
>
> PRIEST: Well sir, I say Amen to that.

After this confession, Straight is ready to meet his brother.

Straight, I suggest, is an old man with a wisdom that is reminiscent of the wisdom of the overman. It is the wisdom to move beyond your accidental history and your conventions for getting better judgments concerning your existence. Nietzsche relates this ability to Zarathustra, and this causes Jung to interpret Zarathustra as an expression of the archetype of the old wise man. We can interpret Straight along the same lines. It is not an accident that Lynch chose to make a film concerning the journey of an old man. Straight is a fictional concretization of a wisdom that usually relates to old people. Though Straight, unlike Zarathustra, is not presented as a moral teacher, he is presented as an old man whose experience leads him to overcome his personal history and conventions for the sake of ethical improvement. That is to say, Straight is an old wise man.

Are Straight's deeds better understood as a result of self-overcoming or as an expression of the collective unconsciousness? From Nietzsche's point of view, one could say that Straight finds the power for self-overcoming. First, he takes upon himself the responsibility for his life instead of blaming his destiny. Second, he does it alone and in his own way. Third, and most important, he tries to overcome his principles and fears for reaching a better mode of existence, a mode of existence in which one's creative power—and not one's principles or fears—is what matters. Yet, from the Jungian point of view, things should be seen differently; his existential crisis and the stroke make him fragile and enable the collective unconsciousness to capture his self. It is this power that sends him on his journey in the name of American codes: family, God, and individualism.

Straight, one might say, expresses the archetype of the old American wise man. He reconfirms American values without questioning them, which makes the comparison between him and Zarathustra very fragile. Whereas Zarathustra declares a war against his culture's values, and actually against the very idea of common values, Straight reconfirms his culture's values through his actions, and his journey is actually an attempt to correct his mistakes. Yet, this difference, which is very crucial from a Nietzschean point of view, could be seen as not so dramatic from a Jungian point of view. Both Zarathustra and Straight are sure that they choose their way consciously and independently, yet, in fact, both are moved, according to a Jungian interpretation, by the collective unconsciousness.

Even without discussing the difference between European and American individualism, it is clear that Lynch's Straight is an illustration of an American individualism. It is an individualism that is embodied in the American ethos, including its values such as family, God, and a "do it your own way" attitude. This is the reason why Straight is not Zarathustra, but, at most, an American Zarathustra. Whereas Zarathustra, as Jung claims, is an individual who tries to challenge the limits of his culture's values (even though he could be conceived as an expression of an old archetype), Straight is an individual who obeys his culture's values. His individuality reflects the American ethos and serves the values of this ethos. Straight is an individual who works hard for his family (and his nation) and ends his story (and, as such, his life) near his brother after a confession to a priest. Zarathustra, on the other hand, does not have a family at all, and one of his recurrent motifs is that of the death of God.

Straight is very different from Zarathustra, though at first glance, and by the mediation of Jung, one can find similarities between them. Straight is indeed an old wise man, and, as Jung argues, one can find in his character a combination of inferiority and megalomania. We see him in the film as a crippled old man on his strange, little vehicle on the wide and endless roads of America; his inferiority is illustrated by his look, and his megalomania by his deeds. Yet, although it is hard not to respect his efforts, in comparison to Zarathustra he appears as no more than a marionette.

This point could be well clarified by Zarathustra's speech on the three transformations of the soul, together with Jung's idea of the archetype. The speech speaks of three modes of existence: what Zarathustra refers to as the camel, the lion, and the child. The camel is Zarathustra's simile for the hero: one who takes upon oneself seriously the values of his or her society and is ready to sacrifice his or her life for these values. The hero, like the camel, has the will and the power to carry other people's burdens without complaining and without questioning the value of this burden. Society appreciates the hero's deeds and repays him or her with prizes and respect. The hero, one can say, should overcome his or her self-interest to serve society. Therefore, the hero is the first model of self-overcoming.

The lion, a higher transformation of the soul, is the simile for the rebel: one who goes against common values and dedicates his life to revolt. It is a higher transformation of the soul, according to Zarathustra, since it is a soul that has the power and the courage to say "no" to orders; that is, to express an independent will. This is a second and higher model of self-overcoming, since the rebel is one who can overcome the human need for reception. Whereas the hero has the support of the collective, the rebel should find his or her power in one's own self. Yet, Zarathustra argues, it is not the highest transformation of the soul.

For Zarathustra, the child is the simile of the highest transformation since the child has an authentic will. It is a soul whose values are determined neither by others nor by resistance to others, but by self-creation. It is the highest expression of an independent will, since it is a will that does not depend, positively or negatively, on given values. This is the highest model of self-overcoming since at this existential stage one overcomes the need to be defined in relation to others. The child, one should remember, is the simile in this context, not the thing itself. That is to say, it is not a Romantic view that advocates the return to childhood, but a thesis concerning the development of the soul according to the idea of self-overcoming.

Though it is clear from this speech that Zarathustra (or Nietzsche) prefers the creator, who is represented by the child, to the hero and the rebel, one should understand all three transformations as different models of individualism.

The hero must be an individualist in order to become a hero; otherwise every normal member of society would be considered a hero. One wins this status by overcoming personal interests and dedicating oneself to society. It is a mode of individualism since it depends on the individual's belief or recognition that one is unique, though one shares common values with other members of society. He or she takes it upon oneself to fulfill these values no matter what others will do.

The rebel is actually the common image of an individualist: one who can not identify with society's values and is willing to pay the price of isolation for staying true to his or her own will. Yet, one's will itself is defined by the rejection of society's values. That is to say, the self-identity of the rebel as an individualist depends, paradoxically, on the society whose values the rebel attacks.

The creator has a different mode of individuality. It is a mode of individuality not for others (hero) and not against others (rebel). The will of the creator is symbolized by the child since the child's will is perceived as one that has not yet been shaped by common values. However, the child is only a symbol. In order to be a creator, one should free oneself from common values. This very process of overcoming common values gives birth to this mode of individuality. Like the child, the creator conceives the world as a wide field of possibilities and not as a structure in which to find one's proper place.

Straight is not a child, either in fact or as a symbol. He is not a creator, but a man who feels that he should perform his duty. Yet, it is not a duty Straight creates in himself for himself, but rather a duty he should perform as an American man. Straight actually conforms to the values of his society, though he feels that he makes a great decision of his own. In fact, even the resistance of his friends to his deeds serves as an approval of his will. He does not challenge them with new values but with his strong determination to conform to the values they all share. His choice of an old machine can be seen, from this perspective, as a symbol of his obedience to the old collective consciousness.

Straight, if so, is a hero who behaves according to the collective values. His existential crisis forces him not to wait any longer, but instead to make a decision. In such a situation, the feelings of inferiority and megalomania coalesce. Straight experiences his fragile mortality and the weakness of his body. His values reject this recognition, and he exerts power from the collective unconsciousness in order to fight against it. Thus, he feels that he knows what should be done and that he has the power to do it. His megalomania is expressed by his deeds; he feels strong enough to go on this pathetic journey, which even a younger man with a healthy and strong body could hardly do.

Jung claims that, at a time of existential disorientation, one is searching for an ethical guide in the image of a old wise man. Sometimes it brings one to put one's life in the hands of another person, but sometimes it causes one to perceive oneself as such a persona. This is what happened to Nietzsche, according to Jung, when he wrote *Thus Spoke Zarathustra*. Zarathustra is the personification of the old wise man archetype. Straight's persona, I claim, is created in the same way and in an even more explicit manner. Lynch presents an old man with an old wisdom that reflects the values of the American ethos. Is it an existential disorientation of Lynch or only of Straight that gives birth to *The Straight Story*?

I do not intend to answer this last question. My goal is not to present, like Jung, an analysis of the artist through his or her piece of art, but to focus on Straight's individualism. This analysis suggests that although we can see Straight as a good example of self-overcoming, his persona is very different from the persona of Zarathustra. Whereas Zarathustra takes us beyond good and evil, Straight reconfirms the values of his society by his deeds and speeches. Therefore, if Zarathustra, as Jung claims, expresses the archetype of the old wise man, one could say that Straight expresses the archetype of the American old wise man. That is to say, whereas Zarathustra expresses the form of the archetype with an original content, Straight's content is common and well known.

Notes

1. Friedrich Nietzsche, *Thus Spoke Zarathustra*, trans. Adrian Del Caro (1884; Cambridge: Cambridge University Press, 2006), 88.

2. Ibid., 89.

3. Ibid.

4. In aphorism 344 of *The Gay Science*, Nietzsche suggests that the will to truth might be revealed as a will to death (see Friedrich Nietzsche, *The Gay Science*, trans. Walter Kaufmann [1887; New York: Vintage Books, 1974], 280–83).

5. Ibid., 90.

6. See C. G. Jung, *The Archetypes and the Collective Unconsciousness*, trans. R. F. C. Hull (Princeton: Princeton University Press, 1990), 42.

7. Nietzsche himself emphasizes this fact in the well-known aphorism 125 of *The Gay Science* titled "The Madman":

"Whither is God?" he cried; "I will tell you. We have killed him—you and I. All of us are his murderers. But how did we do this? How could we drink up the sea? Who gave us the sponge to wipe away the entire horizon? What were we doing when we unchained this earth from its sun? Whither is it moving now? Whither are we moving? Away from all suns? Are we not plunging continually? Backward, sideward, forward, in all directions? Is there still any up or down? Are we not straying as through an infinite nothing? Do we not feel the breath of empty space? Has it not become colder? Is not night continually closing in on us? (Nietzsche, *The Gay Science*, 181).

8. C. G. Jung, *Jung's Seminar on Nietzsche's Zarathustra* (Princeton: Princeton University Press, 1998), 24. It is interesting to note that Giambattista Vico writes in aphorism 62 of his monumental book *The New Science* that "Zoroaster [Zarathustra] is honored as the first wise man among the gentiles" (*The New Science of Giambattista Vico*, trans. Thomas Goddard Bergin and Max Harold Fisch [1744; Ithaca: Cornell University Press, 1968], 38).

9. Jung, *Jung's Seminar on Nietzsche's Zarathustra*, 218–30.

10. Ibid., 239–40.

11. Ibid., 304–7.

12. Friedrich Nietzsche, *Beyond Good and Evil*, trans. Walter Kaufmann (1886; New York: Vintage Books, 1989), 13.

Part 3

THE SELF CONFRONTS THE WORLD: ISSUES IN ETHICS, SOCIETY, AND RELIGION

"THERE'S A SORT OF EVIL OUT THERE"

Emersonian Transcendentalism in *Twin Peaks*

Scott Hamilton Suter

> What is life, but the angle of vision. A man is measured by the angle at which he looks at objects.
> —Ralph Waldo Emerson, *Nature*

> Let nature guide us. Nature is the great teacher.
> —The Log Lady (*Twin Peaks,* season 2, episode 18)

David Lynch's well-known practice of Transcendental Meditation, a form of mantra meditation, and his application of Eastern religious teachings to his work in film and art invite comparisons of the director's work to that of other writers and artists who have approached their crafts with a similar vision. Certainly much of Ralph Waldo Emerson's (1803–1882) thought explores the importance of looking beyond the surface to the unity that lies apart from the apparent reality. Throughout the many hours of work and influence he contributed to the television program *Twin Peaks* (1990–1991), its pilot, and the film *Twin Peaks: Fire Walk with Me* (1992), Lynch offers an Emersonian view of the value of looking further to find the deeper meanings revealed in life. Indeed, as Lynch has proclaimed in words reminiscent of Emerson's, "the mind, being a detective, pieces fragments together and comes to a conclusion."[1]

While a quick overview of the data for the *Twin Peaks* series suggests that statistically Lynch played a small role in the overall production, he and Mark Frost, writer of the well-respected series *Hill Street Blues* (1981–1987), created the show based on Lynch's original concept. It is well documented that Lynch himself contributed to the writing of only four episodes (including the pilot) and directed only six of the total thirty. Still, David Lavery, author and editor of critical works on Lynch's work, and others point out that the look and feel of the series derives from Lynch's vision. Lavery asserts that "non-Lynch/Frost episodes, those directed by their stable or by established filmmakers and written by others, nevertheless perpetuated the show's basic look and feel." Similarly, Lynch biographer Greg Olson notes that "the show maintained a remarkable aesthetic consistency, thanks to the strong example Lynch had set." He comments further: "as in Lynch's feature films *Twin Peaks*'s images gained visual power through simplicity: The frames were uncluttered, so we could get lost in the beautiful shape and texture of a human face or a gleaming black telephone, or the purity of a steaming cup of coffee resting on a red countertop. As always, Lynch wanted to explore layers of reality, the exterior zones and the interior realms of both environments and people (their surface and secret selves)." As Emerson knew, the "angle of vision" determines how we interpret the world, and from the beginning of the pilot viewers are aware that *Twin Peaks* will be presented from Lynch's perspective. Despite the number of directors and writers, the world of the town of Twin Peaks is distinctly a Lynch-envisioned place.[2]

As frequently noted, FBI Special Agent Dale Cooper (Kyle MacLachlan), the inquisitive protagonist of *Twin Peaks,* has an approach to life that can be equated with that of his creator. In fact, some have suggested that MacLachlan himself served as a stand-in for Lynch in *Blue Velvet* (1986) as well as the *Twin Peaks* projects.[3] A focused look at Cooper, then, will reveal Lynch's Emersonian views, demonstrating that Lynch shares much with the nineteenth-century philosopher's conclusion that "as fast as you conform your life to the pure idea in your mind, that will unfold its great proportions. A correspondent revolution in things will attend the influx of spirit. So fast will disagreeable appearances, swine, spiders, snakes, pests, madhouses, prisons, enemies, vanish; they are temporary and shall be no more seen."[4] Despite Cooper's change to the "bad Dale" at the end of the series (more on this later), Emerson's argument that the mind perceives the whole by applying its reason still describes Lynch's vision of how the Twin Peaks world, and perhaps his own, can be envisioned.

Introduced in the pilot, a boyishly grinning Cooper motors along a pleasant Northwest highway, noting to himself: "Got to find out what kind of trees these are." This simple, but significant, utterance immediately suggests that the special agent is not altogether a sharp detective with a quick analytical mind focused solely on the case at hand. Nothing, however, could be more incorrect. In this first view of Cooper, Lynch offers a clue to the character that will be developed throughout the series and in *Twin Peaks: Fire Walk with Me:* the agent is in tune with the natural, and thus the spiritual, world, and this will make all the difference as he deciphers not only Laura Palmer's murder but also the mysterious evil that lurks in the town of Twin Peaks. Throughout the early episodes, directed and cowritten by Lynch, Cooper continues to exclaim about the natural world. He cries out, "Ducks on a lake!" at one point, and, later, after Sheriff Truman (Michael Ontkean) cautions, "There's a sort of evil out there—something very, very strange in these old woods," Cooper, surrounded by the landscape, takes a deep breath and observes, "Life has meaning here." What is it that Cooper sees or feels that others fail to experience?

The application of Emerson's seminal views from *Nature* (1836) offers a clear insight into Lynch's creation of the transcendent detective: "At present, man applies to nature but half his force. He works on the world with his understanding alone. He lives in it, and masters it by a penny-wisdom; and he that works most in it, is but a half-man, and whilst his arms are strong and his digestion good, his mind is imbruted, and he is a selfish savage. His relation to nature, his power over it, is through understanding." Emerson explains that this entails a pragmatic and economic view of nature, one that sees the value of steam and coal as power sources and surgery as a useful way to prolong physical life. Understanding alone, however, is not sufficient for a completely perceptive grasp of life. In fact, he intones, "empirical science is apt to cloud the sight, and, by the very knowledge of functions and processes, to bereave the student of the manly contemplation of the whole."[5]

On the other hand, Emerson explains, one who looks beyond this practical approach will find a complete image of the world and what it offers: "The best read naturalist who lends an entire and devout attention to truth, will see that there remains much to learn of his relation to the world, and that it is not to be learned by any addition or subtraction or other comparison of known quantities, but is arrived at by untaught sallies of the spirit, by a continual self-recovery, and by entire humility. He will perceive that there are far more excellent qualities in the student than preciseness and infallibility; that a guess is often more fruitful than an indisputable affirmation, and that a dream may let us deeper into the secret of nature than a hundred concerted experiments."[6] This dichotomous explanation of ways to explore the world could come no closer to a depiction of how Cooper views life, and his cases, as opposed to the average deductive approach of Sheriff Truman and others in Twin Peaks. At times Lynch utilizes Emerson's ideas in an almost literal fashion. Clues to mysteries are revealed to Cooper in dreams, and the special agent, ever perceptive, recognizes the significance of these portents. Cooper uses both understanding and reason as he applies his dreams to the Laura Palmer (Sheryl Lee) murder case in the early episodes of the program. For instance, with an anxious Sheriff Truman and Lucy Moran (Kimmy Robertson), he discusses the dream in which Laura Palmer revealed her murderer to him. Before Cooper answers Truman's query, however, he asks, "Do you know where dreams come from?" continuing, "Acetylcholine neurons fire high voltage impulses into the forebrain. These impulses become pictures, the pictures become dreams but . . . no one knows why we choose these particular pictures" (season 1, episode 3: "Rest in Pain"). It's his ability to parse the meaning from these pictures that sets Cooper apart from others and imbues him with Emerson's transcendental qualities. After describing his dream, Cooper disappoints the sheriff (and viewers) by admitting that he has forgotten what the beautiful woman "who looked "exactly like Laura Palmer" told him. Undaunted, however, the chipper, Emersonian Cooper exclaims: "Harry, our job is simple. Break the code, solve the crime." In breaking the code, Cooper will employ all his faculties.

If, as I argue, Lynch applies an Emersonian view to the entire world of Twin Peaks, then there must be more to the story than the Romantic hero Agent Cooper. The natural world for Emerson is the source of the "divine," the true revelation of meaning, and certainly Twin Peaks and its surroundings provide a setting for Lynch to apply these ideas. The presentation of image is central to Lynch's art, and he uses this concept to emphasize the value of Twin Peaks's natural setting.[7] Commenting on the value of creating a "real place" in *Catching the Big Fish* (2006), Lynch reflects: "A sense of place is so critical in cinema, because you want to go into another world. Every story has its own world, and its own feel, and its own mood. So you try to put together all these things—these little details—to create that sense of place. . . . While many sets are good enough for a wide shot, in my mind, they should be good enough for close scrutiny, for the little details to show. You may not ever really see them all, but you've got to feel that they're there, somehow, to feel that it's a real place, a real world."[8] Here, Lynch recalls Emerson's reliance on the idea of unity and the importance of comprehending an entire image or view. The philosopher declares that "when I behold a rich landscape, it is less to my purpose to recite correctly the order and superposition of the strata, than to know why all thought of multitude is lost in a tranquil sense of unity." Again, Emerson emphasizes the need to see the world as a whole rather than only in parts, and specific aspects of the *Twin Peaks* series blend this holistic approach with Lynch's keen sense of the sharp, meaningful image.[9]

This approach was emphasized each week as viewers were greeted with the dulcet tones of Angelo Badalamenti's soundtrack and treated to the view of a Bewick's wren on an evergreen bough. While quickly giving way to a typical Lynchian view of industrial "art," the initial peaceful and natural image sets the tone for the world of Twin Peaks. Granted, the world of the sawmill exists here too, but for those first few seconds we are in a beautiful, natural setting. These two images—birds and evergreens (Douglas firs, specifically)—play large roles in the visceral image of the show and reveal Lynch's belief that nature holds significant keys to understanding not only the show but the larger world as well.[10]

Holding true to the opening view, birds feature largely in both the plot and visual world of *Twin Peaks*. Every aficionado knows that "the owls are not what they seem," but other birds, like the Bewick's wren of the opening credits, pop into scenes in unusual places. As noted, for instance, Cooper, expressing a child's delight, exclaims in "Rest in Pain" (season 1, episode 3) "Ducks—on a lake!" Later, in "Drive with a Dead Girl" (season 2, episode 3), the program following the Lynch-directed murder of Maddy Ferguson (Sheryl Lee), we find a close-up of a pileated woodpecker. After the traumatic death of another young woman, viewers are presented once again with the calming, natural image of a bird in a tree. In Lynch's town there is no surprise in finding a bird as a witness to a crime. This bird, however, is a mynah named, quite significantly, Waldo. This nod to Emerson (Waldo is Emerson's middle name, of course, and the name he was called by his family) might be subtle, but it is not surprising given the emphasis placed on Emerson's valuing of nature as a key to understanding life. A truly poetic bird, the nightingale appears in the Road House when Julee Cruise performs the Lynch-penned song of the same title. The lyrics include lines that will become more significant as the show progresses; the bird sings about love:

The nightingale
It said to me
There is love
Meant for me
The nightingale

It flew to me
And told me
That it found my love.[11]

Unlike the owls, these birds are just what they seem—harbingers of nature's value for man, as Emerson proclaims in the final lines of "The Poet": "Wherever snow falls or water flows or birds fly . . . there is Beauty."[12]

Not unlike birds, trees are presented at important parts of the series. As noted, Cooper is first introduced to the audience marveling over the trees. The same trees, however, become Lynch's marker of the onset of ominous activities. Throughout the series, the image of wind swaying the boughs of Douglas firs alerts viewers to the fact that something mysterious may soon occur. Judge Sternwood (Royal Dano), the congenial circuit judge who hears the preliminary trial of Leland Palmer (Ray Wise), cautions Cooper: "Keep your eye on the woods. The woods are wondrous here—but strange." Glastonbury Grove, the entrance to the Black Lodge, lies deep in the forest and consists of a circle of sycamore trees. All arguments, it would seem, that suggest nature might in fact be sinister or, at the least, dangerous. Here, however, it is important to return to the idea of the power of an image to convey what Lynch calls "a real place." Emerson maintains that "this power is in the image because this power is in Nature."[13]

This concept of power shows up in the 1870 essay "Success," in which Emerson declares "Nature knows how to convert evil to good," and cautions readers not to view what might be seen as successful ventures too highly. With descriptions that could stand in for a character list of the television show, he argues: "Nature utilizes misers, fanatics, showmen, egotists, to accomplish her ends; but we must not think better of the foible for that. The passion for sudden success is rude and puerile, just as war, cannons and executions are used to clear the ground of bad, lumpish, irreclaimable savages, but always to the damage of the conquerors." Leo Johnson (Eric Da Re), Hank Jennings (Chris Mulkey), Catherine Martell (Piper Laurie), and Josie Packard (Joan Chen) come to mind as fitting the bill offered by Emerson; however, Ben Horne (Richard Beymer) is perhaps the clearest image of a fanatic, showman, and egotist in the program. He uses people, money, influence, drugs, and his own family to achieve what Emerson identifies as "shallow Americanism," and it is important to note that he literally plots to destroy nature by developing Ghostwood Estates.[14]

Numerous examples of Horne's "talent" exist; how, then, does he contribute to the show's presentation of Emerson's theme of evil turning to good? Quite simply, of all the characters, Ben Horne effects the most complete change. For most of the program's duration, he is a backstabbing, conniving businessman, but when faced with substantial business losses, being jailed for Laura Palmer's murder, and being tricked by Catherine into signing over the Ghostwood lands, he lapses into an insane world where he perceives he is General Robert E. Lee leading the South against the North in the American Civil War. Eventually relieved from this world of imaginary conflict, he resumes his role as Twin Peaks's leading businessman. In "The Condemned Woman" (season 2, episode 23), addressing his brother, Jerry (David Patrick Kelly), his daughter, Audrey (Sherilyn Fenn), and his assistant, Bobby Briggs (Dana Ashbrook), he announces his company has fallen on hard times. But he follows this with: "So, in spite of these reversals and stripped of all the trappings of success, what are we left with? The human spirit." Despite this declaration, the episode writer, Tricia Brock, does not have Ben turn immediately from bad to good; instead she sets him on his way, for his plan for corporate redemption lies in an effort to save the endangered pine weasel, whose habitat will be destroyed by the Ghostwood Estates project. Here, despite the satirical overtones, Ben begins to move toward goodness by launching an effort to rescue nature in the form of the weasel, reflecting Emerson's belief that " 'tis the bane of life that natural effects are continually crowded out, and artificial arrangements substituted." By "On the Wings of Love" (season 2, episode 25), Ben confides: "I am filled to the brim with goodness. Like a Christmas tree all lit up inside me. But at the end of the day, when I look in the mirror, I have to face the fact that I don't really know *how* to be good." By the series' end we have been presented with Ben reading "the *Koran,* the *Bhagavad-Gita,* the *Talmud,* the *Bible, New* and *Old Testaments,* the *Tao-Te-Ching* . . . those holy books that constitute the fundamental framework of man's philosophies of good," books that Emerson often quoted in his essays. We are also teased with the idea that Ben may in fact be Donna Hayward's (Lara Flynn Boyle) father, a shocking revelation for viewers and Donna alike. Motivated by the desire to do good and to tell the truth, Ben wants to reveal his secret to Donna. That truth, however, was never broadcast.[15]

Along with Ben's movement from evil to good, other plotlines in the series demonstrate a connection with Emerson's philosophy. Perhaps the most prominent is Emerson's thought that love is "the affirmative of affirmatives." The idea of love as the opposite of evil shows up throughout the series in characters like FBI Special Agent Albert Rosenfield (Miguel Ferrer), Major Garland Briggs (Don Davis), and most important in Agent Cooper himself. The soap-opera aspect of the program similarly deals with the theme but on a superficial, popular-culture level. The forbidden love stories of Bobby Briggs and Shelly Johnson (Madchen Amick) and Ed Hurley (Everett McGill) and Norma Jennings (Peggy Lipton) are accentuated by the postmodern show within a show, "Invitation to Love"; however, more serious plotlines reveal a closer belief that love beyond the self-love or egotism described by Emerson does "convert evil to good."[16]

For instance, Albert Rosenfield, the gruff, cynical, urban forensics specialist, enters the show as an offensive opposite to the tolerant Cooper. Still, Albert offers a Lynchian, if not Emersonian, view of how love can affect the world. The following exchange occurs in "The Man behind the Glass" (season 2, episode 10):

> TRUMAN: Albert, you make fun of everyone and everything and then act like you deserve an award for it. That's just not right. Get out of here before I do something I won't regret. Again.
>
> ALBERT: While I will admit to a certain cynicism, the fact of the matter is I'm merely a naysayer and hatchet man in the fight against violence. I pride myself in taking a punch and would gladly take another because I choose to live my life in the company of Gandhi and King. My concerns are global. I reject absolutely revenge, aggression, and retaliation. The foundation of such a method is love. I love you, Sheriff Truman.

Albert's approach to life, that of Gandhi and King, offers a stark contrast to his wisecracking, insulting demeanor in earlier episodes, and it offers one more reflection of *Twin Peaks* writers, in this case Robert Engels, incorporating Emerson's thoughts into Lynch's town. Major Briggs, himself a philosophical character, similarly brings the story line to the importance of love when, after being injected with Haloperidal by Windom Earle (Kenneth Welsh), perhaps the show's most malevolent character, he declares that his greatest fear is "the possibility that . . . love is not enough." Upon hearing this, Earle offers an unsympathetic and sarcastic, "oh, Garland, please. I shall weep," later adding to Leo: "We are all love's fools, more or less. But you will learn, as I have, the value of hate. It makes for better company, I assure you." This statement of Briggs's fear, coming near the final episode, leads to the ultimate expression of love, and thus, I argue, the optimistic ending of the television series.

The most important love story in the series is that between Cooper and Annie Blackburne (Heather Graham). Cooper, we have learned earlier, has loved only once, and that experience ended badly when he let down his guard and the woman (coincidentally Windom Earle's wife) was murdered. Upon meeting Annie, however, he becomes truly love struck, and the two embark on a relationship that will lead to Cooper's willingness to give up his soul for her. This is an act that Cooper agrees to perform in the Black Lodge, although one he does not have to complete since Bob (Frank Silva) reacts to Earle's presumptuous request by taking the villain's soul instead.

The interaction of Cooper and Annie in the final shows of the series reveals how an Emersonian thinker might fall in love, and, appropriately, Annie and Cooper first meet when she serves him coffee at the Double R Café. Later, unknowingly contributing to his investigation, Annie identifies Cooper's doodling on a napkin as a symbol found in Owl Cave, an area landmark. Finally, in a rowboat at Easter Park, Cooper and Annie kiss, acknowledging that both can overcome their painful past relationship experiences (Annie's resulted in a suicide attempt; Cooper's in the death of his loved one). Still later, a love-struck Cooper quotes a Hindu proverb (very Emersonian) while discussing love with another love-struck character in the lobby of the Great Northern Lodge: "Love is a ladder to Heaven." Able to match each other's emotions as well as pithy quotations, the characters convincingly demonstrate their mutual attraction. In "Miss Twin Peaks" (season 2, episode 28), for instance, during a discussion at the Double R Café of the upcoming Miss Twin Peaks pageant, the two flirt about Annie's chances of winning the contest.

ANNIE: We're trying to decide who's going to win tonight.
COOPER: No question about it. You are.
ANNIE: You're not exactly objective.
COOPER: I am completely objective.
ANNIE: I think you're not as objective as you think you are.
COOPER: Perhaps that's why it seems so important to me that we kiss.
ANNIE: You impetuous boy. We have an audience.
COOPER: I know this violates multiple laws of physics, but at this moment, Annie, and I mean this quite literally . . . you are the only person in the room.

When Annie visits Cooper's room at the Great Northern to ask for help with her speech, the normally collected detective strays from his analytic path again: "My habit is to construct and control my emotions with great precision. Everything ordered and in its place. What I am feeling now has steamrollered every barrier I've ever, if you'll excuse the expression, erected. I don't know what I know or don't know. I only know . . . I want to make love with you, Annie. That's all I know." Finally, Cooper notes to Diane that his life has been incomplete and that he has failed to realize it. He notes, "I want to make specific mention of Annie Blackburne. Diane, she is a completely original human being. Her responses are as pure as a child's. To be honest, I haven't felt this way about anyone since Caroline. It's taken meeting someone like Annie to realize how gray my life has been since Caroline's death, how cold and solitary." As he does in his professional life, Cooper applies both his Emersonian "understanding" and "reason" to his feelings for Annie.

A final quotation from Emerson's *Nature* again applies directly to *Twin Peaks*'s characters' reactions. Just as Lynch demonstrates Emerson's belief that "a guess is often more fruitful than an indisputable affirmation, and that a dream may let us deeper into the secret of nature than a hundred concerted experiments," his final presentation of Cooper in the television series draws specifically on another of Emerson's thoughts: "The problem of restoring to the world original and eternal beauty is solved by the redemption of the soul. The ruin or the blank, that we see when we look at nature, is in our own eye. The axis of vision is not coincident with the axis of things, and so they appear not transparent but opake [*sic*]. The reason why the world lacks unity, and lies broken in heaps, is, because man is disunited with himself. He cannot be a naturalist, until he satisfies all the demands of the spirit. Love is as much its demand, as perception. Indeed, neither can be perfect with the other. In the uttermost meaning of the words, thought is devout, and devotion is thought."[17] In *Twin Peaks*, the world is returned to its beauty by Cooper's act. By *offering* his soul he *redeems* his soul, and this, to Lynch, is significant. Returning to direct the final episode, Lynch, in the words of his biographer Olson, "could not abide the all-important conclusion of the script his colleagues handed him." The director commented that "it was completely and totally wrong." Although he is not given writing credits for this ultimate episode, Lynch scrapped the script and wrote a new "heartfelt fantasia on what he considered to be the key *Twin Peaks* themes." One of these themes, I argue, is the importance of love in an Emersonian sense—love that restores "to the world original and eternal beauty."[18]

What can be drawn, then, from the final shot of the last episode? After facing and being overwhelmed by his evil doppelganger in the red room, Cooper, with the face of Bob reflected in the mirror, smirks evilly and mimics his good self asking, "How's Annie?" In order to see this in Emersonian terms—terms that require us to see beyond the partial world to the unity of all things—one must, indeed, look further, past the ending of the series itself. Interviewed by Chris Rodley after the program had gone off the air, Lynch had much to say about the final episode. Responding to the thought that Cooper had been possessed by Bob, Lynch reveals his conviction that Cooper is a transcendent character. He notes that "the thing is, he hasn't [been possessed]. It's the doppelganger thing—the idea of two sides to everyone. He's really up against himself. People were really upset that it ended with an evil Cooper who'd been taken over by Bob. But that's *not* the ending. That's the ending that people were stuck with. That's just the ending of the second season. If it had continued . . ."[19] Lynch does not conclude the thought; however, it is clearly possible that the director had a vision of a triumphant Agent Cooper emerging from the Black Lodge. Given the spiritual characterization of Cooper throughout the show, it is not inconceivable that Lynch would have his detective use all of his faculties to reach, as Emerson put it, "the pure idea in [his] mind," seeing not through an opaque glass (or red curtain) but becoming Emerson's transparent eyeball, seeing all.[20]

This resurgence of the "good" Cooper is supported in Lynch's subsequent film *Twin Peaks: Fire Walk with Me.* Although it depicts the final days leading up to Laura Palmer's death, and thus recounts events that occurred before those of the entire television series, viewers are shown Cooper in the red room, for he dreams of meeting Laura there twenty-five years in the future. Arguably more Lynchian than the series, this film provides a more thorough understanding of how the director envisioned Cooper's character. For this argument, the most poignant and important scene comes near the end of the film after Laura has been murdered by her father/Bob. Finally released from the horrors of her life, Laura sits in the red room with a sincerely grinning Cooper by her side. Looking radiant, in stark contrast to her lifeless, gray visage on the banks of the river, Laura expresses her peace and contentment with genuinely joyous laughter. While focused on Laura, the scene also reflects a comforting and satisfied Cooper.

Although some, like Samuel Kimball, argue that *Twin Peaks* is a caricature of Emersonian discourse, the affinities between Emerson's thought and Lynch's beliefs as they are presented in the series and film reveal that Lynch's philosophy parallels much of the nineteenth-century philosopher's.[21] Emerson's foundation in self-reliance and the importance of transcending the physical world to reach the spiritual plane are found throughout Lynch's work and writings. His comment that "Cooper is real close to me; he says a lot of the things I say," requires a look at one final quotation from the agent.[22] Cooper notes to Diane: "It's 1:15 p.m. I've just concluded my second meditation of the day in lieu of sleep. I am completely refreshed and struck again by the realization that we all live at a fraction of our potential." Quirky? Yes, but as viewers we have come to expect such insights from Cooper. His observation assumes more significance, however, as we remember Lynch's admission above and consider his resolute advocacy of Transcendental Meditation. Lynch believes that "everything, anything that is a thing, comes up from the deepest level," and he attains his grasp on that level through daily meditation. His understanding of the world is influenced by, perhaps directed by, this deep delving into his soul.[23]

There is no need to leap, then, to reach the conclusion that Lynch and Emerson are on the same path. Describing his meditation practice, Lynch adopts a prose style reminiscent of Emerson's. In *Catching the Big Fish,* Lynch writes: "I meditate once in the morning and again in the afternoon, for about twenty minutes each time. Then I go about the business of my day. And I find that the joy of doing increases. Intuition increases. The pleasure of life grows. And negativity recedes." When one compares this with Emerson's assertion that "as fast as you conform your life to the pure idea in your mind, that will unfold its great proportions," the similarities are plain. Emerson felt that one could find this intuition in nature; Lynch finds it there, too.[24]

Ultimately, both authors have discovered that this overarching unity leads to a better understanding of life and therefore can make one a better actor in the lives of others. *Twin Peaks* represents a world of David Lynch's imagination, one that can be found in his other works as well, and in that world we find Agent Dale Cooper, a unifying thinker who uses his faculties—mental and spiritual—to contribute to that world. Finally, Lynch ties his world together with Emerson's vision of a world where all "disagreeable appearances" disappear. Lynch's belief as well as his practice sounds ideal: "So compassion, appreciation for others, and the capacity to help others are enhanced when you meditate. You start diving down and experiencing this ocean of pure love, pure peace—you could say pure compassion. You experience that, and know it by being it. *Then* you go out into the world, and you can really do something for people." Emerson's world, Lynch's world, *Twin Peaks*'s world, everyone's world could do no better.[25]

Notes

1. Greg Olson, *David Lynch: Beautiful Dark* (Lanham, Md.: Scarecrow Press, 2008), 276.
2. David Lavery, ed. *Full of Secrets: Critical Approaches to "Twin Peaks"* (Detroit: Wayne State University Press, 1995), 5; Olson, *David Lynch: Beautiful Dark,* 300.
3. Olson, *David Lynch: Beautiful Dark,* 262.
4. Ralph Waldo Emerson, *Nature,* in *Ralph Waldo Emerson: Essays & Lectures,* ed. Joel Porte (New York: Literary Classics of the United States, 1983), 48.
5. Ibid., 46, 43.
6. Ibid.
7. See Olson, *David Lynch: Beautiful Dark,* 254–55, for a discussion of Lynch's art and its connection to his films.
8. David Lynch, *Catching the Big Fish: Meditation, Consciousness, and Continuity* (New York: Jeremy P. Tarcher/Penguin, 2006), 117. For example, in *Twin Peaks: Fire Walk with Me,* as Laura is about to be molested by Bob, Sarah Palmer (Grace Zabriskie) is reading in bed; a close examination of the book reveals she is reading *How to Speak German.*
9. Emerson, *Nature,* 43.
10. The films *Eraserhead* (1977) and *The Elephant Man* (1980) similarly utilize images of the industrial landscape.
11. David Lynch, "The Nightingale," *Soundtrack from "Twin Peaks,"* Warner Brothers, compact disc, 1990.
12. Ralph Waldo Emerson, "The Poet," in *Ralph Waldo Emerson: Essays & Lectures,* ed. Joel Porte (New York: Literary Classics of the United States, 1983), 468.
13. Ralph Waldo Emerson, "Poetry and Imagination," in *The Complete Writings of Ralph Waldo Emerson* (New York: William H. Wise, 1930), 2:732.
14. Ralph Waldo Emerson, "Success," in *The Complete Writings of Ralph Waldo Emerson* (New York: William H. Wise, 1930), 1:708.
15. Ibid., 1:710.
16. Ibid., 1:714.
17. Emerson, *Nature,* 47.
18. Olson, *David Lynch: Beautiful Dark,* 360.
19. Chris Rodley, ed., *Lynch on Lynch* (London: Faber and Faber, 1997), 182–83.
20. Emerson, *Nature,* 48.
21. Samuel Kimball, "'Into the light, Leland, into the light': Emerson, Oedipus,

and the Blindess of Male Desire in David Lynch's 'Twin Peaks,'" *Genders* 16 (Spring 1993): 17–34.

22. As quoted in Olson, *David Lynch: Beautiful Dark,* 359.

23. Lynch, *Catching the Big Fish,* 1.

24. Ibid., 5.

25. Ibid., 169–70.

"In Heaven Everything Is Fine"

Erasing Traditional Morality

Jason Southworth

Like most films by David Lynch, *Eraserhead* (1977) presents a challenge for its interpreters. Any attempt to come up with a coherent interpretation of this film must acknowledge that the film is comprised of several narrative sequences that interweave and interrupt each other and, in doing so, make it increasingly difficult to determine what the film is actually about. This is partly because Lynch makes an intentional effort to baffle and confuse the audience by combining *literal* and *metaphorical imagery*. Literal imagery consists of those scenes, shots, and frames that stand for the reality of the film. In other words, literal imagery consists of what is "actually happening," whether in dreams or in waking life, in the fictitious lives of the onscreen characters. The experienced moviegoer is expected to know literal imagery when he or she sees it and, more important, to be able to distinguish the characters' "real" whereabouts and happenstances from their dreams and fantasies.

Consider how this works in *Twin Peaks* (1990–1991). Most of the series depicts the day-to-day real lives of the residents of Twin Peaks. Sometimes there are scenes that depict the world as it is experienced by a single character, however. Sarah Palmer (Grace Zabriskie) literally saw Bob (Frank Silva) even though others in her place would not have. Likewise, the dreams of Agent Dale Cooper (Kyle MacLachlan) were literally experienced by Dale, even though they are full of symbolism that Dale and the viewer must interpret. Although requiring more cognitive steps than the scenes of day-to-day goings on in Twin Peaks, these scenes are still literal, because they are literally showing us what particular characters in the show (Mrs. Palmer in one case and Agent Cooper in the other) are experiencing.

On the nonliteral side, we find metaphorical imagery. With metaphorical imagery, we view the characters as neither literally experiencing the events depicted, nor as dreaming or fantasizing about those events. Instead, the relation between what we see and what it means is allegorical (i.e., one thing is represented visually as some other thing). In doing this, the filmmaker intends the viewer to come to a specific understanding of the first thing in a way that would be impossible using literal imagery alone. For example, if a man is dressed in a diaper instead of normal clothes, we are meant to see him as a baby, and we can then draw some conclusions about the attitudes and dispositions of this person (you see this happen often in Warner Brothers cartoons). In *Eraserhead,* whenever Henry Spencer (Jack Nance) looks out the window, there is a brick wall just on the other side of the glass. Since it does not make sense that there would literally be a wall so close to a neighboring window (or there would be little point in the window being there to begin with), the only way to make sense of this cinematic fact is to take it as a metaphor, that is, as having a symbolic (and not a factual) role within the film. The brick wall seems to stand for Henry's clustered feelings of awkwardness and suffocation. Henry feels shattered and entrapped; he feels compelled to marry Mary X (Charlotte Stewart) and raise his child, and he feels that the world is closing in on him. The neighboring wall "closing in" on Henry's apartment (via the window, which should normally be the open path for prospects, clear view, and possibilities) must be taken as a metaphorical image that aims to represent Henry's feelings of claustrophobia, and not as something that "really" happens to him.[1]

Most films are fairly simple to interpret, and it is easy to distinguish literal images from metaphorical ones. This is true even for those made by filmmakers often mentioned in the same breath as Lynch. Spike Lee's *Do the Right Thing* (1989) is about the ways in which "the right thing" is context-dependent, and it is obvious that the rising temperature throughout the film is a metaphor for increasing racial tensions. Ingmar Bergman's *Wild Strawberries* (1957) is about the ways we try to rationalize our past behavior as death approaches, and the opening scene of the film, where a skeleton tries to pull a scared Professor Borg (Victor Sjöström) into a casket, is a metaphor for the fact that his impending death troubles the old man. Things are not so easy in the films of David Lynch, and are particularly difficult in the case of *Eraserhead,* where Lynch purposely blurs the lines between what should be understood as real and what is intended to be understood metaphorically. This makes it quite difficult to give a coherent interpretation. In this essay, I focus on giving a coherent philosophical interpretation of the film that accounts for its ambiguous scenes as meaningful, something other accounts of the film have failed to do. To do this, I first give a brief outline of the film and suggest that any adequate interpretation of the film must account for all of the elements of the outline. Following this, I consider several common interpretations of the film and argue that they fall short of our standard for an adequate interpretation. I then offer my interpretation of the film, one that sees it as participating in a long-standing philosophical tradition that rejects traditional conceptions of morality.

Sketching Out the Plot: What Actually Happens in *Eraserhead*

As noted before, *Eraserhead,* much like other films of its type, is comprised of both literal and metaphorical imagery. However, upon watching this film, it becomes apparent that Lynch made a deliberate effort to blend the two together. In other words, Lynch employs a cinematic tactic that makes it hard (and sometimes even impossible) for the viewer to tell the one from the other. What are the aims of such a tactic? And what is *Eraserhead* actually about?

In the most general terms, *Eraserhead* is the story of a man, Henry Spencer, who finds out that he has impregnated his girlfriend, Mary X. Mary's family talks Henry into marrying Mary. The couple lives together for a very short time before Mary decides she can't cope with the child and goes back to her parents. Henry is then left to care for the baby, who soon becomes sick. Ultimately, Henry kills the child.

While this brief synopsis provides a general outline of the film's plot, it is obvious that the film is much more complicated than this simple summary. In addition to the narrative outlined above, there is a series of other scenes that are not part of the main story line of Henry, Mary, and the baby. Because these scenes seem detached from the more straightforward part of the story, and because we are accustomed to movies following one linear story, it can be difficult to understand the role of these scenes in the film. For instance, there are the opening and closing scenes of the film, which depict a man in a shack on what appears to be another planet. The man pulls levers at the start of the film and fails to put the levers back at the end. How are we to understand these opening and closing scenes? If we wish to completely understand this film as a cohesive work of art, we must try to understand what role these scenes play.

Another aspect of the film that can be hard to reconcile with the main narrative is that Henry's child is monstrous. The child has no ears, has two holes in what looks like a snout rather than a proper nose, and eyes on the sides of its head. All in all, the child's head looks more like that of a dinosaur than a human being. How are we to make sense of the baby's appearance? Is this a case of literal or metaphorical imagery?

Stranger still, the camera cuts three times into the radiator of Henry's apartment, revealing a stage on which a woman with enormous cheeks dances and sings. Are we to believe there is actually a woman living in Henry's radiator, or is this a metaphor? If it is a metaphor, what is it a metaphor of? If it is a fantasy, whose is it? It is only in putting all these things together into a coherent story that one can be said to have a good, or successful, interpretation of the film.

So, we now have a standard for judging whether or not we have a good interpretation of the film, namely, to have a good interpretation of *Eraserhead,* you must be able to explain how all the pieces of the story that confuse us fit together. To put it another way, a successful interpretation of this film must be able to not only account for the straightforward linear story line, but it must also be able to explain the series of scenes outside of the main story line through the notions of literal and metaphorical imagery. Now that we have a clearer picture of the content of the film, we can turn to examine the common interpretations and each of their shortcomings.[2]

Criticizing the Critics: What *Eraserhead* Isn't About

Given that *Eraserhead* debuted in very limited release by what was then a completely unknown filmmaker, very little was said in print about the movie at the time of its release. As you might expect from an older film whose success dawned in the digital age, most of its reviews and works of interpretive criticism are exclusively online. Looking over this content, you find three dominant interpretations of the film. The first holds that the film is an argument for a pro-choice position on abortion. On this interpretation, we are supposed to see Henry's life as ruined by having an unwanted child introduced in his life, something an abortion could have avoided. There are two fundamental problems with this interpretation. One problem is that it does not account for many of the alternative narrative sequences. For instance, this interpretation does not address the Man in the Planet (Jack Fisk), or explain the significance of the Lady in the Radiator (Laurel Near). As stated above, any adequate interpretation of the film must make sense of these sequences. Another problem is that it does not account for how sad Henry's life is even before he finds out about the baby. Recall my interpretation of the brick wall outside his window. It sure seems like Henry's life isn't ruined, so much as his bad life is made worse. Why would Lynch present the story this way if he wanted us to believe that it was the child who ruined Henry's life? It would be more reasonable for Lynch to show us a happy Henry at the beginning of the film if we were supposed to conclude that the child's birth was the cause of most of his problems.[3]

A second predominant interpretation is that the film is about suicide. On this interpretation, Henry is supposed to be a paradigm case of a tragic life, one that is only made worse by being forced into an unwanted marriage and by having a freakish child. Things continue to get worse as he tries to escape as best he can. The radiator scenes, on this account, are just the strangest of Henry's attempts at escapism—he can't think of anything in the world that would make his life noticeably better, so he fantasizes about an imaginary woman, awkward and nervous like himself, yet happy. Upon realizing that this woman is not real, he opts for the only escape left to him—suicide. Again, it is unclear what the opening and closing scenes mean on this account. Even worse, however, this interpretation fails to make sense of the scene from which the film takes its name. In this scene, Henry's decapitated head is drilled into in order to produce tubes of brain matter that are affixed to the end of pencils—in other words, his head is turned into an eraser. What does an eraser head have to do with suicide, exactly? Certainly, any interpretation of the film needs to account for the titular scene.[4]

A third common interpretation of the film applies a method that is the exact opposite of the other two interpretations. Rather than find a key theme or idea that serves as the common thread throughout the entire film, this interpretation maintains that the film has no overall theme or message. That is, the film is actually just a collection of scenes or set pieces intended to evoke certain feelings (disgust, angst, confusion) in us. Thus, whatever we are talking about in the film—from Henry, to the baby, to the Lady in the Radiator—this interpretation maintains that there is no theme that connects any of the scenes together. The problem with this interpretation, however, is that it fails to account for the fact that the film has a plot. As we have already seen, the film includes a narrative about Henry, Mary, and their baby. Furthermore, the sequences of events that comprise the narrative are related to one another. This interpretation thus falls short. By holding that no common thread ties any of the scenes together, it ultimately ignores the fact that there is a primary plot that any viewer can follow, even if he can't put it together with all of the other scenes.[5]

Having rejected the mainstream interpretations, it is important to reexamine the film so that we can come to a successful interpretation. In what follows, I explain how we can understand both the main narrative story line, as well as the extranarrative scenes of the film, as presenting an argument for the rejection of traditional morality. I show that Henry has been living a life of traditional morality, buying into the promise that it will lead to a happy life, and that we enter his world during a time of crisis. What we experience through Henry's literal and metaphorical experiences combine to help us learn, as Henry learns, that traditional morality sometimes fails. Some, like Henry, must find an alternative way to live in order to avoid despair.

Bringing It All Back to Henry: The Rejection of Traditional Morality

In the preceding sections, I introduced a distinction between literal and metaphorical imagery, and established a criterion for a successful interpretation of a film. With these elements, I built my own interpretive case for *Eraserhead*. My interpretation centers on the concepts of traditional morality and its demise.

Before offering my interpretation, it is important to get clear on what is meant by traditional morality. First, what philosophers mean by *morality* is any code of conduct that makes claims about how good people should act and how they shouldn't. These codes of conduct tell us how to act, allow us to evaluate the actions of others, and let us know the demands we can reasonably place on others' behavior. The term *morality* itself does not tell us what the code of conduct is—that is the job of particular moral theories. *Traditional morality* refers to the dominant moral code of conduct for a society over a period of time. Again, the term *traditional morality* does not give any indication what the code of conduct is. The code is determined by looking at particular societies at particular times. Examples of traditional moralities range from India under the caste system and feudal China, in which different groups within the population had different rules of conduct, to colonial Britain and ancient Greece, which applied one set of rules to all citizens.

Henry, as well as most readers, lives under the traditional morality of contemporary American values, which is often said to come from the basic precepts of Judeo-Christianity. While there might be some debate about what an exhaustive list of this moral code would look like, some noncontroversial components include: a respect for family, a belief in the sanctity of marriage, a strong work ethic, a recognition of the importance of keeping one's word, an understanding that the right thing to do in many cases involves restraining your actions for the benefits of others, and a belief that a life in accordance with these things will bring you happiness.[6]

With this in mind, we shall go back to Henry. Henry seems to be living a relatively typical, if not slightly awkward life. He has a job that he works dutifully (although he is on vacation for the film), a neighbor toward whom he is polite, and an ex-girlfriend he still loves. All that said, this life does not seem to satisfy Henry or bring him the happiness that is supposed to come from living a moral life (as the brick-wall metaphor is meant to suggest). In spite of this, Henry still tries to live in accordance with social norms, namely, in accordance with the code of traditional morality. He shows compassion and forgiveness to Mary when he accepts her dinner invitation, even though he feels jilted by her no longer coming around. Even though her family is strange, he is polite to them, listening to their odd stories and accepting their idiosyncratic behaviors (for example, he sits in polite silence when Mary's mother has an episode of some kind). Once he finds out that Mary gave birth to his child, he does "the right thing" and marries her. In the first scene in which we see the new family, Henry forces a smile. He knows this is the life he is supposed to want. Even when things start to turn sour in the relationship and Mary leaves, Henry cares for the baby dutifully. There are few things that Henry seems to take pleasure in, but among them are checking the mail and listening to his jazz record. Henry's efforts to do either of these things result in the baby crying, so he stops. To put this in terms of traditional morality, he sacrifices his own pleasure to reduce the suffering of someone he is supposed to care for.

The way the child is depicted in the film is itself further evidence of Henry's unhappiness. As mentioned earlier, the child more closely resembles a monster than a human child. Since humans do not give birth to living things that look anything like this, it is reasonable to see the depiction of the child as a visual metaphor. Since we always see the child after Henry or Mary look at it, his appearance seems to be a metaphor for the way Henry (and possibly Mary) feel about it—as a disgusting creature, not as the little bundle of joy they had been taught to expect. Here we see vividly that, though Henry has blindly accepted the mainstream value structure of his culture, he is unable to relate to that value system in the ways he knows he is "supposed" to. He knows he should see his child as having positive value, but instead, when he looks at the child, he sees only a monster.[7]

This tension between what Henry feels and what he was taught he ought to feel causes him to give up on his search for happiness within the framework of traditional morality. He begins to look instead for happiness in ways that are impermissible according to the traditional morality under which he lives. He fantasizes that his life is different in fairly stereotypical ways for men in the modern age. A prime example of this is that he either dreams or fantasizes (it is ambiguous) about having sex with his neighbor. These attempts to reject traditional morality still are easily understood in terms of the paradigm of that ethic. Henry is not getting what he feels he deserves from life. So, much in the way a child does, he flouts the rule out of dissatisfaction (like a kid kicking his time-out chair). Henry does not go as far as to reject the traditional morality at this point; if he did, he would not feel the need to lash out—he would just do what he wants to do. In other words, he would just leave the marriage (continuing the time-out analogy, there is a certain point where a child will reject the concept of time-out and just walk away).[8]

So, how do all of the strange scenes fit in? Let's take them one at a time. As I mentioned above, the film opens with a man pulling some levers, and it closes with this man not being able to return one of the switches to its original position. In this interpretation, the man is a metaphor for Henry. The scene is meant to show that at the start of the film he is going along in his life in a mechanized, predictable way. At the close of the film, however, his actions have changed him so much that he cannot return to the way things were, even if he might want to (thus, the man can't return the lever to its original spot). One reason to think this interpretation is reasonable, if not correct, is that before the camera pushes into the planet to show us the man, an image of Henry's head is superimposed over the planet. The head then moves offscreen, allowing the camera to move onto the planet. This gives us the impression that the planet is inside Henry's head.

What do we make of the woman in the radiator? It is important to note the similarities between her and Henry. They are both shy and awkward. She struggles to make eye contact with the camera, looking sheepishly off to the side. She is also funny-looking, but not repulsive. While with Henry, what is strange about his looks is his enormous hair, the woman in the radiator has distorted cheeks. The primary difference between them is that she is happy.

She is almost always smiling. She sings a song to Henry composed of just two different, repeated lines: "In heaven everything is fine" and "you've got a good thing and I've got mine." Given the relevant similarities and differences between Henry and the woman, I think she too is supposed to be a stand-in for Henry, to enable him to imagine how things could be different for him. This first time we see her, Henry is just reflecting on the fact that you can have the type of eccentricities that he has and yet actually be happy.

As the film nears its climax, we encounter two fantasy scenes (or one scene that is interrupted for a time) that serve as an allegory for Henry's realization that his previous conception of morality, the traditional conception, is illegitimate. Given the importance of this scene, I explain it in some detail. It begins with another visit to the woman in the radiator. She is once again dancing across the screen. As she does this, creatures that look very similar to Henry's child fall from the ceiling. These creatures are getting in her way, making it hard to dance (something she clearly enjoys, as it makes her smile). This gets bad enough that she finally must either stop dancing or step on the creatures, and at this point she chooses to stomp on one. She continues to stomp on them as she dances across the stage. This scene is interrupted for a time, and when we return, Henry is on the stage with the woman in the radiator. He looks at her, appearing somehow scared and intrigued at the same time. They touch hands, there is a bright light, and then the woman is gone. We see the creatures that the woman in the radiator stepped on blowing across the floor. Henry is scared and attempts to hide to the side of the scene. In watching this, his head comes off, revealing a head that looks like a large version of his child's head. Henry's disembodied head falls through the floor and lands on the street outside. It is picked up by a young boy who brings it to an office. In this office, a man takes the head from the boy and gives it to a machinist. The machinist drills a hole in Henry's decapitated head, puts a cylinder of brain matter in his machine, and turns it on. The machine slices the tube and fixes the brain matter on the end of pencils. After a time, the machinist turns the machine off and tests one of the new erasers. It works, and he wipes eraser dust off the table.

It is at this point that Henry finally comes around to realize that traditional morality is completely bankrupt. We already know that the woman in the radiator is a surrogate for Henry. She is like him in relevant ways, but she is happy. Henry watches her destroy the things that get in the way of her happiness. At first, this thought repels Henry. This is why the scene breaks, and why he hides when he sees the dead creatures after he returns to the fantasy. His head coming off and its replacement with the enlarged version of the monstrous baby head is supposed to tell us that the disgust he felt about the child he now feels about himself. His feelings are further clarified by how things play out at the eraser machine. We see that Henry thinks all of the thoughts, beliefs, and desires he previously had are worthless. Nothing in his head was going to leave a mark on the world. Henry, as we have known him to this point, was completely disposable, and he finally realizes this.

Returning from this fantasy, Henry realizes he does not have to do things he doesn't want to do; he, and no one else, has the power to decide what he does. Because of this, Henry goes to his dresser, gets a pair of scissors, and stabs his child repeatedly, thus taking a first, violent step in rejecting traditional morality. As the child bleeds to death, we see an explosion on the planet from the start of the film. This appears to cause eraser dust to be expelled from Henry's head, showing us that the last of the traditional morality is gone from his thoughts. There is a cut to show that the man with the levers cannot throw the switch back to its starting position, and with this scene we see that Henry can never go back. Everything goes white, and we see Henry embracing the woman from the radiator. Finally, for Henry, it seems everything is fine.

The Philosophy of *Eraserhead*

While this interpretation of the film meets the criteria specified above for a successful interpretation, the ideas and themes I have identified are not new ones. We can see this interpretation as fitting in a more general philosophical tradition of critiquing and rejecting the assumptions made by most writing on ethics. In the following subsections, I explain the three major views of that tradition—*nihilism, existentialism,* and the moral framework of Ludwig Wittgenstein—and I explain how these philosophies relate to *Eraserhead.*

TWILIGHT OF THE TRADITIONAL: HENRY AS NIHILIST

The first philosophical doctrine we will look at is nihilism. *Nihilism* is the term used to refer to the ethical theory espoused by Friedrich Nietzsche (1844–1900) and those that built from his arguments. Like all three of the views we look at in these subsections, Nietzsche rejects traditional morality. His reason for doing this concerns problems he sees with the assumptions that underpin traditional morality. In this subsection, I focus on the most significant one, namely, the belief that there are essential similarities between all humans and that the strong should be subjugated in favor of the weak. These issues are obviously related, and as you might expect, the critique of them is related as well. Nietzsche, while recognizing that there are similarities between all people, points out that there are also essential dissimilarities, which often go undiscussed. These dissimilarities pertain to the conditions under which different people flourish, or become better people. It is true that many people, maybe even most people, do very well under the traditional morality in becoming all that they can be. Others, however, do not. Others require lives that present more reasonable challenges for them. For instance, some people are much smarter than others, and the restrictions of traditional morality prevent them from using this intellect to its fullest extent. In *Twilight of the Idols,* Nietzsche uses an analogy with diet: "The worthy Italian thought his diet was the *cause* of his long life, whereas the precondition for a long life, the extraordinary slowness of his metabolism, the consumption of so little, was the cause of his slender diet. He was not free to eat little *or* much; his frugality was not a matter of free will: he became sick when he ate more. But whoever is not a carp not only does well to eat properly, but needs to." In other words, some people have faster metabolisms than others, and if they are to eat the same diet as people with a slower metabolism, that diet will be bad for them.[9]

If his claims about different types of people flourishing in different ways is true, this calls into question the claim that some need to subjugate themselves for the betterment of other people of a different type. There is no objective reason that can be given, according to Nietzsche. The answer can't be that it needs to be this way so that the people who will flourish under the traditional ethic do so, since calling for everyone to follow that morality will necessarily result in the higher type of people failing to flourish. In *Beyond Good and Evil,* Nietzsche puts it this way: "The question is always who *he* is, and who the *other* person is. . . . Every unegoistic morality that takes itself for unconditional and addresses itself to all does not only sin against taste: it is a provocation to sins of omission, one *more* seduction under the mask of philanthropy—and precisely a seduction and injury for the higher, rarer, privileged."[10]

The rejection of traditional morality is not the end of the story for Nietzsche's nihilism, however. You have to fill the gap left when you reject traditional morality by replacing it with a new morality in order to be a nihilist. This morality has to be fitted to the individual in the same way diets are, and so there is very little for him to say generally about morality. That said, when Nietzsche does go into more specifics, he focuses on what he calls *higher men*. Higher men are the people that are repressed under the constraints of traditional morality. Nietzsche's claims about higher men can be understood in terms of five character traits. These men are solitary, pursue a "unifying project," are healthy, life-affirming, and practice self-reliance.[11]

So, how does the film fit in with Nietzsche's nihilism? Most important, it suggests that Henry has reached the first step in Nietzsche's project; he has come to realize that he had been adhering to an illegitimate morality. As I stated above, this realization comes to Henry in the eraserhead scene. With this realization comes the knowledge that he no longer has to live a life that he finds repressing and constraining. This then leads Henry to kill his child, and he feels justified in doing so since it is the embodiment of all the burdens placed on him by traditional morality. That said, it is important to point out that Henry is not a nihilist in the full sense. Henry meets some of the criteria for a higher man, but not all. He is solitary, healthy, and self-reliant, but he has no unifying project to speak of, and it is ambiguous whether he is life-affirming (since it is left unclear whether Henry has taken his own life).

INTERPRETATION AND NOTHINGNESS: HENRY AS EXISTENTIALIST

As does nihilism, existentialism rejects the framework of traditional ethics, but it does so for different reasons. Existentialism is the name of the moral philosophy of Jean-Paul Sartre (1905–1980), and the anthem associated with it is "existence precedes essence."[12] Understanding what this claim means requires understanding the philosophical tradition Sartre sees himself as opposing. Thomas Aquinas (1225–1274), influenced by the writings of Aristotle (384–322 BC) as well as his own theological beliefs, held that essence came first, and then existence. By this, Aquinas meant that people are born with an innate, fixed essence, placed in them by God. Even as many moved away from a religious conception of the world, the belief that humanity has an innate essence persisted in the claim that we are essentially rational animals. In reversing the order of essence and existence, Sartre is firmly rejecting the prevailing view of human nature. He tells us that humans determine their own essence, and this means deciding what is right and wrong for ourselves.[13]

Since moral rules are invented by humans, there is no reason one should just follow the rules that have been set down by people who came before. You might object, well, if you can stipulate that you need to make up the rules for yourself, I can just stipulate the opposite—that you must follow these rules. Here Sartre points to a general flaw with any theory of morality, even one as unsophisticated as the traditional morality. The flaw is that these theories often fail to give a concrete answer to particular moral questions. Sartre uses the example of a young student who came to him with a question of whether or not to enter World War II. The student, whose brother had already died in the war, felt that he had a duty to join the French resistance and fight against the Nazi occupation of France. But at the same time, he felt he had a duty to take care of his aged mother, something he could not do if he was fighting. Either way, he felt as if he would be abandoning some duty. According to Christianity, the traditional morality to which Sartre is responding, we should "be charitable, love your neighbor and take the more rugged path."[14] The problem now becomes, who should the young man love like a neighbor: the other soldiers in the resistance or his mother? There seems to be no answer. The same concern arises when you consider a principle like "do no harm." If the student goes to war, he is abandoning his mother and doing harm to her. If he stays with her, he will be abandoning the other soldiers, and again doing harm. Sartre's advice to the student is to do what he, himself, feels is right. The reason this is his advice is that no matter which choice Sartre makes, the student will not be deciding his essence for himself; Sartre will be doing it for him. The same holds when anyone tries to follow any standard for what "good people" generally do. If you act based on other people's standards, or what others tell you to do, you necessarily fail to acknowledge your power to ascribe value yourself. Sartre calls this being *inauthentic*. You are being inauthentic by believing that your essence is what someone tells you it is, rather than what you decide. According to existentialism, you must think and make choices for yourself. For those to be good choices, you must recognize that you are the only person who can be responsible for who you are. When this happens, you are being *authentic*.[15]

How does the film fit in with the existentialism of Sartre? As stated above, the culmination of the titular scene leaves Henry aware of the futility of just doing what he has been told is right. With the traditional morality rejected, Henry has no system for determining what he ought to do, and this leaves him in a state of shock (as we can see on his face). Henry then sits down and appears to be thinking about what to do. An existentialist will argue that what Henry is doing when he is thinking is deciding for the first time in his life what *he* cares about, and what *he* finds important, rather than just responding to what he thinks he is supposed to care about. He then gets up deliberately, gets the scissors, and stabs the child. He thought about what he wanted and then he acted on those desires. In the language of Sartre, Henry is acting authentically for the first time in his life.

LYNCHIAN INVESTIGATIONS: HENRY AS WITTGENSTEINIAN

Most people familiar with Ludwig Wittgenstein (1889–1951) know him as a philosopher of language, but his claims about the way language works leads to an understanding of ethics in keeping with both nihilism and existentialism. According to Wittgenstein, concepts like good, right, and just, in the way that they are normally understood in moral reasoning, are incoherent. For Wittgenstein, the meanings of all words are ambiguous. He uses the case of games to make this point. How do you define a game? Is it a competition between two or more players? No, because solitaire is a game with only one player. Are there necessarily winners and losers? No, because ring-around-the-roses is a game with no win/loss conditions. Some games involve physical activity and props, while others can be played while sitting perfectly still. Some are fun, others boring or even scary (think about Russian roulette). There is no rigid definition of "game" that includes all things we want to recognize as games, but excludes all that we do not want to call "games." Yet, we all think we know what a game is. The criteria might differ from person to person, but that's just the way it is, according to Wittgenstein. All definitions are stipulative, and somewhat arbitrary. We want our lists to more or less match up, otherwise it will be difficult to communicate, so we assign definitions that the majority of people can agree to, but there is nothing magic or "true" about the definitions we assign—we could have decided to assign a different meaning to the word "game," or to any word, for that matter.[16]

According to Wittgenstein, the same goes for the word "good." What makes something a good chair is that it meets some preestablished standard for what a chair ought to be. Likewise, when we say a person is a good pianist, what we mean is that this person is able to play musical numbers of a certain difficulty with a certain level of proficiency. It is important to understand that, for Wittgenstein, these standards are arbitrary—we just decide on them, and we can have multiple different arbitrary standards. This is why some fan of classical music (even scholars of the genre) will make the claim that someone like Thelonious Monk (a jazz pianist) is actually not a good piano player. Why? The way jazz pianists play the piano is radically different from the way classical piano is played. You run into the same situation with paintings. In his time, people thought Vincent van Gogh was a terrible painter, and the reason was they did not yet have the evaluative standard for good painting that we now accept.[17]

This all may sound like common sense. However, if you make these types of claims about morality, you quickly find that people become hostile. Morality, what is good, is not supposed to be relative to some arbitrary standard. It is supposed to be absolute—this is why people feel they can make claims about how you ought to behave. If you told Monk he plays the piano wrong and that he ought to play differently, he would, and reasonably should, just ignore you. But if you are telling him he is acting wrong in the moral sense, he can't dismiss you in the same way. We want to believe this about morality. We want to believe that it is true and unchanging and not at all arbitrary. The problem is that there is nothing to make the word "good" absolute, according to Wittgenstein's account of language. The meaning of the word is relative to an arbitrary standard.

So, how does Lynch's story fall in line with the moral writing of Wittgenstein? A Wittgensteinian will take a slightly different view of the ambiguous ending of the film. Rather than seeing Henry as adopting some new moral framework after rejecting the traditional morality, he might be seen as acting at the end of the film in recognition of the futility of moral discourse. He has been trying to conform to a standard that doesn't seem right to him because he was told it was true, but he now realizes that moral claims are only true relative to a context. His actions at the end of the film can be seen as actualizing what he thought the good or right thing to do was all along. Most interesting, this variant interpretation of the ending makes complete sense with the song sung by the woman in the radiator. She can be seen as reaffirming Wittgenstein's point about the arbitrary nature of any definition of "good." "You've got a good thing and I've got mine," and there is no way to impartially find one way to be better than the other.

It should now be clear that the interpretation of *Eraserhead* I have presented can be seen as a part of a tradition within these moral theories. All three theories—nihilism, existentialism, and Wittgensteinian morality—reject the traditional morality, and this is the message of the film. The theories then go one step further than the film and provide accounts for how people should make decisions without traditional morality in place. Since we don't have access to Henry's thoughts, and since he says very little in the film, it is impossible to get very specific about why Henry rejects traditional morality or what he, and by extension Lynch, thinks it ought to be replaced with (if anything). Because of this, each of the three schools of thought can give an interpretation of the film that is consistent with their reasons for rejecting traditional morality, but none of them is better than the others. Given the lack of reasons from Henry, it makes sense to make the more modest claim that the film's meaning simply falls within the same tradition as the three theories.

Notes

I would like to thank Ruth Tallman for her helpful comments on several drafts of this paper.

1. Metaphors can be effective means of conveying complex ideas because so much meaning can be relayed in a very short time through the use of a powerful image. Without the use of the brick-wall metaphor, Lynch would have needed to get Henry's feeling of being trapped across to us through the addition of a whole new piece of dialogue, soliloquy, or narrative overlay. Instead, we gain that information cleanly and neatly, with no dialogue at all.

2. The question of whether there are other standards for judging the quality of an interpretation of a film is a debate for another time and place. Many philosophers and film critics want to give special consideration to claims artists make about their own work while others (myself included) do not. The success condition I have identified is one that will most likely be accepted by everyone in this ongoing debate, however.

3. This interpretation is expressed in the review of the film by Bill Gibron, www .popmatters.com/pm/review/eraserhead.

4. The best-formulated version of this interpretation I have found is given by Ray Wolfe in his paper, "Ray Wolfe's Online Guide to *Eraserhead*," www.geocities .com/~mikehartmann/papers/wolfe.html.

5. This interpretation is best put by Cynthia Freeland in her article "Eraserhead" (see Freeland, *The Naked and the Undead: Evil and the Appeal of Horror* [Boulder, Colo.: Westview Press, 2001]).

6. Some readers might think that Henry does not live in a society with the same traditional morality as I have suggested he does. There are two relevant points to be made in response to this. First, in an interview ("A Fish in the Percolator") with *Philadelphia Weekly* on March 14, 2001, Lynch says that Henry is "living under the influence of those things that existed for me in Philadelphia." This strongly suggests that Henry is struggling with Judeo-Christian morality. Second, even if Henry did live in a society with a different traditional morality, this would not affect the interpretation I am giving past there being a different code of conduct that he would be rejecting.

7. It is noteworthy that Mary doesn't really have a name. Her last name is just a variable X, and Mary is really just the relation he has to the woman: he marries Mary.

8. What is funny and sad about this fantasy is that he needs a pretense for the sex

fantasy. It isn't just the case that the neighbor finds him desirable. Instead, she locks herself out of her apartment too late to call to be let back in. She then asks to stay at Henry's, and things just happen.

9. Friedrich Nietzsche, *Twilight of the Idols,* in *Basic Writings of Nietzsche,* trans. Walter Kaufmann (New York: Modern Library Classics, 2000), 58.

10. Friedrich Nietzsche, *Beyond Good and Evil,* in *Basic Writings of Nietzsche,* trans. Walter Kaufmann (New York: Modern Library Classics, 2000), 221.

11. Nietzsche gives three examples of such individuals: Goethe, Beethoven, and himself. Throughout his writings, Nietzsche extols the virtues of these three men, but there is no single passage or small collection of passages where Nietzsche plainly describes higher men. To come to a reasonable description of these men, one needs to look at all of his writings and make some inferences. The clearest and most academically rigorous account of higher men can be found in Brian Leiter, *Nietzsche on Morality* (London: Routledge, 2002), 116–22.

12. Jean-Paul Sartre, "Existentialism Is a Humanism," in *Basic Writings of Existentialism,* ed. Gordon Marino (New York: Modern Library, 2004), 331.

13. Thomas Aquinas, *Summa Theologiae,* II–II q. 64 a. 7.

14. Sartre, "Existentialism Is a Humanism," 330–31.

15. Jean-Paul Sartre, *Being and Nothingness,* trans. Hazel Barnes (New York: Routledge, 1958), 222.

16. Ludwig Wittgenstein, *The Philosophical Investigations: The German Text with a Revised English Translation, 50th Anniversary Commemorative Edition,* trans. G. E. M. Anscombe (Oxford: Blackwell, 2001), Remarks 68–76.

17. Ibid., Remarks 76–77.

THE MONSTER WITHIN

Alienation and Social Conformity in *The Elephant Man*

Shai Biderman and Assaf Tabeka

In the TV sitcom *Seinfeld* episode "The Pick" (season 4, episode 13), Jerry Seinfeld, the stand-up comedian whose observations on the minutiae of the mundane provide the essence of the show, is caught in his car picking his nose in a traffic jam. More exactly, he *appears* to be picking his nose from the external perspective of the passenger in the car next to him. Unfortunately, that passenger happens to be a model friend whom Seinfeld is trying to impress. When Seinfeld realizes the misconception, he chases the model into the offices of Calvin Klein in order to plead his case. She, of course, is reluctant to accept any excuses. In her eyes, Seinfeld has cut himself off from normative (polite) society by doing something as atrocious as picking his nose in public. She is unwilling to accept that appearances might have been deceiving, and that Seinfeld was actually scratching his upper lip. In her mind, he is forever condemned, and accordingly should be cast out from the social circle. In his (comic) despair, and after an Upper West Side "mob" forces him into the elevator of the Calvin Klein building, he turns to the crowd, spreads his arms, and, with the pathos usually reserved for cinematic parody, states: "I am not an animal!"

Jerry's cry, an obvious parody, offers comic homage to the *J'accuse* of the character John Merrick (John Hurt), the socially outcast protagonist of David Lynch's *The Elephant Man* (1980). Loosely based on the true story of the Englishman Joseph Carey Merrick (1862–1890), the character John Merrick is physically deformed. His deformities and physical limitations are so severe that it is difficult at first to see the human form in him, hence the unflattering nickname "the Elephant Man." We first meet Merrick through the eyes of Dr. Frederick Treves (Anthony Hopkins), a sensible young London physician, in the darkest corner of a local carnival, the coming attraction of a despicable freak show. Locked in a cage, Merrick is being held and treated as an animal. Because of his physical deformities, we initially view his human capacities as limited or nonexistent: he doesn't speak (but only howls); he cannot stand straight or walk properly; he is disfigured; and, most important, as a result, he appears to be a mute imbecile, a creature lacking any human capacities, either cognitive or mental. And so, for all purposes, he appears to be incapable of exercising his humanity. The crowd that visits the circus is fascinated (and horrified) by the site of his monstrosity, and the cruel circus owner, Bytes (Freddie Jones), exploits him by inducing such emotional responses from the crowd.

Our first impression of Merrick is thus one of a circus freak. An outcast of human society, Merrick is perceived as a grotesque curiosity, and he awaits a life no different from that of a circus animal. His luck seems to change, however, when Dr. Treves takes him out of the show and places him in Treves's hospital in order to study his condition. Like the patrons of the circus show, Treves is fascinated with Merrick, albeit for a different reason. Treves sees Merrick from a second social viewpoint: namely, as a guinea pig, or an object of scientific observation. Moved by a certain measure of compassion, but mostly motivated by his scientific curiosity, the doctor asks that he be given the opportunity to examine Merrick as a scientific anomaly. He takes Merrick under his care and brings him to a hospital for further examination and research. Despite the change of scene, Merrick is still a freak-show attraction, albeit on an intellectual and medical scale. Although Treves treats Merrick kindly and with compassion in the hospital, he still treats Merrick as an object of research rather than as a fellow (and equal) human being. He assumes the worst about Merrick's capacities, and therefore is amazed to learn that Merrick's capabilities are much more advanced than what meets the eye. Merrick can speak, mimic verbal behaviors, and communicate (in a rather limited way). But Treves is truly amazed when he realizes that Merrick is capable of not merely parroting the social responses of his benefactor, but also of demonstrating creativity and independence by reciting Psalm 23 in a quiet and gentle voice.

This astounding discovery gives Treves the first opportunity to overcome his first impression of Merrick. Once Treves realizes that there is a gentle human soul behind the monstrous, animal-like exterior, he can no longer treat Merrick as a mere object of scientific curiosity. However compassionate and caring Treves was toward Merrick until that point, the situation now calls for a deep shift in attitude and perception. That is, Treves adopts a third view of

Merrick: Merrick is a human being and should be treated accordingly. He might be (seriously) disadvantaged, but he deserves to be treated as equal. This equal treatment is the focal point of the Merrick story. Throughout the film, he undergoes a transformation from an object of repulsion and vulgar curiosity (due to his deformities) to a subject of equal capacities and rights (despite his deformities). It takes a distinct effort on Treves's part to overcome the impression of Merrick's external appearance and see that, under the nonhuman externality, hides the cognitive essence of a human soul. As the film progresses, we realize that this transformation, which was hard enough for Treves, a medical doctor, to achieve, is even harder for the rest of society. The hospital administrators, the mob as well as the members of high society, find it exceptionally difficult to accept Merrick as an equal. His appearance is always a deterrent, constantly preventing him from being fully and equally accepted into the company of humankind. Nevertheless, a new period in Merrick's life now seems to begin. As rumors about the gentleness and unique abilities of this outrageous-looking creature begin to circulate, high society becomes fascinated with Merrick. He meets and befriends the celebrated actress Madge Kendal (Anne Bancroft), attends tea parties, engages in socially sophisticated events (concerts), and is even acknowledged by Queen Victoria. However, despite this celebrity status, viewers are forced to wonder whether this newfound fame is not just more of the same old thing, that is, whether Merrick is still being observed as an oddity by the curious. While compassion now replaces brutality, and admiration replaces contempt, physicians still keep poking him, and the crowd (whether it's made up of the vulgar masses or high society) still tries to sneak a peek at the freak. Even when Merrick's celebrity status skyrockets and his visit to the opera is greeted with a standing ovation, we still see him as a monstrous freak, constantly falling back to judging him for his inhuman appearance. In other words, despite Treves's efforts, Merrick is still (and might always be) a freak—an outsider, a creature whose membership into humanity will never be accepted. He is forever an object of the sometimes condescending, sometimes fearful, always estranging, look: the look of detestation, curiosity, rejection, or compassion. Whether he is the horror show of the mob or the dancing monkey of the nobility, Merrick is always the object of an unequal look. His look, one might say, determines the way society looks at him.

In this essay, we examine this grim and seemingly unavoidable conclusion. Is Merrick really doomed to be an outcast from society? What can we philosophically learn about the nature and essence of the social order from Merrick's case? What is Lynch trying to say about the nature of the human being, the nature of society, and the relation between these two natures in his adaptation of the real-life story of Joseph Carey Merrick? We discuss and analyze the question of social conformity through Merrick's story, echoing his cry not to be considered as an animal, but as a man, a human being. We show how Lynch, while polishing his unique cinematic style, presents this conclusion as the underlying theme of his adaptation to the Merrick story, and so portrays a grim picture of the social order, with no happy end in sight. To help us understand this Lynchian presentation of social conformity and alienation, we follow Merrick's struggle to gain social acceptance and recognition, both as a human being and as a member of society.

I Am (Not) a (Social) Animal: Between Socialization and Alienation

Merrick's adventures through the looking glass of social conformity make the latter the focal point of the film. In other words, in the heart of the cinematic story of Merrick's misfortunes we find the story of the social order and of socialization. What is the social order? What makes a society, or a social way of life, so distinctively unique? Intuitively, one can explain the term *society* by alluding to a certain kind of cooperation between people, and to some form of order or division of labor. People in a society are bonded together in some way. They are bound by some form of collegiality, and by certain awareness to their equals. In short, the idea of society, or socialization, aims to establish and preserve the unity and cohesiveness of humanity, and to improve and elicit communication and productivity among the members of the social group.[1]

Lynch's *The Elephant Man* is undoubtedly a social film. As much as it is a film about the struggles of the individual Merrick, it is a film about social acceptance and rejection, and, as such, a film that indeed stands as a mirror in the face of society (and a black-and-white mirror at that, cinematically), reflecting and extending society's weaknesses and dark moments. The options seem to be rather limited: one can either be fully accepted by the society (and be treated as equal), or one can be utterly rejected by society (and be treated as a freak). Between an equal member and a freak, a peer and an outcast, we find the heart of the social order. In the following paragraphs, we try to flesh out the roots and nature of this social order.[2]

The social order might be, first and foremost, a natural component of our existence. That is, to live as humans is to live in one social arrangement or another. According to this view, socialization is a defining characteristic of humans and of humanity. Although birds flock and cattle herd, humanity conjoins together for a different reason and in a different way, which is more natural and certainly fundamental to human existence. An early promoter of this view is Aristotle (384–322 BCE), who famously proclaimed that "man is by nature a political animal." In other words, the human being is essentially a social animal. But there is more to that, according to Aristotle. In a later passage, he adds: "it is evident that a city is a natural production, and that man is naturally a political animal, and that whosoever is naturally and not accidentally unfit for society, must be either inferior or superior to man." That is to say, man is indeed a social animal, and this nature has two sides to it. On one side, man strives for cooperation and communication, for inclusion and "togetherness"; but on the other side, this same striving is used to separate and exclude the nonhumans from the order of socialized humanity. That is to say, the superiors and the inferiors, the "gods" and the "monsters," are excluded from the social game because their independent nature is "naturally and not accidentally unfit for society."[3]

But is it really the case that there is an unchangeable, fundamental nature that makes us socialize and exclude from our human society those who, by nature, cannot be socialized? Modern philosophers—such as Thomas Hobbes (1588–1679) and Jean-Jacques Rousseau (1712–1778)—have tried, in various ways, to undermine this assumption. They all promoted one or another version of a political philosophy called *contractarianism,* which stands for an opposing theory to that of Aristotle. According to contractarianism, man is not a political animal by nature, but is born free from any social constraints. In this natural disposition, we fundamentally prefer our individual freedom to membership into society. People in such a state are equally free and equally entitled to any and every resource in nature. They are also equally fragile and constantly prepared to hurt each other in order to get what they want. Since no man is strong enough to maintain himself for a long time in such a state of war, the need for another arrangement arises, and the social contract is born. The social agreement is, therefore, an imminent result of the human's otherwise unsocial nature. The social state is forced upon humanity like chains. As Rousseau notes: "man is born free and is everywhere in chains." In short, man is not a political animal by nature, but is forced into society in order to survive.[4]

Whether by nature or by force, the human's affinity to the social domain appears to be one of its salient characteristics. This seems, on face value, to be a positive and adaptive characteristic of humankind. In his book *I and Thou*, the philosopher Martin Buber (1878–1965) argues that this affinity is actually the only way by which we define and affirm ourselves and each other. According to Buber, the mere notion of selfhood and self-perception (that each of us claims to have) emerges only through encountering and interacting with others. Furthermore, the very nature of this emerged selfhood depends on the quality of the relationship with the other. Buber insists that the first-person perception of one's selfhood (encapsulated in the pronoun "I") does not and cannot exist independently of the others it addresses (signified with the pronoun "Thou"). He maintains "there is no 'I' taken in itself, but only the 'I' of the primary word *I-Thou*." For Buber, the "I-Thou" designates a relationship between two "I"s, two subjects, so that they are not challenging or struggling against one another; rather there is a mutual and equal encounter. This mutual encounter between the "I" and the "Other" affects and affirms them both. The reciprocal relation between them is the condition (and justification) of the social domain.[5]

We need society in order to be, to define ourselves, and to survive. However, there seems to be a downside to this disposition. Whereas we do seem to seek the company of others, we can nevertheless be quite fastidious in picking those with whom we wish to socialize. In other words, whenever we join forces and conjoin to form a society, we almost instantly reject another from the same enterprise. While we define ourselves vis-à-vis the "Other" that we pick, we also, and with the same intensity, define ourselves negatively vis-à-vis the "Other" that we cast aside. The desire for social conformity requires us to raise a flag in unity and to cast aside those who undermine (or fall short) of this unity.

In the early twentieth century, Sigmund Freud (1856–1939) claims that this, in a nutshell, is the predicament of the human condition. Freud holds that the cohesiveness of human society results from its members identifying with one another by putting a common idealized figure in the center of the social circle. Likewise, Freud asserts that this cohesiveness depends on society projecting its own hostility and hatred on those who are left outside the social circle. Those who are cast aside—the nonconformists of any kind (other individuals, other families, other nations, races, or groups)—are denigrated or demonized for no other reason than to strengthen and shape the unity of the social group. This unity is all-encompassing, as it is also the basis of the group's morality, its values and norms. It is the totem around which the group defines its identity and validates the set of norms and values it holds. Accordingly, both the act of unification and the act of casting aside (or rejection) are heavily influenced by this multilayered meaning of the social unity. In other words, people will tend to see their companions and other group members not only as equal but actually as superior to those who do not belong to the group. The membership in "our" society entails that "we" are better than "them." Freud maintains that this pattern of "good us" versus "bad them" is the underlying force that underpins the notion of self-identity of the group members, as it is integral to group cohesion.[6]

Whether it's Aristotle, the modern contractarians, Buber, or Freud, the idea of a social structure explains both the cohesion and camaraderie between fellow men and, at the same time, the constant bickering and animosity among members of the human species. Between friends and foes, members and outcasts, superiors and inferiors, the social domain defines and shapes what can otherwise be referred to as the human condition. The key term that springs out from this condition is *alienation*. Alienation is a prominent term that captures and encapsulates the various social and psychological disruptions that form the shaky and controversial fabric of human existence. Also incorporated in terms like *estrangement* or *externalization*, the feeling of alienation is innately embedded in the social structure and, accordingly, in the nature of human existence. One can typically articulate three directions of alienation or, better yet, the triple role alienation plays in the construction of the social fabric.

First, there is the alienation "horizontally" directed toward other human beings. This role of alienation is to separate me, the "I," from everyone and everything that is not "me." By alienating myself from everyone else, I separate myself from a world of strangers, allowing myself to be distinctively defined and articulated for who I am and what I am. This separation is a precondition that later allows (and maybe even necessitates) the coming together of humankind. In other words, alienating the stranger allows one to first define himself on his own, in order to then be an adequate candidate for socialization and cohesion. This sort of alienation is embedded in the mere existence of a thinking mind in the world, and is, as said, a precondition for any attempt of socialization or rejection. This type underlies Buber's idea of "I-Thou," as well as the idea of the free spirit and its evolution in the writings of G. W. F. Hegel (1770–1831). The latter goes as far as to suggest that any process of individualization has to be, by nature, intermediated by a dividing moment, namely, by a moment of pure alienation (from everything and everyone), in order for the individual to emerge later as a one-man-unity once the alienation is overcome.[7] This moment of division underscores the objectification of the individual insofar as it pinpoints the need to objectify oneself first in order to re-create oneself as a subject when the process of individuation is done. The objectifying relationship (the internal relationship within one's spirit or the external relationship between individuals and society) is therefore the immense tension between subjects and objects, between the active and powerful mindful spirits and the passive and powerless mindless object.[8]

The Hegelian tradition also articulates a second direction of alienation, namely, the alienation directed toward the heavens, or the alienation of the divine. In this type of alienation, we exclude from our human society that which is too perfect and omnipotent to be considered as having the imperfect human nature, and accordingly to be considered as a member of the imperfect and constrained human society. In other words, we create the heavens as different (and alienated) from us, in order to mirror our deficiency and imperfections the way they must be seen from God's eyes. Hegel claims that humans had to "invent" God as the ultimate (all-knowing, omnipotent, and benevolent) alienated "other" in order to redefine and reshape their own mortal and earthly existence again. Humans had to invent God in order to feel once more at home in the world. Deification, as well as objectification, is thus an important direction of alienation.[9]

A third type of alienation is directed downward. In this type of alienation we exclude from our human society that which is too imperfect—commonly too evil, inhuman, vicious, or immoral—to be considered as having the good, compassionate, and moral human nature. Much like the previous type, here too we alienate those whose essence is fundamentally different from ours. Demonization is the mirror image of deification, the "dark counterpart of the utterly transcendent Yahweh," to quote the contemporary Richard Kearney.[10] However, instead of creating the heavens (as a type of "positive" exclusion), we create hell as a type of "negative" difference that separates man from demons, and human being from monsters. We exclude the monsters from our human nature and, accordingly, alienate them from membership in our human community. Following the alienated god, whose alienation stands for "absolute goodness," the monster's alienation articulates and underpins "absolute evil." Evil is to be alienated, and the evil one is the alien.

Both absolutes are, by nature, essentially different from human nature, and therefore can only be subscribed by alienating them from the social realm of human existence.

The threefold typology of alienation fleshes out the centrality of this concept. Whether as a god, a stranger, or a monster, the alien embodies an important (and internal) aspect of the human social nature. The coming together of a society is bound by the constant elimination of "the other." However, more important, that same "other" is an essential counterpart in the mere construction of social identity. The "other" is the litmus test of social conformity. As a god, it articulates inspiring perfection; as a demon, it embodies the uncanny opposite; and in a human form, it stands for social sensibilities like fear, distrust, and suspicion. As Kearney surmises: "The foundational consensus needed for social coexistence is provided by a collective projection wherein some victimized outsider becomes the alleged carrier of all the aggression, guilt and violence that sets one neighbor against another within the tribe. This victimization of the scapegoat . . . enabled the internally divided society to turn away from its own internecine rivalry and focus its hatred on someone outside the tribe."[11]

In all three cases, the alien and alienation are embedded in the heart of humankind's social existence, so much so that, according to Freud, this embedding becomes the distinctive trademark of our own individual humanity. In other words, the external alienation of the "other" is but a stand-in for the real internal act of alienation. Freud writes that "the uncanny encounter with the monstrous is a revelation not of the wholly other but of a repressed otherness within the self." The alien is the "personification of the uncanny," and as such it "stands for that which has broken out of the subterranean basement or the locked closet where it has been hidden and largely forgotten." We look for the alienated other out there in the world, but it is the "monster within" that terrifies us the most.[12]

So far, our discussion unveiled the strong ties between human social nature and the concept of alienation. We have demonstrated how alienation is indicative of social life and social conformity, and how society, by nature, requires that we acknowledge and exclude "others" from our circle of social conformity. This act of alienation is the other side of the same socialization coin. One cannot do one without the other. With this in mind, we can now reexamine the cinematic character of John Merrick, and, while sympathizing with his lonely and alienated disposition, reanalyze his case as a challenge to the nature of human society.

From Monster to God, and Back: The Individuation of Merrick

Throughout the film, and in his many encounters with representatives of human society, Merrick experiences responses and reactions ranging from repulsion to compassion and from horror to sympathy; society is forced to react to the horrid appearance of Merrick's "otherness." His grotesque appearance, by way of its unfitness with otherwise human codes of normality, undermines the fabric of the social uniformity. Therefore, Merrick's alienation is forced on him. Merrick is an alien, a stranger who may not (and probably cannot) ever be considered as an equal member of human society.

Among strangers, gods, and monsters, Merrick's alienation is, most obviously, that of the third type. However, as we will demonstrate, Lynch creates a character in Merrick who embodies all three types of alienation. Merrick is presented in the film as the archetype of alienation, namely, as the paradigm of "other" interacting with the social domain. He is subjected to all kinds of looks and reflections, and so he stands for the multilayered role of alienation and for the way alienation constructs the self-reflective perception of social existence.

The film provides numerous instances that demonstrate the aptness of this conclusion. In most of the film, Merrick is considered a monster, a horrifying and repulsive circus freak who should be avoided, mocked, and look down upon. Right from the start, he is labeled a monster by Bytes, who lures customers to see his show by pointing out the monstrosity of his pet freak: "Life! . . . is full of surprises. Consider the fate of this creature's poor mother, struck down in the fourth month of her maternal condition by an elephant, a wild elephant. Struck down! . . . on an uncharted African isle. The result is plain to see . . . Ladies and gentlemen . . . The terrible . . . Elephant . . . Man." Such an introduction builds the crowd's expectations so that it is almost inevitable that they shriek in horror when they finally see Merrick. The monstrosity of Merrick is not "out there" in the world; it comes to be only when the crowd sees Merrick as a monster.

This type of interaction with the monstrous "other" is a recurring theme throughout the film. One can recall numerous instances where Merrick is treated (and is referred to) as a nonhuman "monster." The most conspicuous instance appears in the final scenes of the film. At this point, Merrick seems to have found a home in Dr. Treves's hospital. He stands in his room, looking at his reflection in the mirror (an action he has previously persistently avoided), when the mob, led by the obscene hospital night porter (Michael

Elphick), bursts into his room. Fueled by his greed, but mostly by his immense and deep detestation of the monstrous "other," the night porter drags Merrick to the window, opens the shades, and presents the horrified Merrick to the crowd gathering outside his room. The image of the deformed Merrick, which moments earlier was the pleasing mirror of Merrick's resolution and reconciliation with himself, becomes once again the vulgar and crowd-pleasing image of "the monster." Ironically, it is Merrick who is utterly terrified by the ordeal, and not the crowd, which the image of "the beast" seems to make more and more ecstatic. The crowd then breaks into Merrick's room, demanding to see more of the freak. Merrick is attacked, mocked, and toyed with. In the heat of the mayhem, Bytes, the old circus owner, joins in, insisting that his star freak rejoin his life in the circus. He kidnaps Merrick, leaving behind only the shattered room (and the tattered picture of Merrick's mother).

The attack on Merrick's room and his kidnapping is a key scene in the film. Lynch presents this scene in a way that emphasizes the dubious nature of the alienated monstrosity. Throughout the scene, it is Merrick who is taken to be the monstrous freak; however, the real monster in this scene is none other than the crowd itself. It is the crowd that acts like a beastly herd, brutally and vulgarly victimizing and torturing the poor Merrick. The viewers are forced to acknowledge this horrifying symmetry when Dr. Treves confronts the night porter in the morning following the attack, after noticing that Merrick is gone:

TREVES: Where is he? Where is Mr. Merrick?

NIGHT PORTER: I . . . I don't know what you mean, Sir.

TREVES: Don't lie to me. I know all about it. You were seen. Where did you take him?

NIGHT PORTER: Take him? Now wait . . . I didn't take him anywhere. We were just having some fun. We didn't hurt him . . . just having a laugh, that's all.

TREVES: HE'S GONE!

NIGHT PORTER: When I left him, he was in his bed, safe and sound.

TREVES: You Bastard! You tortured him. You tortured him, you bastard. Where is he?

NIGHT PORTER: You're not listening to me!! I ain't done nothing wrong. People pay to see your monster, Mr. Treves. I just take the money.

TREVES: You're the monster! You're the freak! Get out! You're finished!

The real monster, to echo the Freudian view, is the monster within. Merrick is only the externalization (and probably the repression) of the alienated monster. Lynch suggests that the true monstrosity lurks in the shadows of each decent member of society and, accordingly, in the heart of the social order itself. We, the members of society, are the monsters. However, failing to acknowledge our horrid nature, we pick on the weak and the deformed who are different from us, labeling our monstrosity in their alienation.

Thus far we have discussed the ways Merrick is portrayed as a monstrous alien. However, Lynch's depiction of Merrick exceeds this type of alienation and also embodies other types, most notably the type of alienation via deification. Three predominant instances support this claim. The first significant mentioning of the deity is also a cathartic moment for Merrick. At this moment, to the great astonishment of Dr. Treves, Merrick reveals himself to be an articulate, expressive, and gentle soul (instead of the mute imbecile he was taken to be). This transformation occurs when Merrick quotes Psalm 23. The significance of this biblical citation is uncontested. Theologically, this hymn presents one of the clearest pictures of God's perfection and, at the same time, a clear picture of humankind's deficiency. The hymn opens with the famous acknowledgment of the human being's mortality. We find our salvation in the guiding and protective existence of God when we embrace our own imperfections: "Even though I walk through the valley of the shadow of death, I will fear no evil, for Thou art with me." The divine intervention in our earthly existence is that of compassion and redemption: "Surely goodness and loving-kindness shall follow me all the days of my life, and I shall dwell in the house of the Lord forever." The divine, as presented here, is the superior "other," whose light is the guiding source of our mortal existence.

It is obvious why Lynch uses this particular citation when he attempts to elevate Merrick from his monstrous alienation. The deified "other," as we already suggested, is but the mirror image of the demonized "other"; God and the monster are the two halves of the same coin of alienation. With this quote, Merrick can no longer be perceived merely as a monster since he now partakes (at least in a symbolic way) in the idea of the divine.

A second example of divine alienation can be seen in Merrick's pastime activity. Throughout the film, Merrick is building a masterwork of detail and shading, a miniature model of St. Philip's Cathedral. Seeing only the main spire of the cathedral from his bedroom window, Merrick is forced to actively partake in the creation of the miniature, relying on his creativity and imagination to complete the work. In other words, Merrick has to create—literally and figuratively—the house of God in order to "feel at home" in it. And though it is later smashed to the ground by the mob that bursts into his room, the cathedral, along with the biblical citation, represent Merrick's alienation vis-à-vis his "divine" superiority.

The final example of Merrick's deification lies in his one-time celebrity status. After recuperating from his social mistreatment, he is embraced by the social elite, most notably by Mrs. Kendal, a famous stage actress. Much like his previous decision to build a miniature model of a cathedral, the theatrical settings also engage the imagination and, as such, have a symbolic meaning. Mrs. Kendal articulates this significance when she realizes that Merrick has never been to the theater. Trying to convey the nature of the theatrical experience, she says to Merrick: "The theater is the shrine of the imagination, where one may suspend disbelief and travel anywhere in the world, to any time you desire. You may look over the shoulders of kings, unobserved, battle with ruthless tyrants, and marry the beautiful princess, all in the space of a few hours. Onstage you may be whoever you wish to be, do anything you please, and always, always live happily ever after. The theater is all the brightest and best things of the world, Mr. Merrick. It is lights and music, gaiety and joy. It's . . . well, it's romance." This sensitive and creative depiction of the nature of the theatrical experience is, at the same time, a metaphysical depiction of the height of human inspiration. In other words, a "shrine of [human] imagination" is a label that can be aptly used to tag the kind of relationship we might have with that which lies outside the normal human capacity and reach. The imagination is unlimited, free, and unbounded, able to carry us beyond the peaks of the common earthly knowledge and so beyond the boundaries of our earthly existence. To expose Merrick to the freedom and wonders of the theater is, at least symbolically, to subject his character to a new scope of feelings and experiences, namely, feelings of admiration, creativity, and awe. Much like his actress friend, who is admired and "worshiped" for her "divine" role in the "shrine of imagination," Merrick undergoes a social transformation, removes his monstrous cloth, and becomes a celebrity.[13]

Merrick's celebrity status is indeed a token of his deification. Flying on the Icarus wings of the collective imagination, Merrick is invited to dinners and tea parties, attends the theater (as the guest of Her Royal Highness

Alexandra, Princess of Wales), and even partakes in a private reenactment of a Shakespeare play (which causes Mrs. Kendal to rejoice: "Why, Mr. Merrick, you're not an Elephant Man at all. . . . Oh no . . . no. . . . You're a Romeo"). However, this love affair with cultured society is, as we previously argued, a two-edged sword. Deification and demonization are two sides of the same alienation coin. Merrick's acceptance by high society is therefore essentially no different from his utter rejection by the common mob. Both attitudes are the result of the same alienated curiosity. They both aim to satisfy the same need to remove the "other" from the realm of normal society, either by demoting it to the depths of monstrosity or by elevating it to the heights of the divine.

Free at Last, Free at Last? Merrick's End

We have yet to examine the third type of alienation, namely, objectification. In this type of alienation, the "other" is neither elevated nor demoted, but instead is stripped of his individuality and given the status of a mere object. Following Buber's distinctions, the objectified other loses his hold in the "I-Thou" relationship and instead is subjected to an "I-It" relationship, becoming the mindless dehumanized "it" in this equation.

Merrick undergoes this type of alienation throughout the film. The first time we see him, he is locked in a cage like a beast. His jailer—his proprietor—Bytes, treats him as if he were a piece of property, an artifact at his disposal. This is, by far, the low point of Merrick's objectification. From then on, things seem to improve. Dr. Treves rescues Merrick from the circus and brings him to the hospital. However, as we suggested, this change is merely superficial. Both Treves and Bytes perceive Merrick as an object that, as such, is there for their use. Whether to satisfy Bytes's greed or Treves's scientific curiosity, Merrick still holds the bitter end of the "I-It" relationship.

The real turning point in Merrick's status occurs when Dr. Treves manages to overcome his feelings of alienation. When Treves realizes that behind Merrick's rugged externality there is the gentle soul of an individual, he can no longer treat Merrick as a mere object. Immediately Treves begins to call him "John," and soon after begins treating Merrick as his friend. Merrick, too, struck by the rapid change in his alien status, refers to Treves as "my friend." The notion of *friendship* thereby becomes the new distinctive title of Merrick's status.

Friendship is, by far, the most conspicuous signifier of the cohesiveness of social relationship. It is the glue that supposedly ties society together. As the paradigmatic structure of social camaraderie and collegiality, friendship is the most desired relationship that undermines and annuls any feelings of alienation. It comes as no surprise, then, that Merrick craves the company and friendship of others. His ability to form friendships and to befriend others is therefore the measure of his success at overcoming his alienation. Throughout the film, Merrick has several experiences with friendship, both bitter and sweet. On the bitter end, we find two dubious instances. The first occurs during the attack on Merrick's room, when one of the attackers refers to Merrick as Bytes's friend. Bytes oppressed Merrick and is now in the midst of ransacking his room. Since neither action is one of friendship, tagging Merrick as Bytes's friend is bitterly ironic. The second instance occurs when Merrick manages to flee his kidnapper and return to England. His escape becomes possible thanks to the kind help of the other circus freaks, whom Merrick calls "my friends." It seems that friendship works only between freaks, the alienated, thus defying the purpose of friendship as the glue of society. In these two instances, friendship seems to work poorly or not at all (thus making friendship an empty word).

On the sweet end, it seems that Merrick acquires two true friends: Dr. Treves and Mrs. Kendal. The sincerity of the latter's intentions can be demonstrated in her introduction of Merrick to the audience when he attends the theater for the first time: "Ladies and gentlemen, tonight's performance was very special to me, because it was very special to someone else, a man who knows the theater and loves the theater, and yet tonight is the first time he's ever actually been here. I would like to dedicate . . . the whole company wishes to dedicate, from their hearts, tonight's performance to Mr. John Merrick, my dear *friend*" (emphasis added).

Is this friendship strong enough to undermine Merrick's alienation? Does this suffice to pull him from his social estrangement and make him an equal member of society? Lynch delves into this question in the film's most dramatic final scene. After his emotional visit to the theater, and the love and friendship he experienced, Merrick is back in his hospital room, attending to his miniature model of the cathedral. Treves, who escorted Merrick to his room, is equally emotional. He looks at the miniature model and wonders, "Will the cathedral be finished soon, John?" "Yes, very soon," Merrick replies, and the two bid farewell and retire for the night.

Merrick is now alone in his room, peaceful and relaxed. He reexamines the cathedral, and with a sigh of contentment, he murmurs, "it is finished."

He then signs his name on the miniature, as if to validate the successful manifestation of his individuality. He then rearranges his bed, removing the mound of pillows that, until that point, was a life-saving element that prevented him from suffocating in his sleep. He now wants to take the final step in manifesting his individuality. He wishes to go to sleep like others do; he wishes to be equal to any other human being. This proves to be fatal. His heart cannot support his deformed body in this position, and Merrick dies in his sleep.

Lynch's ending is, as it were, a grim portrayal of the social domain. Friendship doesn't seem to be enough to undermine alienation. Whether a god, a monster, or a stranger, the alien is excluded from the realm of human society, and is therefore, by nature, forever doomed to be outside the circle. Only death sets Merrick free. He can establish his individuality only through his demise.

Notes

1. For further discussion of the term, see *Routledge Encyclopedia of Philosophy,* version 1.0 (London: Routledge, 1998).

2. The lack of colors in Lynch's film can indeed be taken as a cinematic metaphor for the polarity and extremity of this relationship.

3. Aristotle, *Politics,* trans. Benjamin Jowett (New York: Viking Press, 1957), bk. I, pt. II.

4. See Thomas Hobbes, *De Cive* (Oxford: Clarendon Press, 1983), chap. 1, 2; Thomas Hobbes, *Elements of Law Natural and Politic* (Oxford and New York: Oxford University Press, 1994), chap. 14, 13–14: "no man is of might sufficient to assure himself for any long time of preserving himself thereby whilst he remaineth in the state of hostility and war"; and Jean-Jacques Rousseau, *On the Social Contract, or The Principles of Civil Justice* (London: Penguin Classics, 1968).

5. Martin Buber, *I-Thou,* 2nd ed., trans. R. G. Smith (New York: Charles Scribner's Sons, 1958), 4.

6. For further reading, see Richard Wollheim, *The Thread of Life* (Cambridge: Harvard University Press, 1984); and Cynthia MacDonald and Graham MacDonald, eds., *Philosophy of Psychology: Debates on Psychological Explanation* (Oxford: Blackwell, 1995).

7. G. W. F. Hegel, *Phenomenology of Spirit,* trans. A. V. Miller (Oxford: Clarendon Press, 1977).

8. Hegelian followers and adversaries, most notably Karl Marx (1818–1883), have argued that the concept of alienation portrays the situation of modern individuals—especially modern wage laborers—who are deprived of a fulfilling mode of life because

their life activity as socially productive agents is devoid of any sense of communal action or satisfaction and gives them no ownership over their own lives or their products. For further reading, see Karl Marx, *Capital*, trans. B. Fowkes (Harmondsworth: Penguin, 1976); and Karl Marx "Estranged Labor," in Karl Marx, *Economic and Philosophical Manuscripts of 1844 and The Communist Manifesto*, trans. Martin Milligan (New York: Prometheus Books, 1988).

9. This idea was further supported in the work of Hegel's successors, most notably in the work on religion of Ludwig Andreas Feuerbach (1804–1872). According to Feuerbach, the idea of God is really no more than the idea of our own human essence projected as a supernatural entity distinct from, and opposed to, us. Thus, for Feuerbach, religion is the "self-alienation of the human being, the division of the human being from himself." The real appeal of religion is the appeal of our own self-affirmation, especially our collective or species affirmation, the appeal of a true human community and human love. But in religion this love and affirmation are actually subverted and denied because they are misdirected toward an imaginary being alien to us (see Ludwig Feuerbach, *Principles of the Philosophy of the Future*, trans. M. Vogel [Indianapolis: Bobbs-Merrill, 1966]).

10. Richard Kearney, *Strangers, Gods, and Monsters: Interpreting Otherness* (London and New York: Routledge, 2003), 35.

11. Ibid., 37.

12. Ibid., 35.

13. To further understand the symbolic role of imagination here, we might usefully reflect on a conversation between Dr. Treves and the hospital administrator Carr-Gomm (John Gielgud), held earlier in the film:

CARR-GOMM: Can you *imagine* the kind of life he must have had?
DR. TREVES: Yes, I think I can.
CARR-GOMM: I don't think so. No one could possibly *imagine* it! I don't believe any of us can!

PROPHESIES, EXPERIENCE, AND PROOF

Philosophy of Religion in *Dune*

William J. Devlin

In his film *Dune* (1984), director David Lynch presents us with the religious journey of Paul Atreides (Kyle MacLachlan), son of Duke Leto (Jürgen Prochnow) and Lady Jessica Atreides (Francesca Annis). In this film set in the year 10,191, Paul's parents are the heads of the House of Atreides and serve under Padishah Emperor Shaddam Corrino IV (José Ferrer), the ruler of the known universe. Emperor Shaddam's power rests on controlling the substance called "spice melange," a commodity that extends life and enables safe travel through space. Suspicious that Duke Leto has plans to take control of the spice, Emperor Shaddam sets a trap for the House of Atreides, which ultimately leads to the death of Duke Leto. With the loss of his father, Paul proceeds to carry out two congruent journeys: first, to rebuild the fallen House of Atreides to defeat Emperor Shaddam and avenge his father; second, to come to the realization that he is Kwisatz Haderach, the messiah or hand of God under the prophesies of the religious beliefs of a religious sect, the Bene Gesserit Sisterhood. Through years of training a new army, fighting against Emperor Shaddam and his allies, as well as undergoing religious visions and experiences, Paul achieves both ends of his journeys. By realizing that he is Kwisatz Haderach, he is able to lead the rebuilt House of Atreides against Emperor Shaddam, defeat him, and fulfill the prophesies of the Bene Gesserit Sisterhood.

Though *Dune* is based upon the novel by Frank Herbert (*Dune*, 1965), Lynch himself maintains that his adaptation of the novel to the film exemplifies his own unique creative expression through the character of Paul. As Lynch explains, Paul becomes the focus of Lynch's film qua Lynchian film, as his personal journey to self-awareness as the Kwisatz takes center stage.

Since this journey is the Lynchian aspect of *Dune*, this essay examines Paul's journey to becoming Kwisatz, the prophesized messiah, and the question of how one can know they have a religious calling, through epistemological questions in the philosophy of religion. Such questions include: How do we come to *know* or justify our religious beliefs? Can we have a firm belief in religious ideas without appeal to reason? Must religious knowledge be objective, or can it be limited to subjective, or personal, experiences? Paul's religious journey can be understood through an examination of such questions. He begins to realize that he has a religious calling through the various tests provided by the Bene Gesserit Sisterhood. These tests are religiously and empirically grounded, and accepted as tests to see whether or not an individual is Kwisatz. But though he undergoes these tests and empirically behaves in a manner befitting of the messiah, Paul does not become convinced by these tests alone. Rather, he undergoes a series of religious visions and experiences that help to propel his own understanding and faith that he, himself, is Kwisatz. This series culminates with the final act of drinking the water of life, a substance that has killed every male who has tried to drink it. By drinking the water of life and surviving, Paul fulfills the final prophesy and, through this experience itself, awakens the messiah within him.[1]

I will examine Paul's journey and the philosophical questions that arise through two different epistemic approaches in the philosophy of religion. I will show that the followers of the Bene Gesserit Sisterhood come to understand and justify their belief that Paul Atreides is Kwisatz Haderach through the position known as *evidentialism,* a position that maintains that religious beliefs (such as "Paul is Kwisatz Haderach") are warranted so long as they are grounded in empirical claims. Meanwhile, though the Sisterhood can formulate their beliefs through evidentialism, Paul, himself, takes an alternative approach to understanding that he is the messiah. Paul moves beyond grounding his belief in empirical claims, and toward grounding his belief through personal religious perceptions and experiences. Here, Paul's justification is through what William Alston calls the "perception of God." These two approaches to justifying religious beliefs will ultimately help one understand Paul's long struggle to awaken the messiah within.

"Do You Not Trust Your Own Eyes?": Seeing Is Believing

Paul's journey to discovering himself to be the chosen one is best understood as a personal spiritual awakening, since it is he, alone, who comes to claim that he *is*, in fact, Kwisatz. That is, Paul's awareness that he is the chosen one is a religious belief insofar as he accepts the identity claim, "Paul Atreides is Kwisatz Haderach." But since such a claim is about Paul, himself, his path to accept this claim is unique. Unlike the rest of the characters in the film, Paul must undergo a transformation to achieve the realization that he is Kwisatz Haderach. As such, this means Paul comes to justify his religious belief in a different manner than the others. To understand the uniqueness of Paul's journey and the uniqueness of his justification that he is Kwisatz Haderach, I explore in this section how the other characters in the film attempt to justify the belief, "Paul Atreides is Kwisatz Haderach." From here, I turn to the next section to explore Paul's own method for accepting the claim, in light of the previous method of justification.

Much like our world, the world of *Dune* is blanketed in mythology and legend. In particular, the central myth in the world of *Dune* focuses on a chosen one, or a messiah, who, it is believed, will come to rescue humanity. Reverend Mother Gaius Helen Mohiam (Siân Phillips), spiritual leader of the Bene Gesserit Sisterhood, explains this mythology to Paul. According to legend, the water of life, or the bile of the worms from the planet Arrakis, is a potent liquid that the Sisters use for mystical visions, or "to see within." Furthermore, the Sisters believe that the water of life enables them to see "a place that is terrifying to women," a place that "they dare not go." However, as the myth continues, the Sisters believe that there is a man who is the chosen one, the hand of God. He is known as Kwisatz Haderach. As Gaius explains, according to the religious prophesy, Kwisatz is the one who can drink the water of life, and then "will go where we [women] cannot." Furthermore, though many men have tried to drink this deadly water, every man has died. But, once the real Kwisatz drinks the water, it is believed that he "will come [as] the voice from the outer world bringing the holy war, the jihad, which will cleanse the universe and bring us out of darkness."

With the myth of Kwisatz in mind, a salient and practical concern is raised immediately in the film. Namely, how does one know who Kwisatz Haderach is? Many men may claim to be Kwisatz, but the simple pronouncement "I am Kwisatz Haderach" would not be sufficient in justifying that claim to be a true belief. How, then, can we distinguish the false messiahs from the real messiah? This question of knowing who the real Kwisatz is can be understood through the issue concerning the justification of religious beliefs in the philosophy of religion. Here, we are concerned with how one evaluates religious beliefs. How do we know that a religious belief is true? What makes a religious belief justified?

In *Dune,* we see an answer to these questions readily available. Returning to the myth of Kwisatz, notice that the legend holds that Kwisatz will be a man who is able to drink the water of life and live. Meanwhile, those men who are not Kwisatz who drink the water of life will, ironically, die. The legend thus has an empirical test built into it that allows people to justify their religious belief concerning who is Kwisatz: "x is Kwisatz Haderach if and only if x can drink from the water of life and live." In other words, the inhabitants of the world of *Dune* are able to ground their religious claims in empirical evidence. This method of justifying religious beliefs is known as *evidentialism,* the epistemic position that a belief is justified when it is measured by the evidence at hand. As the modern Scottish philosopher David Hume (1711–1776) puts it, "a wise man proportions his belief to the evidence."[2] In other words, a belief is said to be justified when there is sufficient evidence at hand that warrants acceptance. Using this method, we can rely upon various kinds of evidence: self-evident claims, claims through one's sense-perceptions, claims from memory, etc. Meanwhile, a religious belief, in itself, does not count as evidence. As such, a religious belief is not said to be justified unless it is grounded in a sufficient amount of evidence. Thus, as W. K. Clifford summarizes, evidentialism is the position that maintains "it is wrong always, everywhere, and for anyone, to believe anything upon insufficient evidence."[3]

Now, in *Dune,* we find that all of the characters who consider their religious beliefs, whether publically or privately (through Lynch's cinematic method of revealing a character's private thoughts), apply the method of evidentialism to build their justification. More specifically, when each person evaluates the belief "Paul Atreides is Kwisatz Haderach," he or she appeals to the evidence at hand and determines whether or not it is sufficient for grounding this religious belief. Take, for instance, the Bene Gesserit's "death-alternative test of human awareness," a test concerning one's humanity. The test consists of having the individual tested placing his right hand in a box that causes the psychological (though not physical) sensation of a burning, itching, pain that will generally cause one to instinctively remove one's hand. At the same time, however, the Reverend Mother holds a "gom jabbar," or poisoned needle, at the individual's throat, which she will use to puncture and kill the individual should he remove his hand from the box. Such a test is used to help specify those men who may be Kwisatz Haderach. Those who lack self-discipline, and so lack humanity (and so definitely cannot be Kwisatz), will remove their hand and be killed instantly by the gom jabbar. Meanwhile, those who exemplify their humanity (and so may be Kwisatz) will show self-discipline and keep their hand in the box, overcoming the psychological torture caused by the box.

When Reverend Mother Gaius conducts the death-alternative test of human awareness on Paul, it is initially believed that he will fail the test. Lady Jessica is afraid for her son upon learning that he must be tested. Likewise, Gaius has no confidence in Paul's ability, as she scolds Jessica: "Did you really think you could bear the Kwisatz Haderach, the universe's super-being? How dare you!" However, during the testing, Gaius recognizes that Paul is unlike other men. When she initially uses "the voice," or the manipulation of audio frequencies to control the mind of the receiver, Paul refuses to allow her to control him. Likewise, Paul not only passes the test, but he does so having been able to keep his hand in the box longer than any other human. As Gaius thinks to herself, "No woman child has withstood so much."

The death-alternative test of human awareness, when used on Paul, becomes a portion of the evidence that can be used to justify the claim, "Paul Atreides is Kwisatz Haderach." In this case, we have empirical evidence—namely, witnessing Paul pass the test—which helps to demonstrate that Paul has self-discipline and self-control. Paul's passing of the test thus tells us two things about him. First, Paul did not succumb to animalistic instincts, as so many before him had done. Second, even when compared to those who had passed the test before, Paul was able to do so with greater duration. This elevates him above even the successful human males. These two characteristics thus lend credence to the religious belief that Paul is Kwisatz. Even Gaius hesitantly makes such a conclusion, as she asks herself, "Could he be the one? Maybe." In this sense, then, the use of the death-alternative test of human awareness to help determine if Paul is Kwisatz follows the epistemic method of evidentialism.

But the Bene Gesserits are not the only ones who follow the method of evidentialism when evaluating the religious belief "Paul Atreides is Kwisatz Haderach." Take Thufir Hawat (Freddie Jones), the master of assassins, as an example. When Thufir, Gurney Halleck (Patrick Stewart), and Dr. Wellington Yueh (Dean Stockwell) walk toward Paul's chambers, Paul is able to immediately recognize them solely by the sound of their footsteps. When Thufir hears Paul's declaration that he could tell who was coming, he immediately retorts that those footsteps could have been imitated. Paul quickly responds that he could tell the difference between the imitated and authentic sounds. Here, Thufir thinks to himself that this is, indeed, true: "Yes. Perhaps he would at that." In another scene, when Paul visits planet Arrakis, he is able to naturally place the Fremen stillsuit on appropriately (i.e., in "desert fashion"), without any instructions, help, or guidance. Dr. Liet-Kynes (Max von Sydow), an imperial ecologist who supervises the mining expedition on Arrakis, is skeptical of Paul's actions, as he questions if he had worn a suit before or had assistance. When he learns that Paul did this himself for the first time just now, he is taken aback, thinking to himself, "You shall know your ways, as if born to them."

Both Thufir and Liet-Kynes serve as examples of using the evidentialist method to evaluate the belief that Paul is Kwisatz. Although neither belongs to the Bene Gesserit Sisterhood, they are familiar with the myth of Kwisatz Haderach. As such, they observe Paul's actions and abilities—both his skill to identify one's footsteps and his skill to naturally put on a Fremen stillsuit—as an indication that Paul is more than the duke's son. By providing us audio access to their thoughts, Lynch allows us to follow Thufir's and Liet-Kynes's line of reasoning. Each of them separately takes the evidence before them as being reasons to conclude that the religious belief "Paul Atreides is Kwisatz Haderach" may be correct. Or, at the very least, the evidence is developing in such a way so that it is leaning toward that belief being correct.

While such evidence helps to justify the religious belief "Paul Atreides is Kwisatz Haderach," the ultimate evidentialist justification occurs toward the end of the film where Paul drinks the water of life. When Paul decides to take the final test to determine if he is Kwisatz, his wife, Chani (Sean Young), begs him to not take the test. Like Lady Jessica and Mother Gaius earlier, she is wary that Paul is not Kwisatz and hence will die from drinking the sacred water. She thus warns Paul, "I've seen men who have tried. I've seen how they die." But Paul remains steadfast in his determination to drink the water. In the deserts of Arrakis, Chani provides Paul with the water, giving him a heartfelt good-bye as if he were about to die, while the Fedaykin (the freedom fighters under Paul's leadership) watch on. But Paul does not die; rather, his experience makes his eyes bleed, and the worms come up from the dunes to surround them without attacking. Paul opens his eyes, revealing that he has the "Eyes of Ibhad," the state of having deep blue coloration of one's eyes (the sclera, iris, and cornea).

Having passed the test of drinking the sacred water of life, Paul proves to those around him that he is, indeed, Kwisatz Haderach. He leads the

231 Prophesies, Experience, and Proof

Fedaykin against Emperor Shaddam's army and the House of Harkonnen. When Paul and his soldiers reach the Great Hall of the Arrakeen Palace, he confronts Mother Gaius. As before, she once again attempts to use "the voice" to control Paul. This time, however, it completely fails. Completely unaffected by her power, Paul tells Gaius: "I remember your gom jabbar. Now you'll remember mine. I can kill with a word." With these lines, Gaius is compelled back and ceases her attempt to control Paul. Finally, upon killing Feyd-Rautha (Sting), Paul screams, using his voice to break apart the ground of the palace hall, and rain begins to fall upon Arrakis, a planet that is said to be barren and without rain. When those around Paul stand in astonishment, Paul's sister exclaims: "And how can this be? For he is the Kwisatz Haderach!"

Thus, we can see that the people in the world of *Dune* follow the evidentialist method when evaluating their religious beliefs. No one confirms their belief "Paul Atreides is Kwisatz Haderach" until there is sufficient empirical evidence to justify that belief. The empirical evidence, though mounting throughout the film, culminates in the test of drinking the water of life. There, one applies the claim that "Paul Atreides is Kwisatz Haderach if and only if Paul can drink from the water of life and live." By drinking the water of life and surviving, Paul passes the empirical test built into the myth of Kwisatz, which allows one to conclude, based on empirical evidence, that Paul is, indeed, the chosen one.

"The Sleeper Has Awakened"

Evidentialism helps to explain the method employed by the people in the world of *Dune* for justifying the religious belief "Paul Atreides is Kwisatz Haderach." But this method, alone, doesn't fully encapsulate Paul's own journey toward discovering that he is, in fact, Kwisatz. Although Paul does utilize the empirical method of evidentialism to an extent, I maintain that he ultimately finds that this method, when applied to his personal awareness that he is Kwisatz, falls short. Instead, Paul must switch to an alternative method that is more personal and direct. To help fully expound Paul's journey as a personal journey toward self-discovery, I propose that we incorporate a second method of justifying religious beliefs, a method that allows for religious beliefs to be justifiable in and of themselves through religious experience.

Once Paul learns about the myth of Kwisatz, we can see that, like everyone else, he follows the evidentialist method of determining whether or not he is Kwisatz. He passes the death-alternative test of human awareness, he displays an ability to use "the voice" to manipulate others, and he seems to have naturally gifted abilities unlike any other human being. All of these empirically observable events and skills suggest to Paul that he may be Kwisatz. That is, he weighs these empirical observations as evidence that may justify the religious belief that he is the chosen one. But notice that these observations, alone, do not lead to Paul concluding that this religious belief is necessarily correct. On the contrary, despite these observations, Paul remains skeptical as to whether or not he is Kwisatz. For instance, when he watches his mother drink the water of life, we see that Paul remains nervous and unsure of himself, as he reflects: "One day I will have to do this. Every man who has tried has died. Am I the one?"

It is not simply the case that Paul just hasn't found enough empirical evidence to justify the belief that he is Kwisatz. Even if Paul found an abundance of empirical evidence that would seemingly justify such a belief, Paul still would have his doubts. Rather, the problem for Paul is that the evidentialist method of justifying this specific religious belief—"I, Paul Atreides, am Kwisatz Haderach"—is, itself, an insufficient method of justification. Paul cannot treat himself, through the observations he makes about himself, as an object of inquiry that can make him believe that he is Kwisatz. Instead, Paul must undergo a personal transformation—he must awaken, or become aware of his identity as the chosen one. This transformation is not something externally, or empirically, observed as evidentialism requires. Such a transformation is internal in the sense that it is an entirely subjective experience. In the philosophy of religion, the subjective experience that Paul has as a transformation or a revelation that he is Kwisatz is referred to as a *religious experience*.

The notion of religious experience was most famously discussed by the American philosopher William James (1842–1910). James explains that a personal, or subjective, religious experience is rooted in "mystical states of consciousness." Such states, by definition, necessarily include four characteristics. First, a mystical state has the characteristic of ineffability—"it defies expression . . . no adequate report of its contents can be given into words." The religious or mystical experience is such that it is experienced directly from the subjective point of view and so cannot be transferred or shared with others. It is thus impossible for the individual undergoing the religious experience to place the revelations of such an experience into words that positively reflect a full account of what is revealed. Second, a mystical state has a noetic quality. While a religious experience cannot be accurately expressed in language, it is an experience that imparts knowledge upon the individual: "They are states of insight into depths of truth unplumbed by the discursive intellect." As such, religious experiences are revelatory and illuminating. Third, a mystical state is transient. Though an individual may have many religious experiences, or even recurrences of the same experience, no experience can last very long. Finally, a mystical state is passive. James points out that although one may be active to get into a mystical state, the mystical state, itself, is one of passivity: "when the characteristic sort of consciousness once has set in, the mystic feels as if his own will were in abeyance, and indeed sometimes as if he were grasped and held by a superior power."[4]

Now, some may argue that, given the necessary characteristics that are part of religious experience, the beliefs derived from such experiences do not need to be justified by any empirical evidence. Rather, the experience itself is constituted as evidence for the religious belief. For instance, William Alston (1921–2009) argues that religious experiences should be considered reliable insofar as they are similar to sensory experiences. A sensory experience can be described as a perception that has direct awareness in the sense that it "does not essentially involve conceptualization and judgment." To perceive a given sensory object is simply to say that the object appears to the perceiver in a certain way. As such, one can say that the object that is perceived provides a causal contribution to the perceiver's experience. Furthermore, the object perceived gives rise to beliefs about that object, and these beliefs do not necessarily require evidence beyond the perception itself. Analogously, religious or mystical experiences involve "a direct presentation of God to their awareness." Alston maintains that a religious experience should be construed as a mystical perception, in the sense that one has a "perception of God," or the divine. Like the perception of a sensory object, the perception of the divine gives rise to religious beliefs about the divine. And these beliefs need not rely upon further evidence beyond the perception itself. Thus, the mystical perception of the divine, insofar as it is a direct awareness of the divine similar to sensory perceptions, can provide its own justification for the beliefs that arise concerning the divine.[5]

We can see that Lynch emphasizes this kind of self-justified role of religious experience in *Dune* through his focus on Paul's personal journey toward self-awareness as Kwisatz. As Lynch puts it, this focus is on "the character of Paul: the sleeper who must awaken and become what he was supposed to become." Paul's journey thus begins where he is asleep, unaware that he is Kwisatz. But in order to awaken and to become what he is supposed to become, Paul must undergo a transformation of consciousness. That is, Paul must have a religious or mystical experience that allows him to perceive his own divinity and awaken as Kwisatz Haderach.[6]

Before Paul has his religious experience, however, he must take the necessary steps that lead up to this experience. As his father explains to him, "A person needs new experiences, they jar something deep inside allowing them to grow. Without change, something sleeps inside us and seldom awakens. The sleeper must awaken." We find that, though Paul begins metaphorically asleep, his sleep provides him with the new experiences that will help lead him to his religious experience and ultimate awakening as Kwisatz Haderach. There are two kinds of new experiences that Paul has. First, there is what Paul refers to as his "waking dreams." On several occasions, we see that Paul has prophetic dreams or visions. These dreams are puzzle pieces for Paul—they provide him with information of events yet to come, information of events that have already transpired. For instance, Paul has visions of the future insofar as he dreams of Feyd-Rautha threatening to kill him (an event that occurs at the Great Hall of the Arrakeen Palace) and has visions of Chani, his future wife, whom he will later meet on Arrakis. Likewise, he has visions of past events such as the emperor's plot to assassinate him and his father, and Baron Harkonnen's (Kenneth McMillan) insight, "He who controls the spice, controls the universe." All of this information is presented in snippets and out of context, appearing arbitrary and disconnected. Yet such information serves as clues that help lead to his transformation to, and revelation that he is, Kwisatz.[7]

The second kind of new experience that is an important precondition for Paul's awakening is the spice mélange on Arrakis. When Paul visits Arrakis for the first time, he is taken aback by his immediate awareness of what he refers to as "the pure spice" that is on the suits of the men working with the spice. Later, when Paul eats the spice, he is again astonished by the effects it has on him, as he wonders to himself: "What is it doing to me? Am I the one?" Paul's visions and his relation to the spice help to transform his consciousness. As he explains to Lady Jessica: "The spice! It's in everything here, the air, the soil, the food. It's like the truth-sayer drug. It's a poison! You knew the spice would change me. But thanks to your teachings it's changed my consciousness. I can see it. I can see it."

Paul's dreams and his awareness of the spice are only steps leading up to his religious experience, which is the mystical experience he has through drinking the water of life. After his final waking dream, Paul becomes convinced that he must drink the water of life. As he explains to Chani: "All the images of my future are gone. I have to drink the water of life." For Paul, even though the water of life has killed many men, he realizes that it is his time to come to see if he is, indeed, Kwisatz: "I'm dead to everyone unless I try to become what I may be. Only the water of life can free what will save us. I must drink the sacred water." In other words, through his waking dreams and his experience with the spice, Paul's consciousness has been transformed so that he is now capable of having the religious experience that will complete his transformation into Kwisatz. With his consciousness transformed, Paul drinks the water of life. Lynch cinematically visualizes Paul's religious experience as he drinks—an experience of visions and revelations. Paul goes to the place that Mother Gaius spoke about, "a place terrifying to us, to women," and he tells himself, "This is the place they cannot look." Furthermore, Paul comes to the revelation about the secret connection between the spice and the worms on Arrakis that everyone has missed. As Paul tells himself: "The worm is the spice. The spice is the worm." Through this revelation, he intuitively grasps and applies the mystical ability of "traveling without moving," which allows him to see everything. Once he awakens, Paul sees the world with new eyes, literally in that his eyes are now a deep blue, and metaphorically, in that he sees the world as Kwisatz Haderach.

Now, Paul's experience that follows from drinking the water of life can be understood as a religious experience under James's definition. First, the experience itself cannot properly be explained. Lynch, aware of the ineffability of Paul's religious experience, doesn't attempt to use language to describe the experience. Rather, he attempts to visualize it through a stream of seemingly disconnected images that we, the viewers, are to treat as part of Paul's visions and conscious experience. But Lynch is aware that even this attempt will inevitably fall short of capturing the experience firsthand from Paul's perspective. This is why Paul, himself, doesn't attempt to describe the experience in positive terms. When he refers to the experience, it is only in negative terms. For instance, when he confronts Mother Gaius, he scolds her: "Why don't you go to the place where you dare not look? You'll find me staring back at you!" Here, Paul's mystical experience and religious journey are captured in negative terms—he refers to the place that one dares not go and tells us that that is where he went. But this tells us nothing about what this place is, or what constituted his experience. The reason why Paul makes no such attempt to place it in positive terms is because it is an experience beyond communication.

Second, though it is beyond linguistic, and hence rational, communication, Paul's experience does have a noetic quality to it. Paul has a revelation or insight that the spice and the worm are identical (the worm is the spice, and the spice is the worm). The people of *Dune,* and even we, the viewers, may not be able to understand this revelation, but that is expected since we are not the ones who are undergoing this incommunicable experience. For Paul, however, it is an insight into reality. Third, Paul's experience is transient; it doesn't seem to last too long. Finally, Paul is passive through this experience. Though there is action to help stimulate the experience (Chani pours the water of life into Paul's mouth), Paul is physically lying down when he drinks the water, and relatively inert through the duration of the experience. Though his head moves about and he actively screams, Paul then paradoxically travels throughout the universe without moving. As such, though his experience does allow him to move, he does so while remaining motionless, or, as James would suggest, keeping "his own will in abeyance."

The Hand of God

Lynch's *Dune* thus tells us the tale of Paul Atreides and his transformation into Kwisatz Haderach. But, more important, as we have seen, Lynch suggests through his film that Paul's journey to becoming Kwisatz must be understood as a personal and subjective voyage. Those around him, from his mother to Gaius to us, the viewers, are removed from the experience. As such, at best, we can only epistemically employ the empirical evidence presented to us to infer that Paul is most likely Kwisatz. This method, however, falls short when it comes to Paul's own understanding that he is Kwisatz. Instead, Paul's journey, as a journey of the awakening of the Messiah, must utilize a different method. Paul must have a personal and direct experience. Similar to Alston's "perception of God," Paul perceives the divinity that lies within, and this perception is self-justified through Paul's own direct awareness of the revelation itself. And this revelation is part of a religious or mystical experience that allows him to awaken to the notion that he is, indeed, Kwisatz Haderach.

Notes

1. Chris Rodley, ed., *Lynch on Lynch,* rev. ed. (London: Faber and Faber, 2005), 116.

2. David Hume, *An Enquiry Concerning Human Understanding,* 2nd ed., ed. Eric Steinberg (Indianapolis: Hackett, 1993), sec. X: "Of Miracles," 72–90.

3. W. K. Clifford, "The Ethics of Belief" in W. K. Clifford, *Lectures and Essays* (London: Macmillan, 1879), 124.

4. William James, *Varieties of Religious Experience,* lectures 6 and 7, reprinted in William James, *Selected Writings* (New York: Book-of-the-Month Club, 1977), 401–4.

5. William Alston, "Religious Experience as Perception of God," in *Philosophy of Religion: Selected Readings,* 2nd ed., ed. Michael Preston, William Haster, et al. (New York: Oxford University Press, 2001), 20–22; William Alston, *Perceiving God: The Epistemology of Religious Experience* (Ithaca: Cornell University Press, 1991).

6. Rodley, *Lynch on Lynch,* 116.

7. For further discussion on Lynch's use of dreams in his works, see, in this volume, Robert Arp and Patricia Brace, "'The Owls Are Not What They Seem': The Logic of Lynch's World"; and Simon Riches, "Intuition and Investigation into Another Place: The Epistemological Role of Dreaming in *Twin Peaks* and Beyond."

CONTRIBUTORS

Robert Arp is an ontologist working in the D.C. area with OntoReason, LLC. He has authored numerous articles and book chapters on the philosophy of mind, philosophy of biology, modern philosophy, and popular culture. He is also the author of *Scenario Visualization: An Evolutionary Account of Creative Problem Solving* (2008); the editor of *South Park and Philosophy* (2006); and a coeditor of *Contemporary Debates in Philosophy of Biology* (2009), *Philosophy of Biology: An Anthology* (2009), and *Batman and Philosophy* (2009).

Shai Biderman is a doctoral candidate in philosophy at Boston University, and an instructor at Tel Aviv University, Bet-Berl College, the Open University, and the College of Management, Israel. His research interests include philosophy of film and culture, aesthetics, ethics, and existentialism. His various articles on philosophy and popular culture include chapters on the philosophy of westerns, the philosophy of the Coen brothers, and the philosophy of Steven Soderbergh.

Patricia Brace is professor of art history at Southwest Minnesota State University. With coauthor Robert Arp, she has contributed chapters to *"Lost" and Philosophy: The Island Has Its Reasons* (2007) and *"True Blood" and Philosophy: We Want To Think Bad Things with You* (2010).

Tal Correm is a doctoral student in philosophy at Temple University. Her research interests include phenomenology, aesthetics, moral and political philosophy, comparative philosophy, and eighteenth- and nineteenth-century German philosophy.

William J. Devlin is assistant professor of philosophy at Bridgewater State University and visiting summer lecturer at the University of Wyoming. His fields of interest are philosophy of science, theories of truth, Nietzsche, and existentialism. His essays appear in such volumes as *The Philosophy of TV Noir; The Philosophy of Science Fiction Film;* and *The Philosophy of the Coen Brothers.*

Shai Frogel is a doctor of philosophy at Tel-Aviv University and at Kibbutzim College of Education and is a member of Tel Aviv Institute of Contemporary Psychoanalysis. He has published *The Rhetoric of Philosophy*, on the relationship between the logical and psychological aspects of philosophy; *Rhetoric*, an introduction to the study of rhetoric; and *Ethics: Spinoza and Nietzsche*, a comparison between Spinoza's logical philosophy and Nietzsche's psychological philosophy in relation to ethics of "man without God." He has also published articles on philosophical argumentation, existentialism, and ethics.

Richard Gaughran teaches American and world literature in the English Department of James Madison University. He has taught at Lehigh University, as well as at Allentown College (now DeSales University). He was Senior Fulbright Lecturer for American Studies at the University of Cyril and Methodius in Skopje, Macedonia, where he lived and worked from 1997 to 2000. He has recently published articles on the novelist Larry Brown, the films of the Coen Brothers, and Sam Peckinpah's *The Wild Bunch.*

Sander H. Lee is professor of philosophy at Keene State College. He is the author of *Eighteen Woody Allen Films Analyzed: Anguish, God and Existentialism;* and *Woody Allen's Angst: Philosophical Commentaries on His Serious Films.* He has also written more than thirty essays on issues in aesthetics, ethics, Holocaust studies, and philosophy and popular culture.

Russell Manning teaches philosophy at Yarra Valley Grammar in Ringwood (Victoria, Australia). He is the author of "The Fatal Strategy of the City," "Jean Baudrillard and the Postmodern Re-imagination," and "A Boy Who Swims Faster Than a Shark: Jean Baudrillard Visits the Office."

Jennifer L. McMahon is associate professor and chair of the Department of English and Languages at East Central University in Ada, Oklahoma. Her fields of interest include existentialism, philosophy and literature, aesthetics, and non-Western philosophy. She has published articles in *Asian Philosophy* and the *Journal of the Association for Interdisciplinary Study of the Arts,* among others. She has also published many essays on philosophy and popular culture, including essays in *The Philosophy of Martin Scorsese; The Philosophy of TV Noir;* and *The Philosophy of Science Fiction Film.* Most recently, she coedited, with B. Steve Csaki, *The Philosophy of the Western.*

Ronie Parciack received her Ph.D. from Tel Aviv University's School of Philosophy. She teaches in the Department of East Asian Studies and in the Department of Film and Television at Tel Aviv University. Her research interests include political Hinduism, political and gendered aspects of visual culture in India, Indian literature in English, and India–Israel cultural encounters. Her work has appeared in journals and anthologies, and she is completing a book addressing some philosophical and aesthetic issues of Hindi cinema.

Simon Riches has recently gained a Ph.D. in philosophy from University College London, with a thesis on a priori knowledge, and has taught in its philosophy department for three years. His research interests lie in the philosophy of film, epistemology, and the philosophy of psychology.

Jason Southworth is an ABD graduate student at the University of Oklahoma, and adjunct instructor of Philosophy at Barry University. His dissertation concerns the philosophy of language. He has contributed articles to several philosophy and popular-culture volumes, including *Batman and Philosophy, Heroes and Philosophy,* and *Steven Colbert and Philosophy.*

Scott Hamilton Suter is associate professor of English and American Studies at Bridgewater College. His areas of interest include folk and popular culture. He has published *Shenandoah Valley Folklife,* an introduction to the traditions of that region, and he has published articles and lectured on topics ranging from cottage-style gas stations to the significance of amateur baseball leagues to the humor of the Amish and Mennonites.

Assaf Tabeka is a member of the Israeli Bar Association and a lecturer at the Law School at the College of Management, Israel. His areas of expertise are civil procedure and interdisciplinary studies of law and culture. He has published articles on the legal issues in the works of Heinrich von Kleist, Franz Kafka, and Woody Allen, as well as on legal education and children's literature.

Mark Walling is professor of English at East Central University in Ada, Oklahoma. He has explored the concerns of duality in other essays on Stanley Kubrick, Sam Peckinpah, and Cormac McCarthy.

INDEX

abortion, 192–93
absurdity, 7–9, 113–14, 116–18, 120, 124,
    124–25n1, 146, 148–49
    See also angst; anxiety; despair
Absurd Reasoning, An (Camus), 115
ad hominem argument, 21
    See also fallacy
Advaita-Vedānta, 77, 83, 84, 85
aesthetics, 3, 23, 26, 37, 75, 87, 117, 176
alienation, 4, 132, 141, 210, 213–16, 218,
    220–21, 222–23n8, 223n9
allegory, 155, 190, 197
Alston, William, 226, 233, 236
Amistad (film), 76n10
analytic philosophy, 28, 40
anātman, 88
angst, 115
    See also absurdity; anxiety; despair
anxiety, 115, 117, 120, 123–24
    See also absurdity; despair
a priori knowledge, 33–35, 38, 147
a priori values, 145
archetypes, Jungian, 160, 163–68
argument, 2, 10, 11, 13–17
argument from inappropriate authority,
    18–19
    See also fallacy
Aristotle, 200–211, 213
Armstrong, Karen, 101
ātman, 77, 83, 84, 85, 87
Atreides, Lady Jessica, 225, 229–30, 234
Atreides, Paul, 1, 28, 225–36
authenticity, 113, 123, 145, 201–2
avidyā, 84, 86
awe, 61–62, 219

Badalamenti, Angelo, 45, 74, 179
bad faith, 113–14
Ballard, J. G., 37
Banks, Teresa, 14, 18, 30–31, 34
Baudrillard, Jean, 62, 69, 71, 72
Beaumont, Jeffrey, 16, 26–27, 31, 33, 37–38,
    41n3, 42n17, 43n28, 46–59
beauty, 47, 75n1, 180, 184
Beauvoir, Simone de, 140

Beethoven, Ludwig van, 205n11
Being and Nothingness (Sartre), 50
Bergman, Ingmar, 190
Beyond Good and Evil (Nietzsche), 199
Bhagavad Gita, 181
Bible, 181
big Other, 70–71, 75
birds, 17, 179–80
Blackburne, Annie, 183–84
Blue Velvet (film), 1, 3, 16, 26–27, 31, 37,
    33, 38, 41n3, 42n17, 45–59, 59n1,
    65–66, 74, 99, 176
Bob, 17, 18, 22, 28, 32, 35, 39, 183, 185,
    187n8, 189
body, 4, 27, 95, 98, 128–31, 133–40
    See also embodied subjectivity
Booth, Frank, 1, 38, 41n3, 43n28, 47,
    50–58, 62, 65–66, 74
Borg, Professor, 190
brahman, 84, 88
Briggs, Bobby, 181–82
Briggs, Major Garland, 40, 42n23, 182
Broken Feather, 8–9
brutality, 47–48, 58, 209
Buber, Martin, 212–13, 220
Buddha, 99, 101
Buddhism, 3, 32, 54, 60n6, 77, 88–89,
    91n18, 101, 108
    Zen Buddhism, 3, 95–110
    See also Eastern philosophy; religion,
    Eastern
Bytes, 9, 10, 128, 135, 139–41, 208, 216–17,
    220–21

Camus, Albert, 113–16, 118, 123–24, 146,
    148, 151, 155
"Candy-Colored Clown" (song), 56
Catching the Big Fish (Lynch), 148, 178, 186
causality, 78, 87
Chani, 230, 234–36
chaos, 3, 4, 7–8, 23, 114, 123, 141, 147
Clifford, W. K., 228
commanding, vs. obeying, 161–62
conclusions, drawing, 10–14, 19, 72
    See also argument

243

www.ingramcontent.com/pod-product-compliance
Lightning Source LLC
Chambersburg PA
CBHW030935150426
42812CB00064B/2906/J